Endangered

Cultures

ooooo

Endangered Cultures

Miguel León-Portilla

Translated by Julie Goodson-Lawes

Southern Methodist University Press

Dallas

Originally published as *Culturas en peligro*
Copyright © 1976, Alianza Editorial Mexicana, S.A.

Copyright © 1990, Southern Methodist University Press
All rights reserved
Printed in the United States of America

First Southern Methodist University Press edition, 1990

Requests for permission to reproduce material from
this work should be sent to:
  Permissions
  Southern Methodist University Press
  Box 415
  Dallas, Texas 75275

Library of Congress Cataloging-in-Publication Data

León-Portilla, Miguel.
    [Culturas en peligro. English]
    Endangered cultures / Miguel León-Portilla ; translated by Julie
Goodson-Lawes. — 1st Southern Methodist University Press ed.
      p.   cm.
    Translation of: Culturas en peligro.
    Includes bibliographical references.
    ISBN 0-87074-311-2 (pbk.)
    1. Indians of Mexico—Ethnic identity.   2. Acculturation.
  3. Culture conflict.   I. Title.
  F1220.L4613   1990
  972'.01—dc20   90-52658

Contents

v

Translator's Note

Translating any text is always a difficult endeavor; translating with an eye on both the texture and the meaning at times seemed impossible. I thank Miguel León-Portilla for his revisions of my drafts and for guiding me to what he wanted the manuscript to say and how he wanted it to read. We hope the reader will appreciate the extent to which the original Spanish continues to flavor the English version.

I dedicate this translation to Jane Goodson Lawes, herself an editor of children and of texts.

Preface

Both history and contemporary experience, especially with knowledge derived from anthropological and social research, demonstrate how, under certain circumstances, forces emerge capable of disturbing the integrity and even the very existence of a culture. As with every animate object, a culture, as a living entity, develops in the midst of danger. Our concern here is limited to identifying and, if possible, typifying certain forms of cultural threats. Specifically, we will consider situations where the processes that are generated place the very structure of cultural nuclei in crisis; cases in which damage is done to the values, criteria, and symbols that a culture depends upon in order to orient both its own internal development and its relationships to other societies.

There are numerous examples of what happens when, due to internal or external factors or to a combination of both, diverse types of cultures have entered into such crises. At times the resulting transformations have been positive; but perhaps more frequently, various types of trauma, marginalization, and the dissolution of the culture's very being have been the consequences. Today the number of endangered cultures—made up of minority groups as well as, at times, entire nations—seems to have increased markedly. Among the principal factors that have contributed to this are the rapid acceleration of the processes of change, together with an inability to cope with previously unknown forms of technological development, the global linking of different peoples and cultures through innovative means of mass communication, the violent confrontations of economic interests, and, above all, the boundless ambitions of various types of hegemonic powers.

It is true that there are opposing forces and institutions, such as many of today's international organizations, which condemn all types of aggression and thereby attempt to impede any form of cultural threat or imposition. Nonetheless, the dangers reappear time and again in more subtle ways, keeping the often already-brittle cultural characteristics of many groups and even nations in a state of perpetual crisis.

A culture without its own internal processes of change, capable of both enriching or damaging its own functional integration and dynamism, is unthinkable. It is also evident that there is no people or nation, especially today, that can elude contacts with other states or groups bearing distinct cultural features. However, while there are already numerous risks and uncertainties involved in internal processes of development, the incidence of cultural threats faced by minority groups or by weaker countries—when influenced and even pressured to change by the decisions or interests of powerful states with different cultures—may be even greater.

Reflecting upon these issues brings others to mind: Do students of culture—anthropologists, sociologists, philosophers, and historians—have a professional obligation to investigate cases of endangered cultures familiar to them? Should not their academic knowledge as applied to these matters be made public, especially before those responsible for making decisions in the political, social, and economic spheres of interaction?

This book brings together several studies, each elaborated under diverse circumstances, yet always as a consequence of related interests and preoccupations. In all cases, their themes point to processes of cultural loss or reaffirmation, situations of risk, contacts between different societies and, at times, forms of imposition at the hands of groups or nations seeking hegemony.

The cases that concern me, for the most part, are closely related to my own area of interest in historical research: the cultural sphere of indigenous Mexico. Nonetheless, I have included other essays that go beyond this context. Among them are those that deal with the cultural trajectory of the Northwest of Mexico, not limited to the indigenous populations of that region. And, moving beyond the present-day national borders, I turn to another extremely interesting experience: that of the Navajo Indians in the southwestern United States.

I have attempted to review, enrich, and correlate the studies that now make up this book in light of the concept of endangered cultures. Though diverse situations of the past and present are analyzed, especially with regard to the cultural being of Mexico, I have also left room for reflection upon broader areas, like the truly complex region of Latin America.

Transformations without loss of identity, cases of "spiritual conquest," the cultural traumas suffered by militarily defeated and dominated societies, experiences of cultural groups similar but not identical to the national majorities, crises of cultural collapse or of possible participation in broader cultural contexts—these are the central themes of the essays brought together here. By offering them in the form of a book, I hope somehow to contribute to a deeper awareness of these issues, issues in which all of humankind ought to take interest, in order to discover the answers so urgently needed.

I would like to thank the different publications in which these studies appeared in their original form. Since the bibliography contains their precise references, I will simply list them here: *American Anthropologist, Estudios de Cultura Náhuatl* (National Autonomous University of Mexico),

Revista de Occidente (Madrid), and *Latin American Indian Literatures* (Pittsburgh). I also wish to acknowledge the late Dr. Edward H. Spicer and Dr. Alfonso Villa Rojas for their comments and valuable suggestions with regard to some of the studies, now chapters, included in this book. My gratitude extends to my distinguished translator, Julie Goodson-Lawes, for her patient and friendly understanding in the process of rethinking along with me the contents of this book, having in mind our English-speaking readers.

Miguel León-Portilla
Paris, June 1990
Mexico's Delegation to UNESCO

Endangered Cultures

1.
Conceptual Framework and Case Identification

The aim of this chapter is to outline several major cases that typify contemporary endangered cultures. This implies a need to focus on the meaning of certain concepts, rich in historical and anthropological connotations, that will repeatedly emerge in our study of the different situations under consideration. The concepts to be highlighted are those of culture, "endangered culture," cultural identity, acculturation, and a few other related ideas.

THE SUBTLE CONCEPTS OF CULTURE AND ENDANGERED CULTURE

Two basic concepts that require special consideration are culture and endangered cultures. It is almost redundant to state that the idea of culture, so rich in meaning, has been discussed at length from very divergent points of view. Even within the fields of anthropology and history, of special interest to us here, there is little agreement among the attempts at definition offered by innumerable scholars. Nonetheless, it is possible at least to highlight a set of features or elements that, beyond divergent opinions, have proven themselves to be essential to the basic meaning of "culture."

The universe of culture includes all that human beings have created by living in society, modifying with different

3

purposes and methods the milieu in which they live, pondering, forging institutions, symbols, and values that give root to conduct and to structures endowed with utility. One characteristic that should be underlined is the possibility of transmission, inherent in any culture. Thus it is fitting to speak of a cultural legacy that is communicated to new members of a society who, in turn, have the power to enrich and modify it. Because it is socially transmittable by way of diverse modes of communication, all that can be called culture is fundamentally distinct from what constitutes our biological inheritance.

No culture is genetically predetermined. Though instinct or innate reflex, insofar as they are biological, affect us beyond culture, an important qualification must be made. The behavior and ideas assumed by a certain society with respect to biological requirements—such as sex, nutrition, and self-defense—in fact bestow upon the originally instinctive reactions diverse forms of meaning in terms of the particular cultural context. For example, let us consider the biological fact of sex, which is subject to manifold norms and even taboos. In certain rites it can be converted into something fundamentally sacred; or it can be secularized, on the contrary, and become a favorite ingredient for the communications media, as is frequently the case in modern public announcements. Thus, the realm of the cultural—even impinging upon the purely biological—shapes the integral features of different societies within a seemingly unlimited spectrum of possible behaviors, creations, symbols, values, and structures.

Those who have emphasized the ability for transmission, inherent in all cultures, rightly insist on the fact that all cultural legacies condition, in different ways and to different degrees, the future orientation of the group or society that bears the culture in question. Thus, in terms of the culture itself, and the resulting self-image that a society has, distinct types of initiatives and responses freely emerge to confront situations of contact or exchange with groups of different cultures, or in order to face previously unknown problems.

In this and generally in all kinds of behavior, the lessons offered by global history lead us to recognize that no culture, however rich or developed it may assume itself to be, is the model for accomplishing optimal forms of behavior, creativity, institutions, symbols, modes of preservation, and cultural transmission. Ultimately, these elements should be considered infinitely variable and perfectible in countless ways.

Every society, dynamically structured as a cultural being—distinct from or related to other groups—ought to have access to the resources needed to develop in the environment in which it exists. Its particular legacy and its actual development, however limited these may be, bestow upon it a distinct physiognomy as a people, tribe, minority group, dominant majority, or state, regardless of the forms of political organization that one may attribute to them. Thus, throughout the human trajectory on earth, countless cultures have emerged, some with a perspective that becomes the root for extraordinary creativity, with or without the desire to impose upon or dominate others; other cultures that, marginalized, have had fewer natural resources at their disposal, have been subject to extremely difficult challenges and, in effect, are weaker because of extremely varied and not always clear causes.

An awareness of these facts now brings our attention to the second of the concepts that needs to be defined, that of "endangered cultures." In a general sense we should recognize that as living entities, continuously in the process of change and development, all cultures must inevitably confront sometimes unforeseen problems and influences constituting a challenge or danger to their own integral reality. Several philosophers of history have formulated theories in the attempt to understand the causes and situations that favor either the strengthening and expansion or the decline, disintegration, and death of cultural entities—including, of course, those societies thought of as true civilizations. The causes and motives of such changes have been framed within several different categories, including the challenges and risks posed by the natural environment in which a culture develops, or a wide range of possible internal crises or disintegrative processes. Also, the external pressures and threats exercised by other societies or states, often of fundamentally different cultures, have been cited as a cause of change.

It seems certain—beyond any determinist posture—that these factors are bound to be included among those that can endanger the existence of a culture. What is important to underline is that frequent challenges and risks seem to accompany all cultures, and without them the very being and development of a culture would appear almost as mere abstractions. However, among the multiple forms of confrontation and threat that can loom over a culture, described below are those specifically referred to when using the phrase "endangered cultures."

As a first step, it is useful to enumerate the principal factors that give rise to particular contemporary situations, understood here as endangered cultures. An important place in the list is occupied by the accelerated pressures of the driving forces of change, originating from the exterior. Whether overtly or subtly taxing, these pressures affect the being of weaker or, in certain respects, less-developed, minority societies. The cultural structures of such groups are thus besieged by attempts at homogenization, or by the strength of majority societies and of economically and politically more powerful states. To these factors must be added the growth in communications media, which obliges the many culturally distinct societies and nations that exist around the globe to enter into contact and exchange. Within the context of such global interactions—today more intense and inescapable than ever—a kind of dichotomy has become increasingly clear, reflecting the dual reality of minority or weaker groups versus the cultures of those who constitute social or political entities with hegemonic and even overtly imperialistic aspirations, cultures committed to consolidating and expanding their spheres of influence first through the purely economic, and later embracing the entire cultural context.

Threats of this sort are usually hidden behind various guises. The need for national unity is invoked when referring to minorities living in a country whose dominant groups want to put an end to the coexistence of different cultures, including different languages. When dealing with less-developed nations or peoples, it is proclaimed that the implementation of certain models of change will be the solution to their problems. Thus, the cases of endangered cultures become progressively more common. Obvious examples are the many indigenous groups throughout the Americas, or the diverse minority communities in certain European countries and in the United States, groups that bear distinct cultures as the roots of their unique personalities. Also worthy of note are the current experiences of whole nations that struggle to define their cultural physiognomy within the broad context of the peoples of Latin America, Asia, and Africa, the so-called Third World. The threats—whether covert or openly declared—felt with increasing force in areas like those mentioned above, are precisely the ones that give rise to the cases to be studied in light of the concept of endangered cultures.

CULTURAL IDENTITY

Another concept, also essential to any attempt to understand cultural changes, contacts, and processes of integration or of disintegration, is that of cultural identity. As demonstrated by Richard H. Robbins, among others, much has been said about this concept from very diverse points of view.[1] Its connotation, originally psychological, points to an awareness of the self. The study of the transformations of such an awareness and its operational meaning throughout a person's lifetime are obviously subjects of psychological research. The concept of identity, when applied to the realm of society and cultures, acquires new connotations without losing its original meaning.

Taken by itself, cultural identity also denotes a consciousness shared by members of a society who consider themselves in possession of characteristics or elements that make them distinct from other groups, who in turn think of themselves as having a singular cultural physiognomy. It is not always easy to pinpoint diacritically which are the characteristics or elements that support the appearance and persistence of a particular cultural identity.[2] On the one hand, there is no doubt that cultural identity can survive despite processes of change, with the assimilation of certain foreign elements and the abandonment of others that were once its own. On the other hand, it must be admitted as well that in certain cases these alterations or losses can bring with them, as a consequence, the disintegration of cultural identity.

Nonetheless, it makes sense to demarcate certain elements that have been, and frequently are, the roots of identity—although, of course, they are neither universally shared nor immutable. Among the principal ones are language; sets of traditions; beliefs, symbols, and meanings; systems of values; possession of a certain ancestral land; a world view; and what has been described as an *ethos,* or meaning and moral orientation of a culture. In addition, as a very meaningful feature or element of all ethnic and cultural identity, we must place special emphasis on the historical consciousness shared by the members of the group in question. Such consciousness, as the root of identity, implies the memory—often maintained over generations—of a culture's origin, of certain experiences, and even of a common destiny. In this sense historical consciousness plays a transcendental role in the preservation of cultural identity.

It must also be added that, among the factors that concern the integration of an identity, there are some that relate specifically to its operational and interactive character. Every cultural identity can reaffirm itself, and occasionally also become weakened, as a result of the images that outsiders form of it. When attacked, it may be strengthened by succeeding in its defense through its own values, criteria, and resources. On the other hand, possible confrontations and other forms of contact with societies of different cultures can be clear risks.

The deterioration of self-identity, and even more its total loss, bring with them an acute trauma. They promote the disintegration of the community and place it, in the last instance, in situations of alienation and of easy subjugation, where it is incapable of orienting itself sufficiently to act on its own behalf. In this way, while not implying a negation of the processes of change, possession of a sense of identity is an essential prerequisite for any group to exist and act in its own best interests. This in no way excludes, but rather renders fully operative, forms of interaction and participation or collaboration in the context of other, broader, social entities.

PROCESSES OF ACCULTURATION

Another concept, also basic to our theme, is one that refers to the coming together or contact between different cultural groups. These have been described as processes of acculturation,[3] which, in addition simply to implying contact between distinct cultures, refer to the reciprocal consequences derived from such interaction.

Processes of acculturation can take varied forms, both positive and negative. At times they take place in conditions of mutual respect between the groups that contribute, receive, or exchange cultural elements. But there are also contacts of a violent type, true clashes or confrontations between peoples of distinct cultures. In such cases, the consequences for the vanquished will be, above all, a step toward cultural disintegration, with the imposition of foreign elements and institutions and, at times, also the obligatory surrender of their human and natural resources to serve the victors.

It should also be kept in mind that the concept of acculturation has sometimes included processes of induced change, "induced acculturation," according to the terminology proposed by some researchers.[4] In such cases, the nation or group that initiates these processes has as an objective the introduction of what it considers to be desirable modifications upon the subjugated, culturally distinct, social entity.

However, induced acculturation, even with the best intentions, implies cultural imposition.

NEPANTLISM: "TO REMAIN IN THE MIDDLE"

The words of a Náhuatl Indian from the middle of the sixteenth century refer to the risks, so closely related to cultural identity, that can present themselves in attempts at inducing acculturation. A Dominican friar, Diego Durán, had reprimanded a native for his behavior, pointing out that it was also in discord with the ancient indigenous customs and morals. The wise old native responded: "Father, don't be afraid, for we are still '*nepantla*'"—in other words, "in the middle," or as he later added, "we are neutral."[5] The ancient institutions had been condemned and mortally wounded, while the ones the friars imposed were still strange and at times incomprehensible. Consequently, the Indians found themselves *nepantla,* "in between." The commitment to forcing change had wounded the very values and foundations of the indigenous world.

Cited below is another example that also strongly reflects, perhaps even more dramatically, the trauma of nepantlism. This text is part of a response given by native Mexican sages to the first twelve Franciscans, who held a dialogue with them on religious themes a few years after the Conquest. According to Fray Bernardino de Sahagún, to whom we owe the Náhuatl transcription of this text, the indigenous wisemen, after hearing the words condemning their ancient beliefs, expressed themselves in this way:

> We cannot be tranquil, and certainly we still do not believe, we do not accept as true that which you say, even though this might offend you. . . . It is enough already that we have lost, that it has been taken from us, that our ancient way of life has been impeded. If we remain in this place, we will only be made prisoners. . . .
>
> Allow us to die, allow us to perish, since our gods have already died.[6]

The violent attacks against the indigenous religion and traditions, the death of the gods, and the difficulty in accepting the new teachings as true had already affected the people deeply and had brought about, as a consequence, the appearance of nepantlism. The concept of nepantlism, "to remain in the middle," one of the greatest dangers of culture contact ruled by the desire to impose change, retains its full significance, applicable to any meaningful understanding of similar situations.

THE CONCEPT OF ECOSIS

There is yet another concept pertinent to framing our subject. It refers to the internal structuring of a group or nation endowed with its own cultural identity, as well as its forms of adaptation to the environment in which it lives and to the utilization of natural resources. To express such a concept I have proposed a term that shares the same root as the word *ecology*. The term is "ecosis," used already—on more than one occasion—by the historian Thucydides, who took the word to mean the settlement and mode of interaction with the surrounding area of a group of settlers who arrive at a determined place.[7]

Ecosis originally meant "the process of making or organizing a house." Broadening its meaning and using the concept of house as a metaphor, as did Thucydides, ecosis comes to mean the whole set of transformations that a human community makes for its own well-being, by acting upon the geographic area where it has settled in order to develop there. More precisely, by means of the term "ecosis" one seeks to underline the antecedents and consequences, as well as the forms of development, of the processes of contact between a human group and a particular natural context. Elements that appear common to all ecoses involve the purposeful actions of a group, such as seeking the advantageous exploitation of environmental resources and the establishment of a foundation that transforms the area into a home or place of residence.

The above does not imply the negation of or disregard for the fact that the surrounding environment mitigates and even, to a certain extent, determines these forms of action. But the idea of ecosis emphasizes that, in contrast to irrational animals that merely adapt to their habitat, human beings come to act consciously upon their surroundings in order to benefit from the environment's resources and to create within it what some philosophers have called "one's own place in the world." Thus it could be said that animals live in terms of their habitat, whereas human beings, with their transformative acts, can create a habitat for themselves in the course of their continual search for better modes of existence.

The first forms of ecosis took place in the millennia of the Paleolithic. With their attribute of culture, however primitive it may have been, humans already acted, with resolute plans and purposes, upon the natural surroundings in which they chose to live. Throughout history there have been numerous distinct forms of ecosis. The labors of diverse societies determined to take advantage of their surrounding resources have yielded both positive and negative outcomes. Thus, just as an ecosis can bring about the creation of a "habitat" considered well-suited to human needs, less successful types of actions will bring such consequences as the deterioration of the natural surroundings and the contamination of the environment—damage that is sometimes irreparable. In the future, new and unforeseeable ecoses may come about; worthy of special consideration are those related to the ambitious plans for conquering the universe of outer space.

In the dynamic realization of any ecosis, the community's own world view, system of values, and local institutions play a vital role. The dynamism inherent in a genuine ecosis implies processes of change not only in the surrounding natural environment and in technology and ways to exploit its resources, but also in the internal structures of the society. Since cultural identity is essentially linked to the sense of orientation that guides the behavior of the group, it becomes evident that all forms of ecoses are connected with it.

In our approach to the subject of contemporary endangered cultures, these concepts of cultural identity, acculturation, nepantlism, and ecosis will play an important role. They will allow a better understanding of the processes by which the threats of cultural disintegration are brought to bear. I will include a description, even when limited, of a number of different situations in which contemporary societies and even entire nations may find themselves: societies and nations whose value systems, languages, world views, internal structures, or, in a word, whose very cultural identities exist in a state of crisis or at risk of total disappearance.

THE CASE OF THE "CULTURES OF THE VANQUISHED"

A first type of situation is experienced by the descendants of peoples conquered in the past, whose cultural being somehow endures, embedded within the broader context of an independent national state. Among such groups—of which numerous examples with different variations could be cited—survive what I call "cultures of the vanquished."

A characteristic feature of this type of culture is the subjugation to permanent contact with more powerful hegemonic entities. Even when such processes of acculturation include some positive elements for the nucleus of the vanquished, the great majority translate into factors of disintegration. Frequently, there is a total loss of, or profound alteration in, cultural values, traditions, beliefs, and internal structures. At times, that which the conquerors seek to impose—religion, language, laws, and other institutions—turns out to be incomprehensible to the vanquished; and along with this, often doubt arises among the latter with respect to their own traditions and abilities. This leads them to experience many kinds of nepantlism, as they are in imminent danger of losing their own identity. The ecosis of the conquered ones is also radically modified; they find themselves compelled, for instance, to exploit with new systems and techniques what were once their own resources, this time for the benefit of their conquerors.

Even later, when changes have occurred within the broad national context in which certain "cultures of the vanquished" survived, these transformations were not necessarily positive for them. On occasion, powerful nationalist tendencies have provoked repeated attempts at incorporation, integration, and general absorption on the part of the majority society. These actions initiated and expanded "projects of induced acculturation" in order to change the way of life of those considered less developed and, implicitly, in a state of nepantlism. Even granting that in certain cases, the actions of national governments have brought about positive transformations, it is often the case that the cultures of the vanquished have continued to suffer new traumas.

In the face of this series of events, questions such as the following often emerge: Is it valid to think of such groups as possessing genuine cultures with a distinct sense of identity? Are they not more accurately thought of as marginalized entities, retaining only a deeply fractured structure? Rather than respond directly, I prefer to recall some specific cases, listing some of the best known: numerous indigenous communities of the central region of Mexico; peoples of diverse Mayan languages of Yucatán, Chiapas, and other regions of Central America; Chibcha groups in Colombia; the Aymara, and the large grouping of more than twelve million Quechua-speaking peoples, especially in Ecuador, Bolivia, and Peru. Is there no awareness, in any of these groups, of traditions, ancestral values, world views, languages, and, in sum, varied forms of a sense of identity? Is the continuous historical process that seems to compel them to enter the mixed cultural milieu of the countries in which they find themselves an inevitable destiny? Is their effective participation in the economic, social, and political life at the national level only to be achieved through the radical alteration of their ecosis and the disintegration of their cultural identity?[8]

Other responses are particularly significant among some of those I have described as the cultures of the vanquished, such as the Yaqui, Tarahumara, and others of the north of Mexico, as well as the Pueblo and Navajo Indians in the United States. These groups offer clear examples of cultures that, faced with aggression and induced acculturation, have developed at least partially effective defense mechanisms.

As examples we can recall the drama of the Navajo "Long Walk" and the Yaqui War, which resulted in the deportation and flight of many tribal members. In spite of such facts, as demonstrated particularly by Edward H. Spicer, the Navajo and the Yaqui, surviving even more subtle dangers of assimilation—whether from the mestizo Mexican culture or that of Anglo-America—have readapted their own forms of ecosis and cling determinedly to their cultural identities.[9] To what can we attribute such attitudes, characterized by a more aggressive pursuit of self-defense?

RELATED, BUT NOT HOMOGENEOUS, CULTURES

Let us now turn to other situations in very different contexts, such as the case of minority groups with traits that distinguish them from the national majority within a given country. Here there are no antecedents of conquest by the group that is in power or by any other group. Rather, there are threats, growing at times, derived from political interests that confuse national unity with cultural homogeneity.

The minority groups in question might, in fact, have great affinities with the rest of the population. Their standard of living may be similar and even at times superior to those of the other sectors of society. The differences are derived instead from certain specific characteristics, such as distinct origins, languages, or traditions and beliefs that are shared with the majority. Because of one or many of these factors, such groups maintain a sense of identity that is disturbing to those who insist on the idea of the culturally homogeneous state. To describe the situation of these minorities, I propose designating them as societies with a "culture related to, but not homogeneous with, the national culture."

The defensive attitudes of these groups often inspire arguments used by those who exercise national control in order to justify their own antagonistic actions. Odd forms of induced acculturation are then initiated, whose purpose is to impose the language and other characteristics of the majority as the sole alternatives while at the same time impeding internal and systematic forms of cultural transmission among those who compose the minority nuclei. In extreme cases, such measures can include other attacks, such as possible accusations of separatism and treason to the homeland. Groups like the Catalans, Basques, Bretons, Scots, Northern Irish, and numerous Jewish communities in many countries have experienced such situations, though to varying degrees. Expanding the concept, could it not include even larger groups like the French Canadians?

THE CASE OF THE CHICANOS

One such case can be seen in the situation of different minority groups in the United States. I concentrate here only on the Chicano; however, it is necessary to recognize that there are important distinctions between the various Mexican-origin groups living today in the United States. For instance, the so-called Hispano of the north of New Mexico differs greatly from the Mexican Americans of California, Texas, or even the city of Chicago.

Here we focus on the Chicano groups of California, who, as descendants of Mexican immigrants, have often suffered from the trauma of two cultures in conflict. On the one hand, there is the culture that, as their heritage, was maintained in varying degrees by their parents coming from Mexico; on the other, there is the culture inexorably imposed upon them by the society and the government of North America. Subjected to sometimes violent processes of acculturation, many young Chicanos experience marked forms of cultural nepantlism. Thus in Mexico they were called by the derogatory term of *pochos*, meaning "ridiculously Americanized Mexicans," while in the United States discrimination against them was almost the norm.

The Chicano situation has changed. In the past, in order to mitigate the discrimination against them, Mexican Americans often attempted to pass for persons of Spanish origin; recently, however, and perhaps sometimes with more fantasy than fact, their view has come to rest on their indigenous roots.[10] In an attempt to escape nepantlism, even while amid the dangers that continue to threaten its onset, the Chicanos' response and their aim are to define their identity as a base from which to orient their actions and their interactions, and thus to make their demands heard.

The real challenge for Chicanos is to learn how to take an active part in the socioeconomic life of the United States while preserving, if they wish, their unique ancestral values. Today the so-called Chicano movement seems to have lost some of its original impetus. Prominent Chicanos, including some of those working at the Chicano studies departments in several universities, express doubt about the future of their people's cultural identity.

What can be considered a new threat to such an identity is making itself felt at present. Official records and the mass media are imposing a previously unknown "ethnic" designation that ignores special Chicano identity. Mexican Americans, Puerto Ricans, Cubans, and Central and South Americans from all over are all referred to as "Hispanics." Thus, they are forced to declare their origin and ethnicity in many governmental records: Hispanic vis-à-vis others labeled "American," "Native American," "black," or "Asian." To some, this not only dilutes the Chicanos' identity, but it is offensive in that it obliges people to accept an ethnicity others have forged and imposed upon them. If one can assimilate all those bearing Spanish surnames and describe them as Hispanics, why not do the same with people with English, German, Italian, or Irish family names, pushing them to declare they are "Anglics," "Germanics," "Italianics," "Irishics," and so on? Is this merely a matter of words?

One fact remains: to exist as a Mexican American—a Chicano—is still far from easy. Some have adapted to the mainstream. Those who resist know firsthand that their endurance is besieged by a host of threats. Theirs is indeed an endangered culture.

OTHER SITUATIONS IN THE
SO-CALLED THIRD WORLD

There are many other types of endangered cultures. For instance, we may concentrate on groups who have only very recently become independent nations, like the new African countries, and some of Asia and Oceania. Among the numerous problems they face, one of the major ones is to define, safeguard, and maintain as functional their respective cultural identities.

The dangers that are perceived are very diverse. On the one hand, many vestiges survive of what Georges Balandier has called the "colonial situation," persisting through the influence, whether positive or negative, of the countries that formerly dominated.[11] On the other hand, sometimes subtle threats to the cultural cure—traditions, values, world vision, and a capacity for self-determination—are carried by mass communication, educational systems, missionary activities, the necessity of adopting new institutions and technologies, and the desire to rise above underdevelopment. And even if there may also be positive and necessary ingredients included in all of this, there remains the constant danger of damaging one's own identity with unassimilated elements merely superimposed from Western civilization. Once again, the plurality of native cultures in many of these new countries of Africa, Asia, and Oceania should be remembered. This in itself represents internal risks that derive from the facile confusion between national unity and cultural homogeneity.

Other countries of the so-called Third World are confronted with similar problems and risks. A few questions will deepen the awareness of their situation. Can nations such as those of Latin America achieve their desired economic development without finding themselves influenced by more powerful countries, whether capitalist or socialist?

Do such contacts not unleash, in ever-growing increments, new processes of acculturation, at times covertly induced? Are transformations in indigenous value systems, world views, and the traditional forms of ecosis necessarily to be feared, simply because foreign influences are detectable in the processes of change? Do underdeveloped nations, because of these intrusions, run the risk of seeing their identity fundamentally altered or of falling into new and dramatic forms of nepantlism? As can be seen, it is difficult to escape the dangers that everywhere threaten societies and nations whose existence without identity would soon take the form of alienation.

DANGERS IN THE CULTURES OF THE SUPERPOWER NATIONS

In all of the situations examined above, the factors of possible cultural disintegration have had something to do with the potential influences of more powerful states that attempt to exert hegemonic control. However, it would be overly simplistic to reduce the origin of all such threats to these causes. The best evidence of this is the undeniable fact that the cultures and civilizations of the superpowers themselves are currently in danger.

The United States, the Soviet Union, Japan, and the principal European states, over and above all of their cultural differences—including those of a social and political nature—are now facing threats that were unknown until very recently. Unrestrained technological development, along with constantly changing forms of ecoses, have already provoked imminent danger at times—such as the problems of the deterioration of the environment, pollution, and the foreseeable exhaustion of many finite resources. Also worthy of consideration are the threats presented by the international antagonisms, including the possibility of nuclear war. In addition are phenomena like the current unsettled state of the world economy, the crises of both an ideological and a religious character, student conflicts, and, in general, the growing social instability at the family level. Nor should we forget the situation prevalent in certain countries where individual liberties, such as those of free expression, are extremely limited, or where discriminatory policies are exercised against minorities. No matter what kind of oppression, whether with respect to individuals, minorities, certain social sectors, or other nations—will it not eventually engender a desire for revenge and a danger of mutual destruction?

When we contemplate these situations in the very bosom of nations with dominant cultures, which preach the advantages of the consumer society with its spectacular developments as a remedy for other groups and countries of the Third World, it no longer seems naïve to entertain new types of doubts and fears. However, everything said here does not necessarily imply that our own age, any more than those of the past, will be a mere stage for dark realities, a forewarning of even graver threats. A historical perspective demonstrates that in past centuries and millennia, the human race experienced and survived many instances of endangered cultures. Perhaps the principal differences are that today, more than ever, the forces and processes of change or exchange have accelerated in unrestrainable ways, and that information systems keep us immediately informed about whatever happens in any nation or corner of the world.

Within this context—rich in uncertainty but also in experiences and new methods for research—we have to raise once again the question of responsibility in terms of currently endangered cultures. Anthropologists, sociologists, philosophers, historians, and, in essence, scholars of culture, do they not have an obligation to express their thoughts about the realities that concern the destiny of many peoples, and perhaps of all of humanity? Is professional knowledge of no utility when it comes to pointing out the significance of the deprivation of identity, and of the possible risk of death for not only one culture or another, but for civilization itself in its multiple forms—including, of course, that of the Western world?

It would be ingenuous on my part to attempt to respond here to the problems I have outlined; instead, I will merely think out loud. Is it not true that among the greatest risks that a culture can run is the loss of its universe of symbols, and of all that bears meaning in relation to the culture's very existence and its sense of identity? Such alienation becomes even more tragic when the only compensation offered is the attractions of a consumer society, sex transformed into a commodity, economic ambitions, and the desire for ostentation and power.

A REFLECTION, NOT A CONCLUSION

Historians and anthropologists, who study their own and others' universes of culture, must perceive the increasingly urgent need of endangered societies to deepen from within their knowledge of themselves. In this way they might succeed in surpassing the threats of nepantlism, by recovering their own values, symbols, and meanings. They might even be able to enrich their awareness of their own identity, opposing it to images that others have forged. The opinions of others, elaborated from outside, will then be the object of a more critical appraisal and only with difficulty will they serve as a vehicle for subtle types of induced acculturation.

The discovery of the ways by which a cultural identity can be strengthened is vital in order to face dangers and make room for changes and interactions that truly benefit one's own being. The salvaging of values, symbols, and meanings, with an awareness of cultural self-determination will, in turn, permit participation and collaboration within broader contexts, not in a forced manner, but rather through the pursuit of common goals.

It is the responsibility of those whose profession is to study culture, including cultural dangers and perspectives, to seek new responses. Certainly there are many who, for an extended period, have harbored similar preoccupations. For all of us to bring them to consciousness once again, to transform them into topics for research, will force us to reassess more deeply the capacities of human beings and of human societies, as well as to reappraise the destiny of our only unmistakable creation: the universe of culture.

2.
Transformation without Loss of Identity: The Acculturation of Xólotl's Chichimecs (A.D. 1300–1400)

History offers almost unlimited terrain in which to study contact and reciprocal influences among peoples of different cultures. The aim here is to concentrate on one particularly interesting case, the oldest fully documented example of a process of acculturation beyond the borders of the Old World civilizations. Indigenous codices and texts make it possible to study what took place in the central region of pre-Hispanic Mexico when, in the thirteenth century A.D., groups of nomadic Chichimecs, "barbarians" from the north, came into contact with sedentary peoples of Toltec origin, the bearers of a high culture.

The appeal of studying the acculturation of the Chichimecs lies in the fact that, despite changes and subsequent transformations, the cultural identities of the groups involved endured. The contact between the Chichimecs and the already urbanized descendants of the Toltecs typifies, within the context of the New World, a form of conflict and exchange for which numerous examples can be cited, especially from the history of Asia and Europe. These types of culture conflicts have been frequently described as barbarian invasions or penetrations into the civilized world. Thus, to better frame our understanding of this particular occurrence, a few reflections on cases that have developed

in a parallel manner in other times and parts of the world
are in order.

CONTACTS BETWEEN "BARBARIANS"
AND CIVILIZED PEOPLES

The first high cultures known to history arose, like islands
with undefined margins, within the world of the so-called
barbarians. Over the millennia, the nuclei of high culture
slowly diffused their creations. On occasion they expanded
their borders, while at other times they entered into periods
of decay. Nonetheless, unfailingly, the foci of high culture,
the first urban centers, were encircled and at times violently
attacked by nomadic or seminomadic peoples, peoples often
described as the "fierce ones of the bow and arrow." In this
sense it can be established that, for better or for worse, the
barbarians have formed the shadow and the background of
the civilized.

There were times when the barbarians were a positive
force, as new forms of organization and development were
also given birth through their clash with civilized peoples.
By the same token, occasionally, misfortune and true catas-
trophe resulted when the consequences of the encounter
were the destruction of all that had been developed at great
pains. Thus, recalling two well-known cases, while the Hyk-
sos were the scourge for Egypt, in contrast, the invading
Semites of Mesopotamia absorbed and enriched the culture
of the Sumerians.

The history of the Old World offers countless such examples. During the second millennium B.C. the Mediterranean barbarians are the ones called the "peoples of the
sea," many of whom destroy, while many others assimilate
and merge with sedentary peoples. The ancient and remote
civilization of the Indus Valley, with great centers like Mo-
henjo Daro and Harappa, will succumb, in turn, when the
way is opened for the Aryans who will later give birth to
new forms of culture. The threat of the barbarians, like a
shadow over the civilized, persists over the centuries. The
Mediterranean world becomes the new stage for violent

invasions. The best known of these and the ones that left the deepest roots are the work of the Germanic peoples. Still later, during the thirteenth century, Mongolian hordes will devastate the east of Europe and, almost simultaneously, crossing over the Great Wall, make themselves lords of China.

Anyone conscious of the long series of culture clashes and contacts, involving destruction but also assimilation and new forms of diffusion, is forced to recognize that the study of the reality of the barbarians in relation to the civilized is not of secondary importance, but rather an essential part of the history of culture. Furthermore, anyone who studies the subject, however superficially, will discover that the sequence of these clashes is no other than the impressive succession of the varied processes of acculturation that have, in the end, made possible the birth of a new form of civilization, already incipiently global at the beginning of the modern era. Thus, the fully documented study of the "barbarian versus the civilized" binary constitutes a history lesson that is not only interesting but fundamental to understanding the sequence of all cultural development.

From this perspective let us turn to the study of the acculturation of the Chichimecs, or the "barbarians" of Mesoamerica. Mexico, from pre-Hispanic times to the present, has been the scene of countless processes of acculturation and *mestizaje*. Of all of these, the one of highest contrast, without a doubt, is the one that occurred later between the indigenous and Hispanic worlds, persisting in manifold ways up to the present. The sources of information for its study, besides the documents, are as great and omnipresent as the reality of contemporary Mexico. This is not the case for what concerns the specific forms of cultural diffusion and contact in the pre-Hispanic past.

The majority of these processes are very remote and only knowable in a fragmentary and hypothetical way. Nonetheless, as will be seen, this is not entirely true. While a considerable obscurity remains with respect to the most ancient pre-Hispanic processes of acculturation, thanks to archaeological research, some information is already known about them. Thus, for example, the diffusion of elements from the mother culture of Mesoamerica, the Olmecs, who flourished on the Gulf coasts since the second millennium before Christ, permits us to trace contacts with other groups from the Central Plateau, the Mayan area, the region of Oaxaca, and the area of the Pacific. In the same way, the unearthing of Teotihuacan ceramics and, above all, the discovery of elements characteristic of Teotihuacan art in other Mesoamerican archaeological zones make evident the influence exercised by the founders of the City of the Gods over peoples of remote regions.

But among all the processes of cultural transformation that took place in ancient Mexico, it is the acculturation of the Chichimecs of Xólotl that can be studied most adequately, thanks not only to archaeological discoveries but also to the codices and texts of the indigenous tradition. It is in the cultural context of what occurred to these Chichimecs that the two principal types of indigenous communities present on this continent are represented: those of the hunters and gatherers with very limited or no agriculture, simple diet, clothing, and housing, and with primitive forms of social organization; and those who, in obvious contrast, possessed elements and institutions of a high culture.

When these two ways of life approach one another there occurs, within the Mesoamerican context, something similar to the Old World, as happened in cases like those of the Germans in Europe or the Mongols in China. The barbarians, threatening total ruin in Europe, eventually assimilate to the cultural heritage of the Mediterranean; in China, the Mongols, who ravage and suppress a dynasty, end up making the institutions of a millennial people their own; in Mexico, the Chichimecs, far from destroying what is already in decline, become "Toltecized," that is, civilized, and give rise to the final splendor of the pre-Hispanic epoch.

Germans, Mongols, and Chichimecs typify what can happen when nomads invade the towns and cities where a high culture thrives. From this point of view, the processes of

Toltec-Chichimec acculturation, which began a few centuries before the Conquest, can be seen as the only case of a similar, fully documented clash of cultures outside the parameters of the Old World civilizations. Thus it derives its significance within the broader context of global history.

From a different perspective, looking strictly at the historical development of the American nations, the study of this process has another special meaning. The tenacious resistance to change that numerous indigenous groups continue to demonstrate is spoken of frequently. It would be extremely interesting to compare the diverse forms of acculturation imposed upon the Indians by the conquerors, *encomenderos*, friars, colonists, and even modern independent states, with those in the past that emerged between nomads and sedentary peoples already in possession of a developed socioeconomic and political organization.

This is the double significance of studying the process of Chichimec acculturation. The relative abundance of sources on this historical event permits an analysis of its most outstanding features.

THE SOURCES

Aside from the works of Spanish chroniclers from the sixteenth and the beginning of the seventeenth centuries, among them Motolinía, Durán, Sahagún, and Torquemada, and in addition to the relatively limited archaeological findings in this case, several indigenous documents exist that deal directly with this subject.

There are four principal codices. The most extensive, and the most important, is the one known as *Codex Xólotl*, whose original is preserved in the National Library of Paris. In ten pages, painted on *amate* paper, this manuscript, which seems to be a copy of an older one, offers abundant references to the arrival of groups commanded by the famous Xólotl, as well as their various raids on and contacts with the survivors of Toltec-origin culture in the Valley of Mexico. This codex, which was studied by indigenous historians like Ixtlilxóchitl, is also the documentary source for the study of two centuries of history, until the consolidation of the new states and cities—in particular, Tezcoco, which already enjoyed notable prosperity by the time of Nezahualcóyotl (1402–1472).[1]

The other three codices, also painted in the mid-sixteenth century, though at least in part copies of ancient manuscripts, are those named the *Maps*, or *Codices Tlotzin, Quinatzin*, and *Tepechpan*. All are found in the same National Library of Paris. The first of these, the *Tlotzin* text, is painted on a piece of leather one meter and twenty-seven centimeters long by thirty-five and a half centimeters in width. In it are described, on large bands at the top, the rustic life of the Chichimecs and the types of cultural contact they initiated with civilized peoples; below, some of the results are pictured, among them the slow adaptation to agriculture, specifically mentioning the existence of urban centers like Culhuacán and Azcapotzalco. As the name of this codex indicates, it gives preferential treatment to the description of the events that occurred during the days of Prince Tlotzin, grandson of the great chief Xólotl. Though there are editions of this codex with commentaries, the manuscript remains in need of a new study where other sources and more recent discoveries are taken into account.[2]

The *Codex Quinatzin* can be considered to be the continuation of the preceding manuscript. Painted on a piece of indigenous paper, seventy-seven by forty-four centimeters, in its upper part the description of the life of the nomads is repeated: they are depicted as hunters of birds, snakes, rabbits, and deer, who take shelter in caves, dress in animal hides, and always carry their bows and arrows with them. In this case, the central figure of the codex is Quinatzin, son of Tlotzin, great-grandson of Xólotl. Also, contacts with peoples of a more advanced culture are alluded to several times; it notes the arrival of two groups of peoples coming from the south, the Tlailotlaque and the Chimalpanecas, possessors of more highly developed characteristics and institutions, who would enrich the cultural life of Tezcoco. In contrast to the descriptions in the upper half, what appears below is a consequence of the process of acculturation for almost two centuries: the court of Tezcoco, with its principal characters and organizational units. Reproductions of this codex are included in the same works cited for the preceding manuscript.[3]

The last of the four codices is the one named *Map of Tepechpan*, which, though it also deals with the arrival and acculturation of the Chichimecs, refers more particularly to the history of the province of its name, which would later become a tributary of Tezcoco. While less important to the issue at hand because of its limited focus, this extensive document, painted on a strip of indigenous paper six meters and twenty-five centimeters long by twenty-five in width, should not be overlooked.[4]

Mention is made here of only the most important of the texts written with the Latin alphabet after the Spanish Conquest, in Náhuatl and Spanish by both indigenous and mestizo authors. Occupying a special place among them are the various relations and the *Historia Chichimeca* of Fernando de Alva Ixtlilxóchitl. Though it is beyond doubt that this descendant of Tezcocan nobility frequently exaggerates when speaking of his ancestors, it is nonetheless the case that his work is a rich mine of information about the processes that make up the object of this study. As sources, Ixtlilxóchitl used the codices mentioned above as well as other documents and traditions currently lost.[5]

The early indigenous informants of Fray Bernardino de Sahagún should also be acknowledged, for in what is known as the *Codex Matritense* they provide references in Náhuatl about the Chichimecs' way of life and their encounter with the civilized.[6] There are various other indigenous works on this subject, though they deal not so much with Xólotl's Chichimecs as with other related groups; among them are the *Relaciones* and the *Memorial breve de Culhuacán* written by the chronicler Chimalpahin, as well as two compilations by anonymous authors, known under the titles *Anales de Cuauhtitlán* and *Historia Tolteca-Chichimeca*. It is evident through these chronicles that the process that evolved in the case of Xólotl's Chichimecs, while it remains the best known, was not unique. Chimalpahin writes of a similar sequence of events that takes place among the Chichimecs who settled in the region of Chalco-Amaquemecan. In addition, the *Anales de Cuauhtitlán* describe what occurs around the province of this name and in other neighboring regions. The *Historia Tolteca-Chichimeca*, whose content is clear from its title, includes information about the acculturation of those who founded Cuauhtinchan and Totomihuacan in what is today the Puebla-Tlaxcaltecan area.

Thus the study of the acculturation of the Chichimec groups, in particular those guided by Xólotl, can be carried out not as conjecture but as a fully documented example.

THE ABANDONMENT OF TULA AND THE ARRIVAL OF THE CHICHIMECS

References to the ruin of Tula are numerous. Beyond the legendary tales there is a well-established historical fact: the ancient metropolis of the wise priest Quetzalcóatl was already in decline toward the end of the eleventh century A.D. Not long afterward, during the following century, its abandonment was to take place. Some of the heirs to its culture journeyed to distant regions. The Mayan sources from Yucatán, as well as the Quiché and Cakchiquel of Guatemala, speak of the appearance of Toltec groups in these areas. Archaeological research demonstrates that some established themselves in the lowlands of Michoacán and Guerrero. Some remained nearby, in Cholula. Still others settled in places already "Toltecized" long ago, such as Culhuacán to the south of the Valley of Mexico, and in other areas of the same region, at times in small groups and even occasionally—according to Ixtlilxóchitl—reduced to mere families hiding in fear of the Chichimec invasion.

Recalling the grandeur of the Toltec culture, an eloquent text taken from the *Codex Matritense* offers, by way of

a synthesis, some of what later peoples thought about that
ancient way of life:

> The Toltecs were wise,
> it was said that they were artists of featherwork,
> of the art of affixing them . . .
> This was their inheritance
> thanks to which the insignias were granted.
> They made them beautifully,
> truly they put in them their deified heart,
> what they did was a marvel,
> precious, worthy of esteem.
> The Toltecs were very wise,
> they conversed with their own heart,
> they gave origin to the counting of the year,
> to the counting of the days and of the destinies . . .
> The Toltecs were wise,
> they knew of the stars
> that are in the heavens;
> they gave them their names;
> they knew their influence.
> They knew well how the sky moves,
> how it turns,
> this they saw in the stars . . .
> They were careful of the divine things,
> they had only one god,
> they took him for their sole god,
> they invoked him,
> they petitioned him,
> his name was Quetzalcóatl. . . .
> There were many houses in Tula,
> the Toltecs buried many things there.
> But that is not all that is seen there
> as traces of the Toltecs;
> also their pyramids, their small mounds,
> there where it is called Tula-Xicocotitlan.
> The remains of earthenware pots can be seen
>   everywhere,

those of their bowls, their figures,
of their dolls, of their little figures,
of their bracelets;
everywhere their vestiges remain;
truly the Toltecs lived together there.[7]

In open contrast to the way of life of those who owned
houses and palaces, wise ones who knew the reckoning of
the years and the days, followers of the great priest Quetzalcóatl, there is also a description of the Chichimecs' way of
life in the codices cited, as well as in the texts in the Náhuatl
language:

In the year 5-Reed
the Chichimecs drew near:
they lived as archers [hunters],
they had no houses,
they had no land,
their clothing was not of sewn cloaks,
only animal skins made up their dress,
and they also made them with straw.
Their children were cared for only in small nets,
in *huacales* [wooden frames].
They ate big prickly pears,
big cacti, wild maize,
sour prickly pears.
They toiled much
with all this.[8]

The Toltecs were a civilized people; the Chichimecs lived
as roving hunters, with no more housing than the caves.
As the text says, "they had no houses, they had no land."
The insignia and dress of the Toltecs were famous; the
Chichimecs covered themselves simply with animal pelts and
leaves. The former cultivated the land, possessed an abundance of corn, and had precious cotton brought up from
the south; the latter ate only the fruits they collected, or the
meat of the animals they were able to kill. The Toltecs spoke
the Náhuatl language, which would come to be the lingua

franca of Mesoamerica; most of the nomadic hunters spoke languages like Pame, Mazahua, and at times also Otomí. Thus they were called Popoloca, the pre-Hispanic equivalent of barbarians.

The image of the Chichimec as described in the texts is also given in picture form, abundantly detailed, in the *Xólotl, Tlotzin, Quinatzin* and *Tepechpan* codices, as well as the paintings included in the *Historia Tolteca-Chichimeca*. And it is not a mere coincidence—but rather a result of a parallel cultural phenomenon—that this whole series of descriptions presents extraordinary similarities to the vision held by other ancient historians of the ways of life of the barbarians in their midst. Thus, for instance, the Roman historian Tacitus described the life of the Germans in the following way:

> They do nothing in public or private
> without carrying their weapons in their hands. . . .
> When they are not making war,
> they dedicate themselves to hunting
> and even more to idleness. . . .
> It is well-known that none of the German tribes
> live in cities
> and that they will not even tolerate having their
>   houses together
> among themselves.
> They live separately and dispersed,
> according to what attracts each one
> a source of water, a meadow or some woods. . . .
> They do not know how to use either stone or tiles;
> the wood they use for everything is coarse,
> lacking in beauty and attractiveness.
> They tend to open subterranean caves
> and place big mounds of mud on the roofs.
> There they have their refuge in the winter
> and there they store the fruits they gather. . . .
> They cover themselves with the pelts of ferocious
>   beasts . . .

the women have clothing similar to that of the men,
although they also frequently wear ones of cotton
 cloth. . . .
The upper part of their dress has no sleeves;
they leave their arms and shoulders uncovered,
as well as a good deal of their chests.[9]

Although there is a nuanced distinction, the image of the
different barbarians almost inevitably emerges similarly in
the eyes of those who, by virtue of living in cities, are called
civilized. The codices and texts go on to speak of what happened when the barbarians of Mesoamerica became aware
of the abandonment of Tula. The underlying causes of its
desertion are not clear. The texts mention religious antagonisms, and it is said that sorcerers coming from the outside
attempted to impose new rites and ceremonies. There were
struggles, deaths, and epidemics. The pressure that was exercised by the hordes of Chichimecs to the north probably
also played an important role. The indigenous chroniclers,
already writing within the context of a new culture that
resulted precisely from the process they are attempting to
reconstruct, refer straightforwardly to the attitude of the
Chichimecs in terms such as these:

> The Toltecs had been destroyed and the land was de-
> populated, when the great Chichimec Xólotl came to
> populate it, having news of its destruction from his ex-
> plorers. . . . And having entered the boundaries and
> land of the Toltecs until arriving at the city of Tolan,
> the imperial center, he found very great ruins aban-
> doned and without people, for which reason he did not
> want to settle in Tolan, but rather he proceeded with
> his people, always sending explorers ahead, to see if
> they could find some of the people who had escaped
> the destruction and calamity of this nation, and which
> were the best places and sites to inhabit and populate.[10]

The first plate of *Codex Xólotl* graphically illustrates
what Ixtlilxóchitl describes. In it the Chichimec leader is

Above: A Chichimec hunter (*Codex Quinatzin*).
Below: Xólotl looks down from a hill at a Toltec family that has
remained in Chapultepec (*Codex Xólotl*).

depicted, accompanied by his son Nopaltzin, and both are
contemplating the Valley of Mexico from a mountain sum-
mit, in search of lands in which to settle. Nopaltzin and
several other captains carry out the treks and explorations
mentioned by Ixtlilxóchitl, as indicated by the tracks of
their footsteps leading to the various regions of the valley.
The Chichimec chief, after staying some time in the place
that was called Xóloc in his honor, established himself per-
manently in Tenayuca Oztopolco, which the chroniclers
say was a site of "many caves and caverns."

In Tenayuca, where many different buildings already
stood—among them a famous pyramid that, in later years,
would have new superimposed structures added—was organized in what Ixtlilxóchitl solemnly calls "the court of the
Chichimecs." From this place the prince Nopaltzin and, like
him, different leaders of varied Chichimec origins, approach
other spots like Teotihuacán, Culhuacán, and Cholula with
amazed eyes. In these last two, the ancient ways of life endured; such traditions are represented in *Codex Xólotl* by the
figures of artisans shown to be working metals or sculpting
stone in the region of Cholula. There are many other contacts that, even if casual, are yet more direct. The Chichimecs speak in signs with the few people of Toltec origin who
have remained dispersed outside of the great urban enclosures. Little by little Xólotl's people, and other groups who
by this time have also broken into the area, develop an image
of the resources of the lands they desire to conquer. Their
initial forms of contact will be followed by others, more permanent and definitive, as a consequence of their discovery
that the region was a suitable area to enjoy life.

THE SETTLEMENT OF THE NOMADS

The lake zone was certainly attractive. Besides the possibilities for fishing, the nearby mountains offered—more than
the plains to the north—an abundance of game. The
Chichimecs were less interested, for the moment, in the
vestiges of cultivation and what remained of the ancient
chinampas, or artificial farmlands and irrigation systems, all

of which are represented in *Codex Xólotl.* The fish and game, water and woods were sufficient reasons for appropriating a land that had no master nor defender. The only resistance was to arise from the people of Culhuacán, but even they would cede after the first hostile approaches were transformed into more peaceful contacts and even, at times, into family ties.

By the end of the thirteenth century, whether due to the intervention of Xólotl, as Ixtlilxóchitl repeatedly insists, or independently of him, several Chichimec groups had already settled in different places: the Tecpanecas in the northwest, in Azcapotzalco; to the north, in Xaltocan, the Otomazahuas; and to the east, in Coatlichan, the Acolhuas. Nopaltzin, the successor to Xólotl, will remain in Tenayuca after marrying a Toltec Culhuacán princess by the name of Atotoztli. The ancient provinces of the south, those in which Toltec elements and institutions survived, no doubt looked fearfully upon the settlement of their new Chichimec neighbors. Many decades passed during which the mere fact that the ancient nomads contemplated the vestiges left by a superior culture, constituted a lesson of immeasurable worth.

The birth of Tlotzin, grandson of Xólotl and the first mestizo Chichimec leader—of Toltec ancestry through his maternal line—brought with it new incentives that would lead the barbarians to change their way of life. Tlotzin, following the example of some chiefs who preceded him, founded a chiefdom that emerged from the region dominated by the Acolhuas of Coatlichan. Just as Tenayuca originally was known by the name of Oztopolco, "in the place of many caves," so the appellation of the site chosen by Tlotzin reflects the ancestral affection the Chichimecs felt for caverns and caves. It was named Tlatzallan-Tlallanóztoc, "in the lands and in the caves that are next to it." The Chichimecs—who were said to be natives of Chicomóztoc, "the place of the seven caves"—not only continued to prefer these shelters for their dwellings, but they entertained themselves by keeping the idea of caves in their place-names. The Náhuatl name of many of the places inhabited by the Chichimecs is proof of this: Tenayuca was also Oztopolco, the dominion of Tlotzin was called Tla-llanóztoc, there was also a Tepetlaóztoc, "in the caves of the mountains," and finally in the surroundings of Tezcoco could be found Oztotícpac, "over the caves," and Tzi-nacanóztoc, "in the caves of the bats." Though it is not known with certainty what language was spoken by Xólotl's Chichimecs, it can be assumed that it was not the Náhuatl of the ancient settlers of the region. Pame, Otomí, and Mazahua would have to be included among the many Chichimec languages, generically called Popolocas, or "barbarous." It is quite likely that the place-names origi-nally expressed in these languages were later translated into the lingua franca of the Nahuas, as would be the case for all of the *óztoc*[s], or "places of caves."

With Tlotzin, the mestizo Chichimec-Toltec prince, al-ready established in Tlatzallan-Tlallanóztoc at the begin-ning of the fourteenth century, they now enter the era in which, according to the testimony of the codices and texts, the number of changes from culture contact increased. More than half a century had passed since the arrival of the Chichimecs in the Valley of Mexico, and what was origi-nally a precarious settlement began to acquire very differ-ent features, thanks to the ever-expanding processes of acculturation.

ASSIMILATION OF
TOLTEC-ORIGIN INSTITUTIONS

A main source for the study of what took place in the times of Tlotzin is, as mentioned above, the Tezcocan codex that bears his name. In it is the account in Náhuatl and the his-torical representation of an event that can be advanced as a symbol of what occurred at the time. On one of Tlotzin's treks through the region of Coatlinchan, while giving rein to his love of hunting, a meeting takes place that was to change his life. The person who crosses his path is none other than a man from Chalco, of Toltec stock, who will spontaneously convert himself into Tlotzin's teacher and guide. The Náhuatl text included in the codex states:

Tlotzin had gone there to Coatlinchan, to go hunting. There a Chalca by the name of Tecpoyo Achcauhtli approached him. He seemed frightened when he saw Tlotzin with his bow and arrow. Tecpoyo Achcauhtli then said to Tlotzin: "Oh, my son, let me live by your side!"

Tlotzin did not understand his language because he is a Chichimec. Nonetheless, from this moment the Chalca accompanied Tlotzin during his hunting expeditions. Tecpoyo Achcauhtli carried upon his back the deer, rabbits, snakes, and birds, the other hunted.

Then for the first time Tecpoyo Achcauhtli began to roast what Tlotzin had hunted. For the first time he gave Tlotzin cooked foods to eat, because before this Tlotzin ate what he had hunted raw.

Tecpoyo Achcauhtli lived alongside Tlotzin for a long time. On one occasion he told him, he asked his permission: "Oh, my son! Let me go tell your servants, the Chalcas, the Cuitlatecas; let me go tell them how I have come to see you and how I have lived at your side."

By then Tlotzin understood a little of the language of the Chalca. He sent rabbits and snakes in a satchel with him.

But Tecpoyo Achcauhtli returned to the side of Tlotzin. He told him: "Oh, my son, come visit the Chalcas who are your servants!"

Tlotzin then accompanied him. Tecpoyo Achcauhtli took the lead. He carried upon his back the deer and the rabbits that Tlotzin shot, as he had the first time. When Tlotzin arrived, the Chalcas came out to receive him. They made him sit down; they brought him presents. They gave him tamales and *atole* [filled steamed maize cakes and maize gruel]. Tlotzin did not eat the tamales,

he only drank the *atole*. Then Tecpoyo Achcauhtli spoke
to the Chalcas, he said to them: "Has not Toltzin already come to be like a prince, a son?"

Right away the Chalcas began to make ceremonies;
thus they venerated their gods. Tlotzin, since he was
Chichimec, did not know about the ceremonies of the
Chalcas in honor of their gods. Because the Chichimecs
only occupy themselves with seeking deer and rabbits,
which they immediately eat. They only have the sun for
a god, which they call father. Thus they venerate the
sun, they cut the heads off the snakes, the birds. They
make holes in the ground, they sprinkle the grass with
blood. They also have the earth for a goddess, they call
her their mother.[11]

The same codex that includes this text offers a pictorial
description of the story. It shows the noble personage
of Tecpoyo Achcauhtli, who has taken as his own the role of
educator and missionary to the Chichimecs. To him is owed
the initiation of this new form of friendly contact, which
made possible the changes desired by those who found
themselves forced into having the nomads for their neighbors. Thanks to Tecpoyo Achcauhtli, Tlotzin began to learn
the Náhuatl language, and he also tasted dishes like *atole*
and tamales, classic foods of the civilized peoples of the
Mesoamerican world. Beyond this, in the company of
the Chalcas he had the opportunity to ponder the forms of
worship of an ancient organized religion. Finally, his encounter would lead him to repeat the actions of his father,
since, according to Ixtlilxóchitl, he also chose a woman of
Toltec lineage for his wife: Pachxochitzin (Little Hay
Flower), "daughter of Cuauhtlápal, one of the lords from
the province of Chalco."[12]

It is not at all strange that one who was already so tightly
linked to sedentary peoples would feel an inclination to introduce into his own dominion manners and customs formerly unknown to the Chichimecs. Ixtlilxóchitl reports
what then took place:

Above: Tecpoyo Achcauhtli teaches Tlotzin and his wife how to roast meat (*Codex Tlotzin*).
Below: Corn being sown in holes made by moles (*Codex Tlotzin*).

One of the things in which he [Tlotzin] took most
care was in the cultivation of the land. . . . With the
communication that he had there with the Chalcas and
Toltecs, given that his mother was of Toltec heritage,
he noticed how necessary corn and the other seeds and
vegetables were for the sustenance of human life. And
he learned especially from Tecpoyo Achcauhtli, who
had his home and family at the rock of Xico. He had
been his tutor and teacher, and among the things that
he had taught him was the way to cultivate the land.
. . . And although many of the Chichimecs thought it
was a very convenient thing and began to put it to work,
others who remained in the harshness of their past went
to the mountains of Metztitlan and Totépec and to
other more remote parts.[13]

Corroborating the words of Ixtlilxóchitl concerning
the introduction of agriculture in Tlotzin's dominions, in
the codex of the same name there is a graphic representation of what seems to be the Chichimecs' first attempt at
cultivation. In it is depicted a field of corn that grows precisely from holes made by sticks. The Chichimec people,
who preferred to dedicate themselves to hunting and fishing, developed the idea of leaving the grains of corn in the
holes left by rodents. They thought that they would save
energy this way, because even if the vermin ate the greater
part of the grain, some would still prosper. Tlotzin died
around 1318, according to our sources, and although he
had put great effort into changing the life of his people, he
certainly did not accomplish the full realization of his desire. This task was reserved for his son Quinatzin, and,
more precisely, his grandson Techotlala.

With Prince Quinatzin the hegemony of the region
passed from Coatlinchan, where the Acolhua Chichimecs
had settled, to a new center, Tezcoco—the future metropolis where the process of acculturation would culminate and
where, in later years, the Toltec inheritance would once
again flower. Proclaiming the determined attitude of

Tlotzin's son, Ixtlilxóchitl tells us: "If Tlotzin took particular care that the land be cultivated, Quinatzin was more favored in the time of his empire, compelling the Chichimecs not only in that regard [cultivation], but also that they populate and build cities and places, pulling them out of their rustic and wild lifestyle, following the order and style of the Toltecs."[14]

But even so, the fulfillment of what Quinatzin proposed was not easily attained. This is attested to by some of the schemes of which he availed himself, including the circumstances that were finally favorable to him. Information on this is given by Ixtlilxóchitl in *Codex Xólotl* and also, to an extent, in the Tezcocan codex known as *Quinatzin* in honor of this prince. The first of the tricks Quinatzin employed to call the Chichimecs' attention to the importance of agriculture was the following:

> He made three big fenced-in areas—writes Ixtlilxóchitl—one below Huexotla, toward the lagoon, and another in the city of Tezcoco that had begun to be established. These two were for sowing corn and other seeds used by the Aculhuas and Toltecs. And the other fence in the town of Tepetlaóztoc was for deer, rabbits, and hares; and he gave the charge of its care to two Chichimec leaders, one of whom was called Ocótoch and the other Coácuech, and though they were pleased with the one fenced-in area, the other two of the sown land, as something they had never been accustomed to, was very hard on them.[15]

The idea of setting up enclosures as hunting preserves, put into practice since the times of Nopaltzin, was now applied to the area of agriculture. The purpose was to persuade the Chichimecs that, if hunting were attractive and the preserves had been made to make hunting easier, the cultivation of plants in sown land was at least equally important, since it liberated them from the punishing labor of gathering poor fruits and greens—putting better foods like corn, beans, chile, and squash within their reach.

Enclosed gardens like these spoken of by Ixtlilxóchitl are also represented in the *Xólotl* and *Quinatzin* codices. The experiment gave the desired results in the long run, though not without first having to overcome resistance and even violent rebellions. In the case of the fenced-in areas, the chiefs who were responsible for them—giving vent to their anger—initiated a revolt that brought with it the flight of groups that, before working the land, opted for returning to the northern plains, where they could maintain their old way of life.

But if the discontented withdrew from the setting in which the processes of acculturation were increasingly more intense, there was also, on the other hand, the happy circumstance of the arrival of two groups of culture-bearing peoples, whom Quinatzin received with his blessing. According to the chronicler Ixtlilxóchitl and the codices, around 1327 those known as Tlailotlaques and Chimalpanecas—among whom, it is said, were many craftspeople and wisemen—obtained permission from Quinatzin to settle alongside the Tezcocans.

> They came from the Mixtec provinces [writes the chronicler], two nations called Tlailotlaques and Chimalpanecas, also of Toltec lineage. The Tlailotlaques . . . were accomplished in the art of painting and writing histories, more so than in the other arts; they brought Tezcatlipoca for their principal idol. The Chimalpanecas brought as their captains and leaders two lords named Xiloquetzin and Tlacatotzin . . . Quinatzin married them to his granddaughters. . . And having chosen among the best people that they were bringing and more to the purpose, he had them settle within the city of Tezcoco; the rest he gave and divided up among other cities and towns by neighborhoods, as even today their descendants remain with the last names of Tlailotlacan and Chimalpan, although before these two nations had been in the province of Chalco for a long time.[16]

Above: Artisans of Toltec origin working gold and precious stones (*Codex Xólotl*).
Below: Quinatzin welcomes the Tlailotlaques and Chimalpanecas (*Codex Quinatzin*).

The new immigrants not only filled the gap left by the groups of Chichimecs that refused change, but rather, as could be expected, with their mere presence they accelerated what today would be called the cultural development of Tezcoco. The Tlailotlaques would teach the Chichimecs the highest of the ancient knowledge, "the art of painting and writing histories." The Chimalpanecas, for their part, would contribute to cultural change in different ways, including encouraging agriculture. Thanks also to both groups, the religious practices and beliefs accepted from ancient times by sedentary peoples began to be accepted by the Chichimecs. For the first time, toward the end of Quinatzin's rule, it is possible to speak of widespread and profound cultural transformation. As a symbol of the acculturation of the Chichimecs, it is worth remembering the customs and ceremonies that Quinatzin adopted in his court. No one describes this better than Torquemada:

> Since already by this time the number of people had grown much greater and the dominions were loftier and more authoritative, and the social order of the kingdoms and provinces had become more established, this ruler no longer wanted to be treated in the common or ordinary manner, instead moving out of this, like the one who had been raised in great order and care with the Acolhua and Toltec lords, he made himself be carried on litters, which were extremely and expensively decorated, given that the Toltecs who made them were very skilled in everything they did. . . . And from that he made it a custom, every time he left his house no matter where he went. And from this remained the custom that all those who came after, had of treating themselves with this haughtiness and lordliness.[17]

One can also bring in a testimony concerning the speed with which practices, repeatedly said to be of Toltec origin, are introduced. This one deals with the birth of Techotlala,

the future successor to Quinatzin. Chimalpahin Cuauhtlehuanitzin, in his *Tercera relación,* recalls:

> When the esteemed son was born
> of Quinatzin Tlaltecatzin,
> the one called Techotlala Coxcoxtzin,
> fifty-two years had already passed
> since Quinatzin Tlaltecatzin governed.
> Only in a mesh,
> in a net,
> had they raised their children,
> the Tezcocan Chichimecs.
> But he was raised
> by a noble woman of Culhuacán,
> called Papaloxochitzin,
> "Little butterfly flower,"
> noble person of Náhuatl language.
> She then raised him in a cradle.
> Soon she taught him the Náhuatl language,
> the language of the Toltecs.
> Also she clothed him with her cape,
> with her truss.
> The language that the Tezcocans first spoke
> was the Chichimec dialect,
> they spoke like Popolocas, [barbarians],
> and for the first time,
> he came to speak Náhuatl well,
> Techotlala Coxcoxtzin.[18]

Heir to the accomplishments of his father and now educated in the refinements of his Toltec heritage, Techotlala,
who governed Tezcoco from 1357 to 1409, would have as
his mission to consummate, as far as possible, the already-
long process of transformation among the Chichimecs. Ixtlilxóchitl wisely says, as if he had foreseen the idea and the
reality of the future concept of acculturation, that "already
by this time the Chichimecs were very intermixed with those
of the Toltec nation."[19] The methods that Techotlala came

to enact would accomplish this "intermixing" of peoples, customs, beliefs, and institutions.

THE CONSEQUENCES OF THE
ACCULTURATIVE PROCESS

A brief reflection on the long process of cultural contact and the subsequent Chichimec transformation highlights some of their causes as well as the forms that they took. In the beginning there were only exploratory, generally casual, contacts. Soon afterward the desire was born to own lands with an abundance of water and forests, where the ancient culture had flourished. Thus the first forms of settlement took place in the times of Xólotl and Nopaltzin. The initial contacts would be converted later into the first forms of family linkages. Tlotzin typifies a new type of Chichimec leader, already mestizo through his maternal side, who was of Toltec origin. Another type of encounter then occurs. This time the sedentary peoples are the ones interested in changing the customs of their already-inevitable neighbors. The noble Tecpoyo Achcauhtli of Chalco, who assumes the responsibility of indoctrinating Tlotzin, best exemplifies this attitude. There were conflicting reactions when Tlotzin, who had assimilated these teachings, attempted to transform his people by introducing agriculture, among other things. Many were accepting, but there were others who rebelled and preferred to return to the nomadic life. Quinatzin continued the efforts initiated by his father. He also welcomed the influence and the teachings of those who possessed more developed cultural institutions. After welcoming the Tlailotlaques and Chimalpanecas, new forms of acculturation began to develop in the very bosom of his dominions. He also had to overcome the resistance of those who did not wish to change. Astutely, fully aware that transformations are often derived from contact, but also come from the direction that the sovereign imposes on his people, he commended the education of his future successor to a people of Toltec origin. Thus, this future ruler would understand which steps were left untaken in the full realization of what Ixtlilxóchitl correctly calls the "inter-mixing" of peoples and cultures.

It is known that Techotlala brought the process that his father and grandfather had initiated to a happy conclusion. As a ruler he dictated new laws, forged alliances, and broadened the dominions of Tezcoco considerably. He also welcomed four other groups of immigrants, who contributed to accomplishing the desired "intermixing." The ones recently arrived had suffered persecution on the part of the lord of Culhuacán. Techotlala decided to protect them, and

> he sent them to settle in the city of Tezcoco, because they were a civilized people and convenient for his purposes, for the good government of his republic, and thus they settled in the city in four neighborhoods, because the families of this Toltec people, or as they were called at the time, Culhuas, were so many: in one neighborhood they of the family of the Mexitin settled, whose leader was called Ayocuan; the second neighborhood was given to the Colhuaques, who had for a leader Naúhyotl; the third to the Huitzimahuaques, whose leader was called Tlacomihua; and the fourth to the Panecas, who called their leader Achitómetl.[20]

By joining the already-established groups of the Tlailotlaques and the Chimalpanecas, they increased the diffusion of the ancient practices and religious beliefs that were assimilated by the Tezcocan Chichimecs. From another perspective, their presence was also felt in the ever-increasing use of Náhuatl throughout the region. Considering it to be an instrument and vehicle of culture, Techotlala, who had spoken the language since he was a child, finally decided to impose it upon all of his people: "He ordered that all those of the Chichimec nation were to speak it, especially those who had offices or charges of the republic; nonetheless, he respected all the place-names of the regions and the ruling of the republics, as prescribed in the paintings, and in accordance to other things of civil government."[21]

Thus, to the gradual acceptance of the rites and ceremonies of sedentary peoples was added that of the Náhuatl
language, which, a century later, came to be spoken by the
great majority of the descendants of the Chichimecs established in the Valley of Mexico. The long series of contacts
made many things possible for the ancient nomads: the practice of agriculture, life in villages and cities, the splendor of
the ancient-style court, new forms of religious syncretism,
and a blossoming in the area of the arts. All of this came only
after suppressing natural resistance and even open rebellions on the part of small factions. Nonetheless, this happy
state in the last years of government by Techotlala did not
safeguard the ancient Chichimecs, who, despite the transformations, until then had defended their ethnic identity
from a threat already hovering over their dominion.

THREATENED IDENTITY AND
CULTURAL REAFFIRMATION

The Tecpanecs of Azcapotzalco, who had also experienced a
process of acculturation similar, to a certain degree, to that
of the Chichimecs, had gained hegemony in the valley and in
several other regions at that time. The famous Tecpanec
sovereign, Tezozómoc, a contemporary of Techotlala, had
made the region of Tenayuca his own; he had taken over the
kingdom of Xaltocan and widened his dominions through
the area to the south, including Coyoacán, Chalco, and Ame-
cameca, attaining the payment of tribute by the peoples of
the old dominion of Culhuacán. Tezozómoc had conquered
other areas farther away, like Ocuila and Malinalco to the
east, and Cuauhnáhuac to the south. The arrogant sovereign—who, as noted in the *Annals of Cuauhtitlán,* granted
himself the last name of Xólotl as a title—attempted to unify
under his direction the totality of the Chichimec states, with
the intention of establishing what would today be called
an empire.

His seemingly uncontrollable desire would soon bring
him into conflict with Tezcoco. The defeat inflicted by
Tezozómoc and the death of Ixtlilxóchitl, son of Techotlala,
resulted in a violent interruption in the processes of change

and in the flourishing of Tezcoco. Nonetheless, the transformation accomplished since the days of Techotlala was not something that could be overcome or absorbed by force within a different context. Nezahualcóyotl (1402–1472), the most extraordinary of the already-acculturated Chichimec princes, was to be, in alliance with the Mexicas, the one to restore independence to his people. His fame would later grow, as a wise governor, legislator, architect, sage, poet, and counselor, who was always listened to by the lords of Mexico-Tenochtitlan.

The appearance of men like him and his son Nezahualpilli would have been impossible without the long process of more than two centuries of cultural transformation. The refinement that was to prevail in Tezcoco throughout their reign was the fruit of a new cultural rootedness already achieved by Techotlala before the attack that originated in Azcapotzalco. *Codex Matritensis* gives an eloquent description of the then-incipient cultural maturity of the Chichimecs, and in particular of the Tezcocans:

> These, as it is said,
> named themselves Chichimecs,
> but they were already called "the owners of houses";
> which is to say that they were already like the
>   Toltecs. . . .
> Then they gained strength,
> the dominions, the principalities, the kingdoms.
> The princes, lords, and chiefs
> governed, established cities.
> They made them grow, extended them,
> augmented their cities.[22]

And in supreme praise of these new settlements, Tezcoco standing out among them, the text adds:

> The song was established,
> the drums were fixed.
> They say that in this way
> the cities began:
> music existed in them.[23]

It is not surprising that in these towns and cities, whose origin is related to the beginning of music, in addition to the different groups of artists, from the late fourteenth century the *cuicapicque* appeared—those known as the forgers of songs, or poets. Ixtlilxóchitl describes one such artist, of whom he says, "He always came to the court of Tezcoco to be present for any occasion and to attend to his good government."[24] The man in question, a sample of the refinement achieved in the Chichimec world, is known by the name Tlaltecatzin, a title given earlier to Quinatzin in recognition of his work as "ruler of the land." It seems that the poet Tlaltecatzin knew a great deal about the ancient wisdom of Toltec origin, and of the art of careful expression in the Náhuatl language. It is said of him that "left to yourself, in your house, you expressed sentiments and spoke rightly."[25]

One of his poems reflects an interesting aspect of life in the cities that had begun to exist with music. The Chichimecs were no longer nomadic hunters. They now had a famous singer who proclaimed that, besides the precious flowers, and beyond the chocolate drunk by the princes and the tobacco smoke that gives life to the gatherings of friends, stands the admirable creature, "the precious flower of toasted flower of toasted corn," that is, woman. Tlaltecatzin saw the rebirth of an ancient profession in Tezcoco; he knew that there were groups of *ahuianime* in the city, "courtesans," women of pleasure. It is precisely to one of them that he dedicates his thought and the best of his song. Upon reading his words it is clear, for better or worse, that the acculturation of the Chichimecs had certainly progressed:

> I have a yearning
> —exclaims Tlaltecatzin—
> my heart savors it,
> my heart becomes intoxicated,
> truly my heart knows it:
> Red bird with a neck of rubber!
> fresh and fiery,

you show off your garland of flowers.
Oh mother!
Sweet, delicious woman,
precious flower of toasted corn,
you only lend yourself,
you will be abandoned,
you will have to go,
you will remain lean.
Here you have arrived,
before the princes,
you, marvelous creature
you are an invitation to pleasure.
On the mat of yellow and blue feathers,
there you are swollen with pride.
Precious flower of toasted corn,
you only lend yourself,
you will be abandoned,
you will have to go,
you will remain lean.
The flowering cacao
is already foaming;
the flower of the tobacco has been passed around.
If my heart would taste it,
my life would be intoxicated,
Each one is here,
on the earth,
you lords, my princes.
If my heart would taste it,
it would become intoxicated.[26]

They who had lived as archers with no houses, who
dressed themselves with animal pelts and ate big prickly
pears and cacti, now are an urban people who enjoy music
and have poets who forge songs in honor of the *ahuianime*,
or "courtesans." All of this takes place at the end of the
fourteenth century. Contemplating it in the light of history,
it is not exaggerated to state that the process of acculturation of the Chichimecs was accomplished by this time. As in

Europe, where the Germans were assimilated to the Mediterranean culture, here the ancient hunters came to appropriate the wisdom of the Toltecs. And some, like the poet Tlaltecatzin, are not only acculturated but become the advantaged apprentices to a gratifying new way of life.

This process of change without loss of ethnic identity, depicted in the codices and indigenous texts, is the oldest fully documented example found in the New World of what can occur when cultures at different levels of development enter into contact. The subject is highly worthy of study as a pre-Hispanic experience rich in meaning in the light of universal history.

3.
The Spiritual Conquest: Perspectives of the Friars and the Indians

For the indigenous peoples of the New World, one trauma of the Conquest lay in the enslavement of their villages, chiefdoms, and nations through the force of arms. To this trauma were added others, just as dramatic in nature, which were to develop as a permanent affliction in the consciousness of the vanquished people. Only one aspect of what took place at that time will be considered here: the intellectual confrontation, rather than an exchange of ideas, between the conquerors and the vanquished. Such an event rarely took place in an egalitarian setting. Indeed, the dominant group did not doubt that its mission was to pursue and suppress native beliefs and forms of worship, considered inventions of the devil, in order to impose its own religion as the sole alternative available to the indigenes. In this way, the evangelistic process and the implantation of Christianity implicitly acquired the character of an attempt at "spiritual conquest."

In a later chapter the subject of the first contacts between Indians and Spaniards will be reviewed, including the siege and victory of the latter over the native peoples. There the intent will be to emphasize the importance of a backdrop of military conquest in understanding other aspects of the situation of the Indian, beginning in the colonial period and continuing through to the appearance of "Indianism," as conceived of by anthropologists and modern state organizations.

The study at hand focuses on the central highlands of Mexico and centers on stirring up the meaning of "spiritual conquest" by analyzing not only the point of view of the missionary friars, but also those of several sixteenth-century Mexican Indians. From the outset it must be said that research on this subject presents special difficulties. The Spanish testimonies, especially those of the friars, include abundant references to demonstrations of acceptance or rejection of the new religion among the Indians; in what concerns the indigenous points of view, whether favorable or critical and disdainful, sources have been more difficult to collect. Nonetheless, there are native expressions concerning this issue, some of which are very revealing and have remained unpublished until now.

A first step is to consider the accounts of the spiritual conquest left by the friars. As demonstrated in their most common assertions, the prevailing idea—especially during the first half of the sixteenth century—was that they had achieved a widespread acceptance of Christianity among the natives. Later, in the second half of the sixteenth and beginning of the seventeenth centuries, very different opinions issue from the writings of the missionaries, some of whom harbored serious doubts about the formal conversion of many Indians and described certain attitudes and perspectives of the native peoples toward the new religion.

Next, the study will turn to native testimonies. By adopting as objective a criterion as possible, the examination includes a very broad range of indigenous expressions that relate to the spiritual conquest and to Christianity. On the one hand, there are texts that seem to imply diverse modes of native acceptance. On the other, one finds relatively frequent proclamations by indigenes who demonstrate their hostility to the new religion and who make specific criticisms of it and of the procedures that were followed in order to impose the Christian faith.

More than attempting to gain an external perspective, what is of interest here is to approach the two faces of the mirror—the consciousness of the friars and that of the Indians—in which events were reflected. Above all, these reflections derived from divergent, and sometimes antagonistic, ways of conceiving of human destiny and the mystery of divine things.

VIEWS OF THE MISSIONARIES CONCERNING THE INDIGENOUS ATTITUDES TOWARD CHRISTIANITY

The first decade following the military conquest gave rise to a number of testimonies, reflecting what could be described as the "euphoria" of the missionaries with regard to the native conversions they believed to have accomplished. Three such statements will be quoted below; they are credited to Fray Pedro de Gante, Toribio de Benavente Motolinía, and to another group of Franciscans, among whom were Jacobo de Tastera, Martín de Valencia, Francisco Jiménez, and Luis de Fuensalida.

The first testimony is included in what Gante wrote on June 27, 1529, to the fathers and brothers of the province of Flanders. Among other things he declares:

> And now, thanks to the Lord, many have begun to follow the natural order, and having already converted to Christianity, with great longing they seek out baptism and confess their sins.
>
> In this province of Mexico I have baptized, with other companions, more than two hundred thousand, indeed so many that I myself do not know the number. Frequently it happens that we baptize fourteen thousand people in a day, sometimes ten, sometimes eight thousand.[1]

Father Motolinía wrote on the same theme in his *Historia de los indios de Nueva España*, with particular emphasis on the great numbers of Indians baptized. Among other statements he includes the following: "I believe that after the land was won, which was in the year 1521, until the time that I am writing this, which is in the year 1536, more than four million souls were baptized, and how I come to know it will be stated later."[2]

A few paragraphs later Fray Toribio reflects upon the events that, in his opinion, lay the foundation for his earlier assertion. He recalls that around this same date there were nearly sixty Franciscan priests in New Spain, to which he adds another twenty who had died earlier, and an equal number who had returned to Spain. He goes on to admit that "of the sixty that at present are here in this year of 1536," twenty must be subtracted for not baptizing the Indians because they were new in the land or because they did not know the language. Of the forty who remained, it should be recognized, according to Motolinía, that they had each baptized one hundred thousand or more, "because some of them must have baptized nearly three hundred thousand." His conclusion is that in fact "there should be nearly five million baptized up to today."[3]

But farther below, extending his consideration to those called "peoples of the South Sea," he does not seem satisfied with the previous figures and, once again widening his calculations, he writes the following without hesitation: "In my judgment and truly there will have been baptized during this time that I am speaking of, which will be fifteen years, more than nine million souls of the Indians."[4]

One last example of the euphoria of the first evangelists is provided in a letter by Fray Jacobo de Tastera and other friars, some of whose names have already been mentioned, sent to the emperor Charles from the convent of Huexotzinco on May 6, 1533. In this case, rather than alluding to numbers, they deliberate on the extraordinary way in which the natives, especially the youngest ones, have received Christianity:

What shall we say of the children of the natives of this land? They write, read, sing plain chants, and of the organ and counterpoint, they write songbooks and teach others the music; they particularly rejoice in ecclesiastic singing; and preach to the people the sermons that we teach them, and they say them with great spirit; the frequency of the confessions with weeping and tears, the pure and simple confession, and the accompanying penance, *nos qui contractavimus de verbo vitae* [we who made a pact of the word of salvation] know it, and that sovereign Lord, who works hidden miracles in their hearts, knows it, even in the external acts it will be able to be seen by those who have not been blinded by ignorance or malice.[5]

There is no need for lengthy commentary about these testimonies. They demonstrate in themselves the clearly optimistic attitude in the exhilaration of those first friars, as much in the references to the great numbers of converted as in the many forms of acceptance of Christianity. Let us now turn to what other equally distinguished ecclesiastics expressed in later years concerning what they had been able to verify on this matter. Their testimonies date from the second half of the sixteenth century and the beginnings of the seventeenth. They are taken from Bernardino de Sahagún, Diego Durán, and Jacinto de la Serna.

In the prologue to book IV of the *Historia general de las cosas de Nueva España,* which speaks of the art of divination of the ancient Mexicans, there is a sort of synthesis of Sahagún's thoughts concerning the conversion of the natives. I will just mention in passing that it is odd that this very extensive prologue does not appear in the modern editions of the works of Sahagún. Because of this, I cite it from the manuscript conserved in the National Library of Mexico:

They [the first evangelists] did not forget in their preaching the warning that the Redeemer left his disciples and apostles when he told them: *estote prudentes sicut serpentes et simplices sicut columbae:* be prudent like serpents and simple as doves. And though they proceeded with caution in the second, they failed in the first, and even the idolaters themselves noticed, in that they [the first evangelists] lacked that serpentine prudence and thus with their sly humility they quickly offered themselves to receive the faith that was being preached to them. But they remained deceitful in that they did not detest or renounce all their gods with all their customs, and thus they were baptized not like perfect believers but as fictitious ones, who received that faith without leaving the false one they had of many gods. This cover-up was not understood in the beginning, and the main reason for this was the opinion that the above-mentioned preachers had of their perfect faith, and thus they affirmed it to all the ministers of the gospel who happened to preach to these people. . . .

All of us were told (as had already been told to the Dominican fathers) that this people had come to the faith so sincerely and were almost all baptized and so wholly in the Catholic faith of the Roman Church that there was no need to preach against idolatry because they had abandoned it so truly. We accepted this information as very true and miraculous, because in such a short time and with so little preaching and knowledge of the language, and without any miracles, so many people had been converted. . . . It was discovered after a few years very evidently the lack of serpentine prudence that there was in the founding of the new Church, because they were ignorant of the conspiracy that had been made among the principals and native priests, to receive Jesus Christ among their gods as one of them and to honor him like the Spaniards honor him, according to their ancient custom wherein when foreigners arrived to settle near those who were already settled, when it pleased them they would take as a god the one brought by the recently arrived and in this manner they say that Tezcatlipoca is the god of those from Tlalmanalco, because they brought him with them, and Huitzilopochtli is the god of the Mexicans because they brought him with them. . . .

In this fashion they easily accepted as a god the god of the Spaniards, but not in order to leave their ancient ones, and this they hid during the catechism when they were baptized, and during the catechism when they were asked if they believed in God the Father, the Son, and the Holy Spirit, along with the other articles of the faith, they would respond *"quemachca,"* yes, in accordance with the conspiracy and custom that they had; and asked whether they disowned all the other gods they had adored, they would also respond *"quemachca,"* yes, deceitfully and lying. . . . and thus this new Church was established over a false foundation, and even after having put some buttresses, it is still damaged and ruined.[6]

This is certainly not the only place where Sahagún expresses his views in these terms. Further testimony can be found in his "Adición sobre supersticiones" [Postscript concerning superstitions], included as a kind of appendix at the end of book X of his *Historia*. [7]

Expressions of doubt as to the total conversion of many of the natives are equally abundant in the works of the Dominican Diego Durán. For instance, referring to the way in which the natives celebrated some of the festivals of the Christian religion, he insists that in them many of the ancient rituals covertly endured: "Today they use [the pagan ritual] in some celebrations, particularly in the feast of the Ascension and that of the Holy Spirit, which fall in May, and in others that correspond to their ancient feasts. I see it and I remain silent because all go through it, and so I pick up my staff of roses like the others and go reflecting upon our great ignorance."[8]

And speaking in more general terms about what he considers to be the feigned attitude of the Indians in the festivities of Christianity, he comments:

I will take note of what is most essential and necessary for the office of the ministers; it is our principal intent to warn them of the mixing that there might be concerning our feasts and theirs which, while pretending to celebrate the feast of Our Lord and of the Saints, they intermix and blend and celebrate those of their idols when they fall on the same day. And during the ceremonies they will bring in their ancient rites, which would not be a surprise if it were still done today. . . . Feigning that the rejoicing is made to God, when their object is the idol. I would not venture to pronounce such a fearful judgment if we did not have so much fear of it and warnings from others. . . . We are no longer as blind and ignorant as we were until now.[9]

After such considerations by Durán, it is interesting to turn to the explanations given by men like the Franciscan Jerónimo de Mendieta and the Dominican Bartolomé de las Casas for the survival of native idolatries and the lack of rootedness of Christianity among the Indians. According to the first friar, one cause could be attributed to the terrible examples given and the many abuses committed by the Spaniards who lived with the natives. For the second friar, on the other hand, the primary reason lay in the methods adopted in the process of bringing the natives to the new religion. In the opinion of Fray Bartolomé, the "only manner of conversion" was very much opposed to the common, almost immediate, imposition of the new faith, assuming as it did a truly slow path of teaching and persuasion—inviting and attracting, according to his own words, "like the rain and the snow come down from the sky, not impetuously, nor violently, nor suddenly, but with care and gentleness."[10]

Certainly many of Las Casas's contemporaries did not share his views, as seen when, at the beginning of the seventeenth century, several other friars and clerics wrote works directed—as indicated by their titles—toward the radical "elimination of the idolatries." Such is the case, among others, of Jacinto de la Serna, who around the year 1636 concluded his *Manual de ministros de indios para el conocimiento de sus idolatrías y extirpación de ellas*, a "Manual for the Ministers to Indians for the Knowledge of their Idolatries and the Elimination of Them." Serna, who had been the parish priest of Xalatlaco in the Valley of Toluca, maintained that the ancient beliefs persisted even after more than a century of New Spanish life, and thus opened the first chapter of his book with the following appraisal:

> So many years having passed since, with the coming of the Spaniards in 1521, the light of the Gospel was brought to New Spain, one could reasonably think that just like the darkness of night departs with the coming of the sun to our hemisphere, so the abysmal darkness of paganism and idolatry had been totally exiled with the light and knowledge of the true sun of justice, Christ Our Lord.
>
> Because after so much light, so much preaching and labor, when they should have been full of light, they are in such abysmal darkness . . . and when it could have been expected of them that they are children of the light, it is seen by experience that they are of the darkness: because the darkness of idolatry grows from them, that they have, and have had, covered up, that they have never abandoned, which they have from the time that they were first preached the faith. . . .
>
> And they go beyond this, they accept their darkness for light; since they hold as very necessary their superstitions and idolatries, that without them nothing good will happen to them; and the reason they give is *"Ca iuh otechilhuitiaque in huehuetque, totahuah, tocolhuan."* "Because thus they left it said to us, the ancient elders, our fathers and grandfathers," and they are so committed to this tradition, which is transmitted from fathers to sons, that they show great emotion when they see that it is being forgotten, and they say: *"Auh quen? Cuix ilcahuiz, cuix polihuiz in otechmachtitiaque huehuetque?"* "But how? Are you going to forget and lose what the ancient elders taught us?" Seeming to them that this is sufficient reason and convinced of it, they learn the ceremonies and superstitions that are so numerous that there is no thing, office, or interaction for which there isn't one that needs to be learned.[11]

With his sights fixed on the elimination of idolatries, Jacinto de la Serna not only recognized the survival of what he
called the "abysmal darkness," but went so far as to collect
Náhuatl expressions that are in themselves a reflection of
the native thought dedicated to preserving the ancient
ways. And Serna, upon entering the seventeenth century,
was not the only one to perceive such attitudes; there are
analogous testimonies in the works of authors like Fray Juan
de Torquemada, Hernando Ruiz de Alarcón, and Pedro
Ponce.

The evidence presented up to this point implies conflicting perspectives. On the one hand, there are the testimonies
of men like Gante, Motolinía, and the other Franciscans who
speak euphorically about the miraculous conversion of millions of Indians. On the other hand, we have the assertions
of those who, during the second half of the sixteenth and
beginning of the seventeenth centuries, not only put into
question the attainment of such goals, but resolutely declare
that the old paganism is still alive. As Fray Bernardino de
Sahagún noted, the "serpentine prudence" was greatly lacking, and the native rites and beliefs, seen as the inspiration
of the devil, had covertly endured. Their judgment, though
it may seem extreme, should nonetheless be seriously considered: "And thus this new Church was established over a
false foundation, and even after having put some buttresses,
it is still damaged and ruined."[12]

INDIGENOUS EXPRESSIONS
CONCERNING CHRISTIANITY

Missionaries like Gante and the first twelve Franciscans
were untiring in their New World activities. They took it
upon themselves to learn the indigenous languages and to
establish schools, hospitals, churches, and convents in order
to make the introduction of the Christian faith possible in a
world that, through eyes not yet clear of medievalism, ultimately looked like a field of idolatries inspired by the devil.
If we also consider that many of these apostolic men were
unflagging defenders of the Indians against the frequent

abuses to which they fell victim, any facile condemnation of
their actions against such idolatries would certainly reflect a
profound ignorance of the historical moment that they occupied. In this sense I can borrow the words of Robert
Ricard, who wrote in the conclusion of his book *The Spiritual Conquest of Mexico:* "It would be a strange mistake to
ascribe to me the intention of denigrating this [Christian]
work, admirable in so many ways."[13]

It is clear that objective criteria should be used to acknowledge the actual accomplishments that, in one way or
another, were the results of religious proselytizing. Thus,
due attention will be given first to testimonies that reflect
certain forms of native acceptance of Christianity. To assert, for example, that a good number of the indigenous
youth who studied in the College of Santa Cruz of Tlatelolco
had sincerely embraced the new faith seems to be a legiti-
mate assumption. In the collections of songs in the indigenous language we also find—citing here one source in
particular—several poems, written by the natives, that ex-
alt specific Christian mysteries. Such is the case with a
"Song about the Resurrection of Christ," composed by the
governor of Culhuacán, Don Baltazar, for Easter, 1536.
The following verses are representative of his poem:

> For two counts of days,
> for eight times there has been fasting,
> the penance has been completed.
> They have been afflicted,
> they have been distressed,
> all your creations,
> here on the earth, surrounded on all sides by water.
>
> But now let us quickly leave,
> you, my little sisters, little girls,
> let us go see, let us go contemplate:
> He has revived, he has life, he is rising,
> His heart now has come to life: Jesus Christ.
> May it come out hither,

let the heart let it out,
your precious song, to Our God,
let us raise our song,
with him, with him,
our hearts will be gladdened.[14]

Other examples, similar to the one above, are preserved in the same manuscript of *Cantares mexicanos* in the National Library of Mexico. For instance, the text includes a fragment of a hymn about the "Redemption of Men," credited to Don Francisco Plácido, governor of Xiquipilco.[15] Also common, especially in communications directed toward the royal authorities from certain indigenous leaders, are reiterations of their acceptance of Christianity and even proclamations of having collaborated with the friars in their missionary tasks. Although in some cases such expressions of acceptance could be seen as influenced by a veiled self-interest, they should not be left aside as mere reflections of indigenous postures of accommodation.

One example of such indigenous writings is the letter of March 17, 1566, sent by Don Pablo Nazareo de Xaltocan to Philip II. It includes a blatant solicitude of favors and, as well, a reminder of what he, Don Pablo, who presents himself as a sincere Christian, had done for the proselytizing effort:

> In the same way, I, the above-mentioned Don Pablo Nazareo, having made to disappear with no little and diverse effort many evils provoked by the idolaters, pacified during more than forty years in the company of others, and primarily by means of the Christian doctrine rather than by the sword of the Spaniards, these Mexican provinces, teaching the sons of the Indians the Christian doctrine, as well as to read, to write, to sing in the churches and to assimilate the Christian customs, thus pacifying the Mexican provinces.[16]

Finally, recognizing that such testimonies undoubtedly demand careful analysis and evaluation, let us turn to another form of writing that also contains open proclamations of an acceptance of Christianity. Here reference is made to some of the many wills, primarily of the upper-class indigenes, that have been preserved. As an example I cite, from the somewhat later date of July 28, 1623, the words of the Indian María Alonso, native to San Martín Izquitlan. Explicitly professing the Christian faith, María Alonso declares:

> In the first place I leave forever my soul in the hands of the Lord God, of whom I am a creature redeemed by the precious blood of our respected Lord Jesus Christ in whose faith I will die. . . . In the second place I state that I have a house located at the edge of the water toward the region of Xochimilco. . . . I say that, when I die, it should be sold and its value should be destined in favor of our souls: mine, that of my esteemed husband, Domingo Hernández, and of my mother-in-law, María Xúchil and my father-in-law, Agustín de Escalona.[17]

Though it is clear that in some documents where Indians appear to be professing the Christian faith various forms of fear, self-interest, or accommodationist postures can be assumed, the existence of sincere expressions cannot be denied. The will cited above seems to be an example of this last.

But just as some native words reveal acceptance, other very different texts demonstrate the intellectual stance of Indians who were openly hostile to the friars' preaching and the new religion that the Spaniards attempted to impose. In such documents the attitudes of many ancient wisemen and native priests, possessing more articulated consciousness than the commoners, come to light. Through the texts it is clear that they put themselves at risk to confront the systematic eradication of what they considered to be the deepest roots of their culture.

The earliest of these testimonies predates the fall of Mexico-Tenochtitlan. Its source is the *Codex Ramírez*, which conserves fragments of ancient indigenous communications.

In it, among other things, is a description of the welcome given Hernán Cortés by Prince Ixtlilxóchitl of Tezcoco before he made his first entrance into the Mexican capital, in November of 1519. Ixtlilxóchitl, who found himself at battle with his brother Cacamatzin and with Motecuhzoma, wished to seal his friendship with Cortés and consequently accepted baptism. In order to provide further proof of his good intentions toward the foreigners, he attempted to prod his mother, the Lady Yacotzin, into submitting to the ritual of the new religion as well. The violent reaction of Yacotzin upon discovering his intentions in many ways typifies the attitude of those who, like her, would reject the change that was being imposed upon them as unthinkable: "Ixtlilxóchitl then went to his mother, Yacotzin, telling her what had occurred, and that he was coming for her to baptize her. She responded that he must have lost his mind, for so quickly he had let himself be defeated by a few barbarians such as the Christians."[18]

Another example of a similar view of Christianity is contained in the Náhuatl text, gathered by Sahagún, of the *Coloquios,* dialogues held in 1524 among some of the native wisemen with the twelve Franciscans who had recently arrived in New Spain. After listening to the missionaries' strong challenges to their native religion, the *tlamatinime,* wisemen and priests of the ancient culture, show that they are deeply disturbed and, contradicting the words of the friars, demonstrate that their thought and practices with regard to divinity could, and should, be respected. The following are the truly dramatic words of the *tlamatinime:*

> Our Lords, very esteemed lords:
> You have endured hardships to arrive in this land.
> Here before you, we ignorant people contemplate you.
> . . . And now, what shall we say? What shall we raise to your ears? We are merely common people. . . .
> Through an interpreter we respond, we return the breath and the word of the Lord of the Near and of the Surrounding (Tloque Nahuaque). . . .

Because of Him we put ourselves at risk, for Him we put ourselves into danger. . . . Perhaps we are to be taken to our ruin, perhaps to our destruction. [But] where are we to go now? We are common people, we are destructible, we are mortal. Let us die now, let us perish, since our gods have already died.

Calm your hearts and your flesh, our lords! Because we will break open a little now, we will open the secret a little, the ark of the Lord, our [god]. You said that we know not the Lord of the Near and of the Surrounding (Tloque Nahuaque), the One to whom the heavens and the earth belong. You said that our gods are not real gods. This word that you speak is a new one, and because of it we are distressed, because of it we are frightened. Indeed, our ancestors, those who came to be, those who came to live on the earth, did not speak in this manner. They gave us their ways of life; they believed them truly, they worshiped them, they honored them, the gods. They taught us all their forms of worship, their ways of honoring [the gods]. Thus, before them we eat earth [kiss earth to make an oath], for them we bleed ourselves, we fulfill our promises, we burn *copal* [incense], and we offer sacrifices.

It was the doctrine of our elders that we give thanks to our gods, that they merited us [with their sacrifice they gave us life]. In what way? When? Where? When it was still night.

It was their doctrine that they grant us our sustenance, all that we drink and eat, all that which maintains life: corn, beans, wild amaranth, sage. They are the ones from whom we request the water, the rain, from which the things of the earth are made. They themselves are rich, they are happy, they possess things; in such a way that always and forever things germinate there, and grow green there, in their house . . . there, where somehow there is life, in the place of Tlalocan [the paradise of the Rain God]. Never is there hunger there, never is there sickness, there is no poverty. They

give courage and authority to the people. . . . And in
what way? When? Where were the gods invoked, be-
seeched, accepted as such, revered? It has already been
a very long time: it was there in Tula, it was there in
Huapalcalco, it was there in Xuchitlapan, it was there
in Tlamohuanchan, it was there in Yohualichan, it was
there in Teotihuacán. . . .

And now, are we the ones who will destroy the ancient rule of life? That of the Chichimecs, the Toltecs,
the Acolhuas, the Tepanecs? We know to whom life is
owed, to whom birth is owed, to whom conception
is owed, to whom growth is owed; how we must pray.

Listen, our lords, do nothing to our people that
would bring about their disgrace, that would cause
them to perish. . . . Peacefully and calmly consider,
our lords, what is necessary. We cannot be tranquil, and
certainly we still do not believe, we do not accept your
words to be true, even though we may offend you. Here
are the Lords, those who govern, those who carry, who
have in their charge the whole world. It is enough that
we have already lost it, that it has been taken from us,
that our governance has been impeded. If we were to
stay in this place, we would be but prisoners. Do with us
what you will. This is all that we respond, that we answer, to your breath, to your word, Oh, our lords![19]

Lengthy commentaries on this dramatic response of the
indigenous wisemen are unnecessary. Instead, the following
is a very similar reply, given nearly a century later by natives
from Xalatlaco, in the Valley of Toluca. Jacinto de la Serna,
cited earlier, transcribed the Indians' answer to the insis-
tent Christian preachings. The reasons offered for their
continuing ties to ancient beliefs resound like an echo of
what the *tlamatinime* had put forth in the *Coloquios*: "*Ca iuh
otechilhuitiaque in huehuetque, totahuan, tocalhuan.* Because
thus they told us, the elders, our fathers, our grandfathers.
Auh, quen? Cuix ilcahuiz, cuix polihuiz in otechmachtitiaque

huehuetque? But how? Will it perhaps have to be forgotten,
to perish, what the elders taught us?"[20]
The essence of these responses lies in the clash between
what is one's own and has given root to one's very existence,
and what is perceived as an incomprehensible imposition
from the outside: it is the first form of native reaction in the
face of the new religion. Further, these texts encompass a
kind of admonition against what would come to pass if,
finally, the ancient beliefs and rituals were abandoned without being replaced with a sincere acceptance of the doctrine
of the friars: "Do nothing to our people that would bring
about their disgrace, that would cause them to perish.
. . . It is enough that we have already lost it, that it
has been taken from us, that our governance has been
impeded."[21]
The misfortune that could befall them by abandoning the
old without assimilating the new was even more explicitly
stated by the elder Indian mentioned in chapter 1. It is
pertinent to cite here, in full, what Fray Diego Durán wrote
with respect to this:

> Once I questioned an Indian regarding certain things,
> particularly why he had gone dragging himself about,
> gathering monies, with bad nights and worse days, and
> having gathered so much money through so much trou-
> ble he put on a wedding and invited the entire town and
> spent everything. Thus reprimanding him for the evil
> thing he had done, he answered me:
> Father, do not be frightened because we are still
> *nepantla,* and since I understood what he meant to say
> by that phrase and metaphor, which means to be in the
> middle, I insisted that he tell me in what middle it was
> in which they found themselves. He told me that since
> they were still not well rooted in the faith, I should not
> be surprised that they were still neutral, that they nei-
> ther answered to one faith nor the other or, better said,
> that they believed in God and at the same time keep

their ancient customs and demonic rites. And this is what he meant by his abominable excuse that they still remained in the middle and were neutral.[22]

The answer given by the elder Indian virtually amounts to a theory of cultural nepantlism—remaining in the middle, the old obfuscated but the new not yet assimilated. His words also implicitly convey an appreciation of what the distortion of native roots, as a consequence of the preaching of the friars, had meant to the indigenous world. Some of the preachers themselves, particularly Sahagún, while not developing the theory of nepantlism so concisely, had nonetheless perceived the magnitude of the problem. Precisely because of this, they insisted on a fundamental knowledge of pagan beliefs and practices in order to truly replace them with Christianity.

But while the missionary effort directed itself to such an end, the attitudes of many indigenous priests, who covertly preserved the pre-Hispanic traditions, remained the primary obstacle to the process. In the eyes of the Indian sages, their duty was to revive in the people the religion of their fathers and grandfathers. They also believed it necessary to work as preachers, in this way imitating the missionaries. There is evidence of this type of activity that, through its very nature, inevitably put the dissidents at risk of detection. The sources speak of numerous cases, from a very early date, in which native priests and other prominent Indians persisted, both covertly and overtly, in rescuing those who had already accepted the baptismal waters. The texts, which have survived in various ways, about those natives whose goal was to restore the validity of the pre-Hispanic religion, undoubtedly reveal the most significant indigenous views concerning Christianity.

First there are the original cases of this type of activity on the part of the old native priests. Shortly after the Conquest, according to Motolinía, one of the priests, or *teopixque*, of the cult of the god Ometochtli appeared in the province of Tlaxcala. Upon arrival at the *tianquizco*, the marketplace, he declared the following in the name of his god: "That soon all would die because they had made him angry and had left his house and gone to that of Santa María."[23]

The priest of Ometochtli who spoke in this way paid with his life, as Motolinía again writes, for his desire to bring those who were being won over by the missionaries back to their beliefs. Another description of a similar event, which took place in the year 1526, is offered by the indigenous chronicler Juan Ventura Zapata. The following is the version of his account in Náhuatl:

It was then also that Nécoc Yautl appeared, "Enemy of one part and another" [a priest of Tezcatlipoca].

He said, he went about deceiving the people, he went about betraying: no one should become indoctrinated, no one should get baptized. He would ask them for the ancient books, for the *copal* [incense]. One time Nécoc Yautl was captured there in San Sebastián in a trap like a wooden crate. In the marketplace they beat him, in the presence of Fray Luis [de Fuensalida], in front of the people. Then began the search for wizards there in Tlaxcala. It was undertaken by the disciples of the priests.[24]

The ones who exposed themselves in this way must have been fully conscious of the risks they ran of all sorts of punishments—even death—for continuing to profess and to preach the beliefs condemned by the friars as the inspiration of the devil. The wisemen had already clearly recognized these dangers when they replied to the twelve Franciscans: "Because of Him [the Lord of the Near and of the Surrounding], we put ourselves at risk, for Him we put ourselves into danger. . . . Perhaps we are to be taken to our ruin, perhaps to our destruction. . . . [But] where are we to go now?"[25]

For those who chose to carry on as bearers of the pre-Hispanic religious message, the enterprise they took on was risky in the extreme. Now not only the friars but also the royal authorities, and the beginnings of the Holy Office of the Inquisition in New Spain, would launch campaigns against them. One well-known case is that of Martín Océlotl, native of Tezcoco, who was taken for a sorcerer in 1536, put in prison, divested of his worldly goods, and thrown off his land. From the denunciations solicited through the procedure followed by the Inquisition, something is known of his preachings—including, among other things, an appeal to the idea of the imminent end of the world due to the abandonment of the ancient religion. Speaking with a prominent Indian of Acatzinco, he had expressed this belief in a veiled way: "I have called together everyone from this hamlet, and what I want to do for them is to make them quickly put all hands available to work in the fruit trees, like maguey [century plant], cherry trees and apple trees and all the other fruit trees because due to a lack of water a great hunger will come and the corn will not grow."[26]

Announcing portents in the heavens, he then went on to connect belief in the possible end of the world with the fate the friars would then confront, as "they would be turned into *chichimicle*," that is, *tzitzimime*. This was a clear allusion to what was believed could occur in the feast of the new fire, when "if they could not bring forth fire, the human lineage would end. And that night, and that darkness would exist forever . . . and from above would descend the *tzitzimime*, who were extremely ugly and terrible creatures who would eat all the men and women."[27]

Thus, to Martín Océlotl, the friars, bent on destroying everything that had given root to the people, were in essence little more than disguised *tzitzimime*, devouring all that is good. Furthermore, the missionaries were hostile to all happiness, since they were truly ignorant of the fact that "we are born to die and that after, when dead, we do not have pleasure or joy."[28]

A similar form of criticism made of the friars, touching on the last point, was expressed by other prominent elder lords of Tlaxcala. To their eyes, professing Christianity implied negating precisely all that gives pleasure to human beings on earth:

These poor fellows must be sick or must be crazy, let these miserable ones cry out: their craziness has seized them; let them be, let them pass their sickness such as they can. Do not harm them, since in the end these and the others must die of this sickness of insanity. And look, if you have noticed, how in the middle of the day, in the middle of the night, and at dawn, when all are enjoying themselves, they cry out and weep. Without a doubt it must be a great pain that they carry because they are men without sense, since they neither search out pleasure nor joy but rather sadness and solitude.[29]

In fact, criticisms such as these, with a sense that the followers of Christianity "neither search out pleasure nor joy," constitute another indigenous view of the new religion that has been clearly documented in the sources. And though it could be argued, of course, that the native priests of the pre-Hispanic religion also constantly insisted upon the necessity of sacrifice and abstinence, it is interesting to note the way the friars' attitude was specifically judged and classified here as the "sickness of insanity." Once again such an appreciation reflects the surprise and resistance provoked by what was seen as a cultural imposition, incomprehensible and even absurd, despite its apparent similarities with customs and traditions of the indigenous culture itself.

Another case in which arguments directed toward challenging the new doctrines are highlighted is presented by the procedure followed by the Inquisition against the *cacique*, or local leader, of Tezcoco, Don Carlos Ometochtzin Chichimecatecuhtli. In his trial, which achieved great renown, several people of some notoriety participated: Fray Juan de Zumárraga as bishop and apostolic inquisitor, and Alonso de Molina, Bernardino de Sahagún, and Antonio de Ciudad Rodrigo, in the role of interpreters.

It is through the declarations of the many natives who testified against Don Carlos that we know of the charges that were leveled against him. Dispensing with accusations that, after being baptized, Don Carlos covertly continued his idolatry and invited others to do the same, let us concentrate on the arguments he formulated, according to the witnesses, with regard to the Christian religion. Since there is full agreement across several of the testimonies, it is enough to transcribe the words that were repeatedly attributed to him:

> Brothers, listen. Who order us and lord over us and prohibit us and destroy? Because here I am, I who am lord of Tezcoco, and there is Yoanizi, lord of Mexico, and there is my nephew Tetzapilli, who is lord of Tacuba; and we should not tolerate that anyone should come between us and make themselves equal to us. After we are dead then maybe it can be so. But now we are here and our grandfathers and ancestors left it to us. . . . What are you doing? What do you want to do? Perchance do you want to be a father? These fathers, are they our parents? Were they born amongst us? If I saw that that which my parents and ancestors held was in accordance with this law of God, I would guard it and respect it. Well, brothers, let us guard and keep that which our ancestors had and guarded. . . .
>
> Let everyone follow what he wishes because also the preaching fathers say that, and that what the preachers teach us, let us hear it and set it aside, and let us not attend to them, and let no one put his heart in this law of God nor love this God. What certitude do you see and find in this law? I do not understand it.[30]

In few words he offers a reiteration of the already-known argument: the Indians must not leave their own beliefs nor their old way of life in exchange for something that is not even understood. A different tactic was to quote the testimony of wisemen from the past, in particular Nezahualcóyotl and Nezahualpilli, the former rulers of Tezcoco who, according to Don Carlos Ometochtzin, had said nothing about a new faith like the one the missionaries now came to preach:

Look, listen, my grandfather Nezahualcóyotl and my
father Nezahualpilli did not say anything when they
died, nor did they name anyone nor those who were to
come; listen, brother, that my grandfather and my father saw everything behind and to come . . . and they
knew what was to take place a long time hence, and
what had taken place, like the fathers say and call the
prophets, because truly I tell you that my grandfather
and my father were prophets who knew what was to
take place and what had been done. Thus, brother,
understand me, let no one put his heart in this law of
God and divinity. . . . What is this divinity, what is it
like, from whence did it come?[31]

If the wisest among their forefathers had said nothing
concerning the new religion and the new divinity, there was
no reason to change their way of thinking—no matter how
much the friars insisted in the new schools and books. They
were compelled to remain firm in the ancient beliefs:

Well listen, brother, because truly I tell you that that
which is taught in the school is all a mockery. . . .
Nor will they be able to make one believe with what they
teach there, like you or others, that law and that which
you say and teach from their books and doctrines. By
chance is it true or is it finished . . . ? Well listen,
brother, that our fathers and grandfathers said when
they died that truly it was said of the gods that they had
and loved that they were made in heaven and on the
earth, thus, brother, let us follow only that which our
grandfathers and fathers held and said when they died.[32]

Another, rather subtle, manner of criticism consisted of
highlighting the fact that even among the Christian friars
themselves there were different variants of religious practice, and thus it followed that the pre-Hispanic beliefs and
practices should also have their own place and validity.

Look how the friars and clerics each have their own way
of doing penance; look how the friars of Saint Francis

have one kind of doctrine, and one way of life and one way of dressing and one way of praying; and those of Saint Augustine have another way; and those of Saint Dominic have another; and the clerics another, just as we all see; and thus it was among those who guarded our gods, those of Mexico had one way of dressing, one way of praying and of offering and of fasting, and in other towns, another way; in each town they had their own mode of sacrificing and their manner of praying and of offering, and such is what the friars and clerics do that no one coincides with the others.[33]

To all of this Don Carlos would further add, according to the witnesses, the idea that the new doctrine would directly interfere with what individuals could do with their personal lives, in the pursuit of contentment and pleasure. Thus, among other things, he stated: "What does a woman or wine do to men? Don't the Christians have many women and get drunk without the religious fathers being able to impede it? Well, what is it that the priests do to us? It is not our duty or our law to impede one from doing what they wish. Let us leave and put over our shoulders that which they tell us."[34]

According to the corroborating testimony of several witnesses, these were Don Carlos Ometochtzin's principal forms of argument. With few words he objected to what he saw as an obvious imposition, and which, furthermore, contradicted the teachings of the ancient wisemen, among them Nezahualcóyotl and Nezahualpilli. On the other hand, he insisted that the native religion and traditions should at least have a place beside the many differing forms of religion as practiced by the Franciscans, Dominicans, Augustinians, and the other clerics. Finally, he discussed the condemnatory attitude of the Christians, opposing much of what gave pleasure in life. He reinforced this last point by emphasizing the fact that the prohibitions seemed directed not so much toward the Spaniards as upon all of the natives.

Don Carlos Omechtochtzin, as is well known, lost his life over the freedom he had given to his thoughts. However, neither his death—made as an example—nor the increasingly intense persecution of religious practices and beliefs of pre-Hispanic origin, prevented numerous other Indians from striving to preserve and even disseminate what they took to be the roots of their culture.

I will cite a final example from the unpublished *Journal*, in Náhuatl, of the Indian Juan Bautista, conserved in the Capitular Archive of the Guadalupe Basilica in Mexico City. Written during the second half of the sixteenth century, its author recorded a multitude of particularly interesting facts. Speaking about what happened in the year of 1558, he describes the behavior of another of the native priests spoken of above. The name of this preacher was Juan Teton, neighbor to Michmaloyan, in the Valley of Mexico. Juan Teton insisted on the need to return to the ancient faith. To this end he demanded that the baptism be renounced, and that the heads of the "converts" be washed, thus rising above the influence of the Christian ritual. As a particularly strong argument, Teton announced that the date was very near when "the binding of the years" should be made at the end of the cycle of fifty-two, which fell precisely in that year, since 1559 corresponded to the last year of the cycle of 2-Reed according to the pre-Hispanic calendar. At that time, those who had not "washed their heads" would be transformed into all sorts of animals. Here is the story written by Juan Bautista, with the words attributed to Juan Teton:

> Juan Teton, a neighbor of Michmaloyan, tricked and coaxed those of Coahuatépec and those of Atlapolco, he mocked their baptism. And the way in which Juan tricked them and coaxed them to in order to wash their heads [to make them renounce baptism] was the following. . . . Those of Coahuatépec first reneged on their baptism, washing their heads, and when they had washed their heads they sent a paper to those of Atlapolco: with this he tricked the people of two places. . . .

First he tells them, he tricks them, those of Coahuatépec: listen you, what do you say? Do you know what our
grandfathers are saying? When our binding of the years
has come there will be total darkness and the *tzitzimime*
will descend, they will eat us and there will be transformations. Those who were baptized, those who believed
in God, will be changed into something else. He who
eats the meat of a cow will be converted into that; he
who eats pork meat, in that will be converted, and will
go about dressed in its skin, he who eats the meat of the
rooster into that will be converted. Everyone, into that
which is their food, into that from which they live, into
the [beasts] they eat, in all of that they will be converted, they will perish, they will no longer exist, because their life will have come to an end, their count of
years. . . .

Look at those from Xalatlauhco, those who first believed, Don Alonso: his children and the principals were
turned into three capes and three hats. All of them were
transformed into something else, all went about graz-
ing. They no longer appear in the town where they
were, but in the pastures, in the forests is where they are
on their feet: they are cows. Now I have fulfilled my
responsibility with you; it will not be long before the
marvel takes place: if you do not believe what I tell you,
then just like them you will be transformed. . . . I will
make fun of you, because you were baptized. I will pardon you, so that you will not die and with that everything can end. There will also be hunger: take care of
your squashes, and the *tlalamate,* and the *jaltomate,* and
the fungus on the trees, and the silk on the corn, and the
leaves of the *jilotes,* and the ears of corn. . . .

When you are shouted at in Chapultepec, you will
go about crawling on your belly on the sand; then you
will be seen by the Old Lady with hard teeth and with
this you will be frightened, with this you will not be
eaten, you will be left alone. Thus this is, such as you
hear it. And it will happen that only there will the Lord

of the land make the things of our sustenance grow. Everywhere on the earth what is edible will dry. . . .

This happened in Coahuatépec, Atlapolco, and here are the names of those who washed their heads [reneging on the baptism]: the governor of Coahuatépec, Don Pedro de Luna, Francisco Zacayóatl, the judge of Huexotla . . . . Nicolás, the fiscal, governor of Atlapolco; Don Pedro Xico, fiscal; Juan Tecol. And they were apprehended there in Xalatlauhco when our dear father Pedro Hernández was present there; then he brought them here to Mexico, he presented them to the archbishop and to the provisor Francisco Manjarráez. And this took place in the year 1558.[35]

Actions and preachings like these of Juan Teton, in which the ancient beliefs are appealed to as arguments against Christianity, are not rare in the available documents. The cases discussed above make it possible at this point to formulate something of a conclusion.

A FEW REFLECTIONS

According to Sahagún and Durán, among others, the euphoria of the first missionaries, who proclaimed the sincere conversion of millions of indigenes, came in large part from their lack of "serpentine prudence." They frankly believed that they had built the faith upon solid ground, when in reality Christianity, in the words of Fray Bernardino, "was established over a false foundation."

Thus, the critical perspective of some of these same friars brought them, in the second half of the sixteenth and beginning of the seventeenth centuries, to observe that the ancient paganism had survived in the indigenous soul, though at times it was hidden by a cloak of elements from Christian ritual. Of course, some of these apostolic men could console themselves with certain instances that implied authentic conversion, as in the case of the youngsters educated in the College of Tlatelolco, who intoned Christian songs that they themselves had composed. Still, the antagonistic expressions that were voiced as frequently among the Indians provoked serious doubts about the achievement of the work that the early friars had believed already accomplished.

The indigenous testimonies presented here are examples of various native points of view, openly hostile to an acceptance of the new faith. Among them are found expressions of surprise and disgust when confronted with the idea of abandoning what was considered to be the roots of their native culture. Another frequent response was to harbor Christian beliefs and practices—but only superficially. There were also challenges to the new faith formulated by comparing the doctrine of the native forefathers to the incomprehensible preachings of the friars, at times considered worthy only of ridicule. They remembered the words of their wisemen, and from them both advice and threat were taken: the count of the years would come to an end, darkness would reign, and the *tzitzimime* would descend upon the earth.

From another perspective, the indigenes feared remaining *nepantla,* "in the middle," having lost the old yet not assimilating the new. Further, they saw the friars as people whose religion opposed all that gives happiness on earth. To this they added that the friars' preachings seemed to be directed toward the Indians rather than the Spaniards, given that the behavior of the latter did not modify itself at all to such priestly admonitions. With respect to the friars themselves, upon discovering that not all of them are of the same religious order, the native of New Spain argued that there are many forms of religiosity and that, therefore, the one of pre-Hispanic origin also had its own meaning.

The texts that bear the words of the Indians allow us to learn something of their thoughts when faced with what they took to be the overwhelming imposition of Christianity. Thus emerges the trauma of a people whose roots are slated for eradication by the conquerors, considering them grounded in the work of the devil. Certainly there were conversions, but many indigenes remained caught in the middle, *nepantla.* It was a small victory for the native priests and wisemen to facilitate the safeguarding and partial preservation of native ways of life beneath the outward appearance of the new rites and beliefs, rejected by the heart as incomprehensible.

This process of acculturation—the so-called spiritual conquest—is very different from what took place long before, between groups like Xólotl's Chichimecs and the heirs to the Toltec culture. Though that encounter was also witness to profound transformations, the cultural personality of the ancient nomads did not remain traumatized. These are two truly divergent experiences of contact and confrontation in which the indigenous society participated: one within the context of pre-Hispanic Mesoamerica, the other the inevitable continuation of the Conquest.

The testimonies cited here in no way exhaust the subject. To analyze and assess the contents of other existing texts will involve an effort to comprehend a past whose reality lives on, in a multitude of forms, in the very being of Mexico.

4.
Bartolomé de las Casas in the Indigenous Consciousness of the Sixteenth Century

Reference has been made to the core of Fray Bartolomé de las Casas's position with respect to the Christian conversion of the Indians—or, put another way, to the so-called spiritual conquest. The friar clearly condemned the widely accepted procedures for proselytizing the natives not only through his actions but also in his numerous writings, such as the well-known *Del único modo de atraer a todas las gentes a la religión de Cristo* (Of the Only Way to Attract All Peoples to the Religion of Christ). What he considered to be the "only mode of conversion" had little in common with the hurried forms of Christianizing employed by many religious of the time, who lacked a careful understanding of the indigenous mentality and, indeed, bore little respect for it.

Above all else, Fray Bartolomé had insisted, with the entire strength of his spirit, in the need to remain fully conscious of the dignity of human beings, their inalienable freedom—and also the inherent worth and the right of different peoples and cultures to exist. Thus he condemned all cultural imposition, referring explicitly to what many attempted to justify under the pretext that a necessary precursor to spreading the Christian faith was the suppression of idolatries, which in turn could only be accomplished by forcefully subduing the Indians.

To subdue them first through war—wrote Las Casas—
is contrary to the law and the soft yoke and light and
gentle load of Jesus Christ; it is the same as practiced by
Mohammed and practiced by the Romans, with which
they harassed and stole from the world; it is what
the Turks and Moors have today . . . it is terribly
wicked, tyrannical, dishonorable to the mellifluous
name of Christ, it is the cause of infinite new blas-
phemies against the true God and against the Christian
religion, as from great experience we know was done
and is today done in the Indies.[1]

To Fray Bartolomé, all subjugation and hostility, "terribly
wicked and tyrannical," formed an obstacle that, by its very
nature, impeded authentic conversion: "and thus it is an
impediment to the conversion of any pagans and it has made
it impossible that an infinite number of people in that orb
will ever be Christians, after all of the irreparable and
lamentable wrongs and damages."[2]

A logical corollary to the above in Las Casian thinking is
the thesis—another result of his comprehensive and respectful attitude toward different cultures—that any proselytizing process should follow an unhurried path of
rapprochement, teaching, and dialogue. From one of his
numerous texts in which he presents or reiterates this in-
variable position comes the following passage found in the
Tratado cuarto, published by Las Casas in 1552:

The kings of Castille are obligated because of divine
right to make sure that the faith of Jesus Christ is
preached in the manner in which He, the Son of God,
left decreed in his Church . . . that is to say, peacefully, lovingly and sweetly, charitably and affection-
ately, through gentleness and humility and good
example, inviting the unfaithful and especially the
Indians who are by their nature very gentle and peaceful. . . . And thus they will have as a good and gentle
and just God, the God of the Christians, and in this
way they will want to be His and to receive His
Catholic faith and holy doctrine.[3]

It is well known that with regard to this issue, as well as with many other questions he posed, Fray Bartolomé's perspective gave rise to criticism and violent antagonisms. Ultimately, it is clear that the Dominican held a vision far ahead of its time and, in global terms, was able to grasp the so often tragic significance of all violent cultural confrontations. Such a meeting between distinct peoples was particularly tragic when the desire for cultural imposition on the part of the dominant group inspired excuses and subterfuges that were used to sweep aside the dignity of the indigenous people, bearers of different cultural institutions and values.

The opinions of many of Fray Bartolomé's contemporaries about his ways of thinking are generally well known; they were almost never stated without vehemence, and were usually expressed against him as a person, against his thought, and in opposition to his work. Nonetheless, in the long succession of views put forward during the sixteenth century and frequently cited by the followers of Las Casas, the perspective of the people who were themselves at the heart of this polemic has been overlooked. What opinion might the indigenes themselves have held with regard to Father Las Casas, his thoughts and position? Certain events have been cited demonstrating native recognition of the friar or providing evidence of assistance they lent to him; however, as far as is known, these references have not related directly to the existence of opinions formulated by Las Casas's indigenous contemporaries that would indicate their view of him from the perspective of their circumstances as a vanquished, and ultimately subjugated, people.[4]

Are there no explicit testimonies of Las Casas's significance to the indigenous consciousness of the sixteenth century? One such statement, quoted below, is extremely eloquent and though not totally unknown, it has not received the attention it deserves.[5] It is the testimony of several prominent Indians: governors, mayors, and rulers of different regions of Central Mexico and of the capital itself, among them a distinguished chronicler, Don Hernando Pimentel, the grandson of Nezahualpilli. To present

their words within the appropriate historical context, it is
useful to reflect upon a few circumstances of the moment.
It is very likely that one or several of these Indian lords
could have met and dealt personally with Father Las Casas
during one of his stays in the capital, whether in 1532,
1538, or his last during the year of 1546. It would be
helpful as well to remember some of the most celebrated
opinions expressed by prominent Spaniards from Mexico
during these years, especially those attacking Las Casas,
whose meanings literate Indians and principal lords must
have grasped.

The positions of the most famous antagonists were already well known. Needless to say, Juan Ginés de Sepúlveda
occupied a principal role among them, and his reactions to
the actions of the friar were soon known in Mexico. It had
been his privilege to discover "rash, scandalous, and heretic
propositions" that he himself had noted "in the book of the
Conquest of the Indies that Fray Bartolomé de las Casas
printed without license."[6] The *cabildo* of Mexico City had
been so overjoyed with the attitude of Sepúlveda that on
February 8, 1554, they decided to manifest their gratitude
by sending him some "jewels, and other goods" of this land.[7]
All of this was as a consequence of the alarm that the Dominican's ideas and labors had caused in Mexico among the
authorities and Spanish residents. Another example of this
uneasiness is offered in a letter that shortly before, in April
of 1553, was sent to the emperor by surviving conqueror
Don Ruy González. In it, he gave voice to what was thought
and said in the city, writing "that a Fray Bartolomé, who
passed through this land . . . known as a cleric and friar
and now bishop by Your Majesty, who calls us, the conquerors, tyrants and thieves and unworthy of the name of
Christians . . . and other things that create scandals, as is
attested to by his confessional and by what we heard of him
here."[8]

To the reactions of the *cabildo* and people like Ruy González, who must have been well known in Mexico City, was
soon added the already-public one of the good Franciscan

Motolinía, surely esteemed by many Indians, both *mace-huales* and principals. His letter to the emperor, dated in Tlaxcala on January 2, 1555, is to a great extent an echo of the attitude of those who, in the regular and secular clergy, still remembered with resentment the presence of the bishop of Chiapas as a consequence of the meeting of prelates of 1546 in Mexico City. Gathering evidence to refute the accusations of Las Casas, among other things Motolinía says: "I marvel at how Your Majesty and your advisers have been able for so long to tolerate a man so worrisome, restless and boisterous and bothersome and quarrelsome, in the habit of a religious, so anxious, so ill-mannered and so offensive and damaging and so without calm."[9] The condemnations of the city *cabildo* and of people like Ruy González and friars like Motolinía were no secret in the atmosphere of Mexico between the years 1553 and 1556. The indigenous leaders, especially the literate ones like the Tezcocan Don Hernando Pimentel, must have been thoroughly familiar with them.

Perhaps, by way of compensation, they were also aware that the Royal Council of the Indies at least had agreed to hear the list of Fray Bartolomé's denunciations, complaints, and accusations. Further, the principal Indians noted the arrival in 1544 of the inspector Tello de Sandoval, who had come to make public the new laws abolishing *encomiendas,* an institution against which the then-bishop of Chiapas had struggled so strongly.

In spite of this, however, it was clearly dangerous to express a divergent opinion about Las Casas in the year 1556, especially for Indians. Nonetheless, it is precisely at this moment that a select group of them met in the town of Tlacopan (Tacuba), as if in the capital itself, to demonstrate openly to Philip II the injustices to which their people are the subject, "the many wrongs and damages that we receive from the Spaniards, because they are amongst us and we amongst them," and to ask for a defender, a man who was "very Christian and of good will." Further, they explicitly petition him to designate "the bishop of Chiapas, Don Fray Bartolomé de las Casas, to take on this charge of being our defender and that Your Majesty order him to accept."

Those who wrote these words on the second of May, 1556, in Tlacopan, "where we are all assembled for this," were far from unknown townspeople. The letter's tenor alone, with the arguments presented, reveals the fact that it was written by lords who included among them one or more "literate Indians." They seem to be familiar with some of Las Casas's writings, speaking as he does of the wrongs that have made their destruction and end imminent.

The lords surely met in order to elaborate on what had been discussed in earlier talks, for that same day, May 2, 1556, their letter was ready to be sent to the "very high and very powerful King and Lord, Don Philip." The group probably gathered in the house of Don Antonio Cortés, who, as he himself says in another writing, is a "*tlatoani* [ruler, governor], or *cacique,* of the town named Tlacopan."[10] Among those who will endorse the petition that Fray Bartolomé be designated as their defender are the *caciques* and lords of important places in the central region. Thus we encounter none other than Don Pedro Motecuhzoma Tlacahuepantzin, son of the last great *tlatoani,* or lord, of Mexico, who, aside from claiming the dominion of Tula through inheritance from his mother, had been distinguished by Cortés immediately after the Conquest with the governorship of the Atzacualco quarter in the capital itself. Despite the shadow cast upon him by Gómara, who claimed that he "liked wine," according to popular belief, Don Pedro enjoyed the recognition of the Crown of Spain and was granted the title of count of Moctezuma.

Also famous among the participants was Don Hernando Pimentel Ixtlilxóchitl, son of Coanacotzin and lord of Tezcoco, who, as is well known, kept up correspondence and relations with the count of Benavente and the viceroy Luis de Velasco. As his relative Fernando de Alva Ixtlilxóchitl would do later, Don Hernando Pimentel wrote on historical subjects and had provided the viceroy with information about the descent of the kings of Tezcoco, as well as many other facts about the ancient Acolhua kingdom. Another of those present was Don Diego Mendoza, governor of the town of Axacuba, who had served in the pacification of the Chichimecs and had received a coat of arms from the Crown in return for his efforts. Don Juan Ixtolinqui from Coyoacán, governor of that very important town, also had come to sign his name. He was another who maintained a friendship with the viceroy Don Antonio de Mendoza and included among his merits having participated in the pacification of New Galicia. Finally, their ranks included the lord of Itztapalapa, Don Alonso; Don Miguel Sánchez, at that time judge and *cabildo* member of Mexico; Don Esteban de Guzmán, a judge from the same city; Don Cristóbal de Guzmán, Don Baltasar de San Gabriel, and Don Pedro de Lati, councilmen of the *cabildo* of Mexico, who were in the company of all of their colleagues, the other councilmen; and finally Don Jerónimo del Aguila, judge and *cabildo* member of Tlacopan, and Don Pedro de Elman who had brought with him as well all the councilmen of this town.

This summary description of the prominent persons brought together for what I call "the assembly of Tlacopan," reveals that the gathering comprised the most illustrious of the indigenous nobility of the central region during the mid-sixteenth century. There is no sure indication of exactly who had the responsibility of drawing up the letter. Two who might well have done so among those who attended the meeting are Don Hernando Pimentel, the chronicler, and Don Antonio Cortés, author of other missives to the king. What does seem clear is that those indigenous leaders who endorsed it, and in particular the one who formulated it, had ample knowledge of the thinking and character of Las Casas. They knew that at that time (1556) he was already a man of advanced age, and in fact he was eighty-two years old. Thus they express their fear and, interestingly, mention that "if by chance said bishop were unable [to assist us] because of his death or sickness" upon the arrival of the letter in Madrid, they would ask that another prominent person "of good will and very Christian" be appointed. These attributes, which to their eyes Fray Bartolomé possessed to the highest degree, were urgently needed. They knew that the priest had plainly devoted his life to the defense of the Indians, and because of this they ask that he officially be given "this charge of being our defender."

Appropriating what they considered to be the heart of the friar's thinking, the writers present their reasons in an orderly fashion, including the following points: "we are in such great need of protection and aid"; "we receive many wrongs and damages from the Spaniards"; it is necessary to give "notice and true accounts of all of them"; "otherwise we will suffer daily so many needs and we are so aggrieved, that soon we will be ended, since every day we are more consumed and finished"; "they expel us from our lands and deprive us of our goods." And all of this is true "for ourselves (the principals) and those whom we have in our charge."

All of the above, particularly the idea of the end and destruction caused by damages received from the Spaniards, is certainly an echo of the already-familiar denunciations of the friar whose official protection is being solicited. In sum, it could be said that in the letter as a whole, the principals of Mexico demonstrate that they have made many of the ideas of Las Casas their own. In those passages that refer directly to the father, their view and opinion of him is clear: they seek him out as a defender because they are persuaded that he, more than anyone else, will be able to approach the king in search of a remedy. This is due to the fact that, in addition to being a wise man, he is "a very Christian person and of good will."

Such is the image of Fray Bartolomé forged by this select group of men of Náhuatl lineage. Since, as Indians, they were precisely the object of the polemic that made up the Dominican's life, their awareness of him is a crucial demonstration of his significance for them. Amidst the myriad interpretations and images that exist of Las Casas—those "irreconcilable enemies," as O'Gorman says, "that uselessly attempt to affirm themselves each at the exclusion of the others"[11]—an important place is occupied by this one held by the Indians themselves, whose feelings, albeit predictable, are far from unimportant. This is particularly the case if one remembers the historical moment in which the letter was written, and that without any reservation they revealed their opinion to the king. This act, as well as the denunciations of Las Casas, provide evidence for the existence of a certain freedom of expression in the Spanish milieu of the sixteenth century, a liberty that many have denied a priori.

Their solicited defender, Fray Bartolomé, was a man "very Christian and of good will." To those who participated in the "assembly of Tlacopan," the following are the features that characterized him: in moral terms his goodness as a priest and defender, and in an intellectual sense his wisdom as a true Christian, so like the ideal that had been preached to them and that they had so seldom seen put into practice. In this way, basing the image of their sought-after protector in wisdom and goodness, the words of the Indians—expressed at a time when Las Casas was showered with insults—constitute a bold foreshadowing of future recognition of the friar. It might be added that the indigenous perspective would coincide in an unforeseen way with the lapidary eulogy by Agustín Yáñez, who saw him as the "supreme father and doctor of Americanness": with the goodness of a father and the Christian wisdom of a doctor in what concerns the being and "the ethos of the New World."[12]

The image formulated by Don Hernando Pimentel, Don Pedro Moctezuma, and the other principals is, ultimately, an expression of the same indigenous consciousness that originally conceived of the "vision of the vanquished" and later developed the "vision of the defender." The evidence lies in the letter transcribed in its entirety below.

To His Majesty, from the lords and principals of the peoples of New Spain, May 2, 1556.

To our very high and powerful King and Lord, Don Philip, king of Spain, etc., thanks be to God.

Our very high and very powerful King and Lord:

The lords and principals of the peoples of this New Spain, of Mexico and its surroundings, subjects and servants of Your Majesty, we kiss the royal feet of Your Majesty and with dutiful humility and respect we implore You and state that, given that we are in such great need of the protection and aid of Your Majesty, both for ourselves and those whom we have in our charge, due to the many wrongs and damages that we receive from the Spaniards, because they are amongst us and we amongst them, and because for the remedy of our necessities we are very much in need of a person who would be our defender, who would reside continuously in that royal court, to whom we could go with them [our necessities] and give Your Majesty notice and true accounts of all of them, because we cannot, given the long distance there is from here to there, nor can we manifest them in writing, because they are so many and so great that it would be a great bother to Your Majesty, thus we ask and humbly beseech Your Majesty to appoint to us the bishop of Chiapas Don Fray Bartolomé de las Casas to take this charge of being our defender and that Your Majesty order him to accept; and if by chance said bishop were unable because of his death or sickness, we beseech Your Majesty in such a case to appoint to us one of the principal persons of your royal court who is very Christian and of goodwill to whom we can appeal with the things that would come up, because so many of them are of such a type that they require solely your royal presence, and from it only, after God, do we expect the remedy, because otherwise we will suffer daily so many needs and we are so aggrieved, that soon we will be ended, since every day we are more consumed and finished, because they expel us from our lands and deprive us of our goods, beyond the many other labors and personal tributes that daily are increased for us.

May Our Lord cause to prosper and keep the royal person and state of Our Majesty as we your subjects and servants desire. From this town of Tlacupan, where we are all assembled for this, the eleventh day of the month of May, the year one thousand five hundred fifty-six.

The loyal subjects and servants of your Royal Majesty, Don Esteban de Guzmán, judge of Mexico. Don Hernando Pimentel. Don Antonio Cortés. Don Juan of Coyoacán. Don Pedro de Moctezuma. Don Alonso of Iztapalapa. Don Diego de Mendoza. Cristóbal de Guzmán, *alcalde mayor*. Miguel Sánchez, judge and *cabildo* member of Mexico. Don Baltasar de San Gabriel. Don Pedro de Lati, councilman of the *cabildo* of Mexico. And all the other councilmen. Don Gerónimo del Aguila, judge and *cabildo* member. Tlacuba (Tacuba) Pedro Elmán, *cabildo* councilman, and all the councilmen.[13]

Once its most obvious meaning is understood, reading this letter provokes reflections of another type. Were those men who wrote and signed it, as distinguished persons closely tied to the Spanish authorities, already resigned to the imposition of all kinds of cultural transformations, including that of religion? Or in their search for a defender, and in the opinion that they held of Fray Bartolomé, was their sole purpose to seek a remedy to the damages, deprivations, labors, and tributes that ceaselessly burdened them and the indigenous people in general?

In asking these questions, it would be ideal to have the means to inquire profoundly into the meaning of this letter sent to Philip II. The point in question would be whether, in the case of these prominent Indians, their preoccupations were circumscribed to gain the assistance of the one who could put an efficient end to the most patent humiliations; or if the resolution of needs beyond this still remained in the minds of the solicitors, needs that they dared to refer to only obliquely, saying "nor can we manifest them in writing." Specifically, the question concerns the nature of such "necessities"—whose revelation, it seems, was not wisely confided in a letter. Did they perhaps relate to the defense of what are today called cultural identity and

respect for ancient traditions, all of which is in accordance
with what Fray Bartolomé expressed in "Del único modo de
convertir a los gentiles" (Concerning the only way to convert the pagans)?

If it seems out of place to attribute to these Indians a
familiarity with what Father Las Casas so often proclaimed
and reiterated, it is worthwhile to underline that repeated
in their letter transcribed above are forceful denunciations
such as that of "the destruction of the Indies," whose translation through indigenous lips becomes, "We will suffer
daily so many needs and we are so aggrieved, that soon we
will be ended." It is well known, on the other hand, that
among those who wrote this letter were several who had
been students in the famous Colegio de Santa Cruz in
Tlatelolco. Thus it is not unrealistic to assume that just as
they had come to master the Latin language and knew the
Bible and certain texts of Greco-Roman antiquity, they also
had the opportunity to read some of Las Casas's writings
and to hear him during his stays in Mexico City. Keeping
this in mind, it is possible that at least insofar as necessities
that "cannot be manifested in writing," some could only be
heard and understood, without risking punishment, by a
"very Christian" man, premier expert on the indigenous
cultural trauma: Fray Bartolomé de las Casas.

5.
Cultural Trauma, *Mestizaje,* and Indianism in Mesoamerica

At the time of the Spanish invasion the native groups of Mesoamerica—whether from the central region of Mexico, the Gulf zone, the Pacific and the area of Oaxaca, or the vast expanse of the Mayan world— were in possession of essentially one culture, which they had developed over several thousands of years. Throughout their pre-Hispanic cultural evolution, they had achieved complex forms of social, economic, political, and religious organization; they built great religious and urban centers; and they created an unmistakable and extraordinary art. Many accomplishments that were once considered to be the sole territory of Old World civilizations were also attained by the peoples of the Mesoamerican culture: calendric systems of surprising precision, diverse forms of writing, rich literatures, and sophisticated conceptualizations that are still evidenced in the indigenous codices and texts that have been preserved.

The invasion, or "conquest," signified, above all, the violent confrontation of this indigenous universe, almost magical in many aspects, with the cultural reality of the Europeans—expansionists with a technological base that at least partially explains the relative ease of their penetration and predominance in the New World. Various accounts of this dramatic encounter are available to us. Several were left by the conquerors themselves, testimonies that contrast strongly with the stories of the vanquished, told in various indigenous languages shortly after their defeat. In both types of chronicles, though much appears worthy of opprobrium, Hernán Cortés and some of the other Spanish captains reach the rank of epic figures, and there are also indigenous heroes who have nothing to envy in the conquerors' exploits. Thus, if Cortés comes to be the prototype of the conqueror of modern times, Cuauhtémoc becomes deserving of the title given him by a poet, as "the only hero worthy of art."

The ancient ideal of the universal Christian empire endured. The men of Castilla were members of a society that believed it had a special mission in the world. This implied broadening the dominions of the monarch, making conquests, exploiting for their own benefit the riches of the New World, and changing the ways of life of the defeated natives—ensuring above all their conversion to the Christian faith. The vitality of this new crusade, as a living reminder of the wars with the followers of the crescent moon in Spain and the Turkish Empire, kept the spirits of the conquerors and, later, those of the first missionary friars high.

This may help to explain why the Spaniards' posture was never one of indifference with respect to the indigenous realities that confronted their eyes. Thus, from their first contacts with the Aztecs, or Mexicas, they expressed a violent aversion to everything that appeared to be linked to the indigenous religion. In the minds of the Europeans, repugnant sacrifices and abominable idolatries constituted the essence of the Indians' system of worship. Their immediate response was to attribute to these ancient beliefs and rites—and to many other cultural elements—the character of being works of the devil that, as such, should forever be eradicated from the face of the earth. Thus, in the case of the Conquest in the New World, cultural confrontation gave free rein to all kinds of acts of destruction. For the conqueror and the friar, such a mode of operation meant the culmination of religious fervor and a claim to fame in light of their own Christianity; for the Indian, the trauma of the

Conquest deepened and was transformed into the inde-
scribable anguish of a culture threatened with death.

Besides the more obvious manifestations of native temples
and images of the gods, the destruction perpetrated by
the conquerors went on to embrace many indigenous monuments and artistic creations, calendric inscriptions, and
"codices," or books of paintings. Also, the records of the
deeds of the past were prohibited, the poems and songs; in
sum, they banned all that had constituted the core of the
rich indigenous cultural inheritance.

The trauma of the Conquest left such a deep emptiness
that in today's Mexico there are many, whether Indian, mestizo, or even of pure Spanish lineage, who fix their gaze
time and again—not for intellectual reasons but instead
with a passion that may seem anachronistic—on that past
over 450 years ago, either to reiterate condemnations or to
claim different kinds of defense, rekindling phobias that
others might think had already been overcome.

THE ANCIENT AWARENESS OF "ACCULTURATION"
THAT WAS CULTURAL TRAUMA

Contemporary testimonies of the events of the Conquest,
much more meaningful than any possible form of later consideration, were left by surviving indigenous wisemen and
the first friars who arrived in Mexico. The first text to be
cited here is from an anonymous Indian chronicler of
Tlatelolco, who wrote in 1528:

All of this happened to us,
we saw it,
we were astonished by it.
By this lamentable and sad fate
we saw ourselves anguished.
Broken spears lie in the roads.
We have torn our hair in our grief.
The houses are roofless now,
and their walls are red with blood. . . .
The water has turned red, as if it were dyed,

and when we drink it,
it has the taste of brine.
We have pounded our hands in despair against the
    adobe walls,
for our inheritance was only a net made of holes.
The shields of our warriors were its defense,
But they could not save it.[1]

An awareness of their fate forced the chronicler to lament
that their cultural heritage was now merely "a net made of
holes." Another very dramatic rumination is owed to Chilam
Balam, "Tiger," elder priest of the Mayan people:

Life is wilted
and dead is the heart of its flowers;
those who dip their *jícara* [gourd] to the bottom,
those who stretch everything until it breaks,
damage and desiccate the flowers of others. . . .
Pugnacious by day,
conflictive by night,
assailants of the world. . . .
There is no truth in the words
of those who have come from beyond. . . .
They Christianized us
but they exchange us between them
as though we were animals.[2]

In order to survive, an indigenous people was forced
to accept the foreign doctrines and rites. For quite some
time—until laws were issued to prevent it—many Indians
were enslaved. Others remained under the tutelage of *encomenderos* who made the Indians work for their own profit.
Culturally decapitated, bent under the burden of forced
labor, and scourged by previously unknown diseases, the
natives began to decrease in number at an alarming rate.

The enormous accumulation of misfortunes that, one
after another, had befallen the Indians were described by
Fray Toribio de Benavente Motolinía as "plagues crueler
than those of Egypt." Among them, according to the friar,

were the diseases and pestilence "that in some provinces killed half of the people and in others but a few less, because since the Indians did not know how to remedy it . . . by it they died like flies."[3]

Plague, which sometimes goes unmentioned, was what Motolinía goes on to describe with the following words:

> [that of the] farmers and blacks, who soon after the land was distributed the conquerors placed in their *repartimientos* [labor drafts] and towns that had been given to them as an *encomienda* [as a grant of tribute payers], servants or blacks to collect the tributes and to attend to the profits. . . . Which I say aggravated the natural lords and all of the people and thus they make others serve them and fear them more than if they were lords themselves. . . . they inflame and corrupt everything, stinking like flesh riddled with flies . . . , drones that eat the honey produced by the laboring bees, that is, that they are not satisfied with what the poor Indians can give but rather they are always nagging like bothersome flies. . . . In the first years they were so despotic . . . in abusing the Indians and in sending them heavily laden to far-off lands and making them do other works, that many of them died.[4]

The list of misfortunes recorded by the Franciscan, always in comparison to the plagues of Egypt, included the tributes, labor in the gold and silver mines, the forced rebuilding of Mexico City, and the abominable use of branding irons to mark the faces of slaves: "because each one that bought the slave, put his name on his face, so much so that his entire face was covered with writing."[5]

If Motolinía's accounts of this situation themselves constitute a full denunciation, we hear with yet more force another voice that compels a deeper awareness of what took place in Mexico and in many other areas of the New World. The obvious reference here is to Bartolomé de las Casas, the bishop of Chiapas. His words were as violent and radical as the trauma imposed upon the Indians. He preached but also

acted, excommunicating *encomenderos,* speaking with the
emperor, writing books, treatises, and booklets—using, in
effect, every means within his reach to validate his defense
of the Indians.

To deepen our understanding of the meaning of the confrontation—and, ultimately, the acculturation—of Indians
and Europeans, it is important to reflect upon the actions of
Las Casas. Undeniably, he along with others—but Las Casas
most of all—had an extremely influential role in the series
of events that held the fate of the Indians in the balance.
And it should be remembered that the subjects of his
actions, as we have already seen, were fully aware of the
efforts and struggles of Fray Bartolomé. In what concerns
Spain—where it was not rare to hold the Dominican as an
enemy and even as mad—it ought to be a matter of pride to
count him among its most illustrious sons.

Through the work of Las Casas something took place in
the milieu of the Hispanic world that has never been repeated. The same people who brought about "the destruction of the Indies" had among them the greatest censor of
their activities. If soldiers or *encomenderos* used violence, the
Dominican, himself a Spaniard, condemned the injustice
with an even greater violence. That enemy powers should
have made use of his clamor and his works to forge a black
legend does not diminish from the fact that the thought
of this unlikely censor, even beyond the particular circumstances, has a universal resonance and validity.

In addition to his denunciations, Las Casas sought a remedy to the wrongs that he perceived. With the help of others, he won the enactment of the famous New Laws (1542),
developed to rescue the Indians from the hands of their
exploiters. Earlier he had initiated projects of reconciliation
with the indigenous communities—like that of Vera Paz in
Guatemala—that today astonish ethnologists and anthropologists interested in the problematic of cultural change.
In his view, the forced conversions to Christianity had to be
eliminated forever. The only way to proceed was to ensure
that the natives, after learning of the message of the Gospel,

would then accept it freely if they wished to do so.[6] What could be described as an essential feature of the thought and action of Las Casas was his profound respect for the indigenous cultures. He gives evidence of this in his *Apologética historia*, the encompassing work he wrote in order to record and appraise the accomplishments of the pre-Hispanic civilizations, especially those of Mesoamerica and the Andean area.

ATTEMPTS AT UNDERSTANDING THE INDIGENOUS CULTURE AND AT MAINTAINING THE NATIVE COMMUNITIES IN ISOLATION

There were other humanists among the missionaries who, both in thought and deed, committed themselves in various ways to supporting the cause of the indigenous peoples. Some, from an early date, initiated research directed toward deepening their knowledge about the ancient institutions and values of the pre-Hispanic cultures, especially the one that had flourished in the central region of Mexico. The purpose of such activities was precisely to preserve as much of value as possible, while making their reconciliation with the vanquished that much easier and more human. The Franciscan Gerónimo de Mendieta provides a clear explanation of the goal of the first of these investigative efforts:

It is worth knowing that in the year one thousand five hundred and thirty three, when Don Sebastián Ramírez de Fuenleal, then bishop of the island of Española, was president of the Royal Audience of Mexico, and the holy Fray Martín de Valencia, being guardian of the order of Our Father San Francisco in this New Spain, by their joint decision the father Fray Andrés de Olmos, a member of the same order (and for being the one with the most knowledge of the Mexican language at that time in this land, and being a learned and discreet man), was charged with writing a book about the ancient things of these natural Indians, especially of Mexico, Tezcoco, and Tlaxcala; so that there would be some memory of

them, and so that that which was bad and out of place
would be better refuted, and so that if something good
were found it could be noted, just as many of the things
of other pagans are recorded and held in memory.[7]

In fact, the work accomplished by Olmos was the point of
departure for systematic investigations concerning the indigenous cultural legacy. The piece he ultimately wrote on
the basis of his research was unfortunately mislaid, and is
only known of through references. Nonetheless, it is important to remember that at least some of the texts that Father
Olmos collected remain preserved in the Náhuatl language,
including several *huehuehtlahtolli,* or discourses of the elders, testimony to the wisdom that had flourished before
the Conquest.

The renowned Fray Bernardino de Sahagún would come
to continue, broaden, and improve upon the work carried
out by Olmos. It is to him that we owe the most extraordinary attempt at understanding, from within, the culture of
the vanquished. In his view, it was a very dangerous and
inhuman error to proceed with the aim of introducing
changes without taking into account the differences in cultural realities. Thus, over a course of forty years, with the
assistance of indigenous disciples and surviving native wisemen, Sahagún dedicated himself to saving something of the
New World treasure, made up of ancient literature, history,
traditions and—in a word—all that was essentially related
to the institutions, values, and ideals of this culture threatened with death.

The fruits of his long and well-planned investigation were
a great collection of texts in the Náhuatl language, taken
from the lips of the Indians, and copies of paintings originating from the codices, or pre-Hispanic books. Such texts,
preserved up to the present, provide firsthand information
about, among other things, the following subjects: beliefs,
rites, festivals and customs, the ancient world view, calendric systems, education, art, business, medicine, law, flora
and fauna, and ethnic origins. In addition, some of the texts

are transcriptions of moral and sacred discourses, hymns and songs, and even what can be described as a purely indigenous vision of the events of the Conquest.[8]

Sahagún often repeated his goals in such a task. Fully conscious of the fact that the object of his investigations was a people whose culture was in a critical moment of disintegration, his preoccupation was to underline the capacities of the Indians, as well as the situation in which the natives found themselves. Only in this way would it be possible to seek authentic conversion.

> This work will be very useful in order to understand the true worth of this Mexican people, which is still not known, because there befell them the condemnation that Jeremiah on behalf of God hurled against Judea and Jerusalem, saying, in the fifth chapter, "I will make it fall upon you, I will bring against you a people from far away, a very robust and forceful people, an ancient people skilled in war, a people whose language you do not understand and have never heard before; people strong and aggressive, very willing to kill. This people will destroy you and your women and children, and everything you possess, and will destroy all of your towns and buildings." This to the letter has taken place against these Indians by the Spaniards: they and their things were so overrun and destroyed that no semblance remained of what they once were. Thus they are held as barbarians and people of very little worth, while, in truth, in what concerns social order they are a step ahead of many other nations that have great pretensions of being very ordered, putting aside some of the tyrannies that their way of ruling entailed. From this little that has been discovered with great effort, it appears that there could be much advantage if all of it could be uncovered.[9]

An awareness of the "true worth" of the Indians who were "a step ahead of many other nations" had brought Fray Bernardino and other friars, like Gerónimo de Mendieta, to conceive of an idea that must have seemed, to many, strange and even extremely dangerous. In their view, the natives could only be freed from their most tragic experiences if they managed to live—while preserving all of the good of their ancient culture—isolated and free from contact with the Spanish. One somewhat similar approach had already been successfully applied thanks to another true humanist, Vasco de Quiroga, member of the second Audience of New Spain and later the bishop of Michoacán. Bringing to fruition a type of utopia, he had organized among the Tarascan Indians of Michoacán new forms of organizing their communities in which, by promoting economic development and paying great attention to health and social and religious aims, the changes were propitiated based upon the participation of natives free from coercion, abuses, and threats.

Juan de Zumárraga, Bernardino de Sahagún, and other Franciscans, shortly after the arrival of the first viceroy, Antonio de Mendoza, achieved the first steps toward their goal. Early in 1536 the Colegio de Santa Cruz in Tlatelolco was formally inaugurated, a school created so that the best of the indigenous youth could be educated. In the school, authentic communication and an interchange of knowledge and values was sought, both of Europeo-Christian and pre-Columbian origin. The institution, which carried out its mission during its first decades of existence, had not only friars for teachers but also some Indians. Later, on more than one occasion, the rector of the school was chosen from among the latter.

The aim of the Franciscans—as we are led to understand in various parts of the chronicle by Gerónimo de Mendieta—implied taking yet another step. Their final objective was to organize, no longer in name only, genuine "Indian republics" where a new version of primitive Christianity would be allowed to flourish without the dreaded contact with the Spanish colonists. In order to lay the foundation for such aspirations, the friars repeatedly discussed the dangers of cohabitation or, as we would say today, of this disastrous form of acculturation: "It is clearly known that the Spaniard has the bad intention and determination to finish with all the Indians of New Spain if they were left in their hands . . . thus when in doubt it must always be assumed that the Spaniard is the one who offends and the Indian is the one who must suffer."[10]

Ultimately, and in spite of efforts to understand the depths of indigenous culture and make possible the isolation of the Indians, the steady will of the viceregal authorities dispelled the hopes of realizing such ideals. Though some works have survived that rescue the texts of the spiritual legacy of the indigenous world, the deeds of friars like Mendieta and Sahagún—as well as the denunciations of Father Las Casas—did not manage to put an end to the prevailing imposition of a society that, finally, was the one that exercised power.

ETHNIC AND CULTURAL *MESTIZAJE*

The efforts at isolating indigenous communities to allow them to develop ways of life emulating those of primitive Christianity quickly faded into oblivion, especially in the central region of Mexico. Instead, the contacts—that is, the processes of acculturation—with both positive and negative results, intensified and widened with the passage of time. Thus, from the second half of the sixteenth century the transformations were visible everywhere, in cities and in towns. Over the ruins of the ancient ceremonial centers where the pyramids, temples, and palaces had been, the new plans of a town based on the Spanish model were laid out, with its main plaza, cathedral and churches, civic buildings, and new types of monuments. The symbol and reality of multiple forms of Spanish domination became obvious. The institutions of *corregimientos* and *encomiendas,* Spanish forms of civil government and the labor of the Indians in agriculture, mining, public works, and all types of private or domestic services, were now prevalent, sanctioned by the authorities, and every day becoming more widespread.

In the ancient indigenous towns great monasteries arose, introduced as signs of the new religion, a kind of fortress where certain elements of a final manifestation of Spanish gothic survived. But at the same time, as if anticipating the later cultural *mestizaje,* vestiges of the creativity of indigenous hands remained. Although toiling beneath the labor that went into such buildings conceived of by the friars and other authorities, the natives managed to capture in them subtle traces of their ancient artistic sense.

Sometimes forcibly and at other times spontaneously, as it often happens in life, the reciprocal influences between the Indians and the Spanish were making their effects felt. George M. Foster, in his *Culture and Conquest: America's Spanish Heritage,* deals with the most important cultural elements that, as a consequence of the Conquest, were introduced by the Spaniards: the new forms of laying out and planning cities, towns, and villages; different agricultural technologies; domesticated animals; dress that, one way or another, came to be an imitation of European clothing; foods and plants previously unknown in the Americas; systems of business, social, economic, and political organization; and, of course, as a fundamental factor, the Christian religion to which all of the natives were to be converted.[11]

The reality of cultural *mestizaje* was that the large majority of those cultural elements originating from the Old World, upon coming into contact with indigenous traditions and ways of life, had to adapt themselves until taking on unforeseen features. As an example, there is the fusion of elements in the field of religion, the sometimes-subtle blendings of pre-Hispanic beliefs and rites with the doctrine preached by the friars. Some of the priests were aware of the situation and did not waver in making it public. Such was the case with Fray Bernardino de Sahagún, who, among other things, vehemently declared his suspicions concerning the rise of the new cult of the Virgin of Guadalupe precisely where the sanctuary of Tonatzin, the goddess mother, had been located.[12]

For their part, the Spanish, especially the children born in Mexican lands, were also seen as being influenced in many ways by the indigenous culture. This was obvious, especially to those recently arrived from Spain, who on more than one occasion demonstrated their surprise at seeing how forms of behavior became milder and more polite among the Criollos, already differing to a large degree from what was considered to be the Hispanic way of being.

Even those who did not know the indigenous languages acquired a distinct accent and frequently employed many native words. Other cultural elements of considerable importance, such as those related to diet, had also been adopted by the population of Spanish origin. To offer some examples, there was the adoption of corn, beans, chile, squash, tomatoes, avocados, and different types of *moles,* or sauces, prepared—with all of the adaptations one might expect—with a base of the original cuisine of indigenous cookery.

Parallel to such reciprocal influences and consequent transformations, something of enormous transcendence was taking place. The coming together of Indian and Spaniard had brought about the appearance of a new type of human being, the mestizo, who, with the passage of time, would come to play a key role in the fate of the Mexican nation. In fact, this ethnic mixing had begun very shortly after the arrival of the Europeans.

Women coming from Spain to the New World were scarce during the first years. This helps to better explain the attitude of the conquerors who, from the beginning, welcomed with open arms the tribute of women offered them by certain *caciques.* Thanks to testimonies such as those included in the *Diccionario autobiográfico de conquistadores y pobladores de Nueva España,* published by Francisco A. de Icaza, it is known that by the middle of the sixteenth century, children of Spaniards and indigenous women were already numerous.[13] These early mestizos were frequently born of women seduced and later abandoned. As many scholars have noted, the unhealed trauma of the vanquished was bound to become inflamed with the awareness of one's descent from a fleeting union, perhaps one of violence, and certainly not one of equality.

In New Spain the *mestizaje* between Spaniards and indigenes, testimony at least to the absence of racial prejudice,
continued to such an extent that toward the middle of the
seventeenth century there were more than three hundred
thousand mestizos. It is interesting to cite a little-known
testimony of an Indian who, at the beginning of the seventeenth century, expressed in Náhuatl his views concerning
mestizaje. The following are the words of the chronicler
from Chalco, Chimalpahin Cuauhtlehuanitzin:

> Of these mestizos we do not know from which Spaniards
> they came, or how they kept their lineage. Perhaps their
> grandparents there in Spain were nobles or common
> people, from whom they came, from whom those named
> mestizos originated.
>
> Here the daughters of the indigenous men of New
> Spain, some of noble origin, others from plebeian peo-
> ple, came to find themselves with Spaniards. Thus were
> born and continue to be born mestizos and mestizas.
>
> And others only through cohabitation, as hidden
> sons, thus on our part we are born here, we come out
> mestizos, mestizas.
>
> Those who are worthy men, be they mestizos, or mes-
> tizas, recognize that they come from us [the Indians].
> But others without reflecting, mestizos and mestizas,
> do not want to recognize that they have some of our
> blood, some of our color. Only vainly do they attempt
> to pass for Spaniards, they look down on us, they mock
> us. Also some Spaniards do that.
>
> But just as any Spaniard of noble blood was made by
> Our Lord God, so also did he favor us, did he grace us,
> though we do not have similar blood and color.
>
> Above all things we must remember that at the start,
> at the beginning of the world, only one was our first
> father, Adam, and only one our first dear mother, Eve,
> from whom we came, even though today our body ap-
> pears in different forms.[14]

Chimalpahin's perception of the complex theme of *mestizaje* was very keen. From Indian women and Spaniards,

whether noble or plebeian, "were born and continue to be born mestizos and mestizas." He then candidly accepts that some came to the world "only through cohabitation, as hidden sons." And herein lies the consciousness of trauma: some of these mestizos "do not want to recognize that they have some of our blood, some of our color. Only vainly do they attempt to pass for Spaniards." There are others, in contrast, who *do* accept what they truly are. But above all, Chimalpahin believes that with regard to *mestizaje,* a coherent and just attitude should be adopted.

Chimalpahin was an extremely religious man who lived as a *donado* [one who works as an unpaid servant of the Church without formal entrance into the religious profession], dedicated to serving in the hermitage of San Antonio Abad on the outskirts of Mexico City. The chronicler, who had researched and written several historical pieces about the ancient indigenous cultural legacy, appeals to his Christian conscience and discovers in it an argument that seems to him without retort. As noble as may be the blood of any Spaniard, he, the Indian, and the mestizo have the same origin in the final instance: all derive their true selves from the same God and all have in common a father and a "dear mother," the biblical figures of Adam and Eve, "from whom we came, even though today our body appears in different forms."

Chimalpahin's Christian argument, a belated echo of proclamations made by men like Bartolomé de las Casas, was unfortunately not something that would always be accepted in practice. It has been said that there were no racial prejudices when it came to sexual unions. However, the same could not be said for those who, mindful of the social structure of the colonies, made way for the implantation of a caste system. This was formed over the base of the ethnic heterogeneity of the different population groups: Spaniards, Criollos, Indians, mestizos, and black slaves. Later mixes between people of these groups were the object of more or less precise categorizations with their corresponding designations: descendants of Spaniard and black, mulattoes; of black and indigenous, *zambos;* of Spaniard and mestiza, *castizos;* of Spaniard and mulatta, *moriscos;* of Spaniard and morisco, *albinos;* of Spaniard and albino, *salta-atrás* ("jump backwards"); of Indian and *salta-atrás, lobos,* etc.

The inevitable discrimination inherent in the caste system did not, however, alter the fact that three centuries of Spanish domination were ultimately a forge that compelled the fusion of peoples and cultures. This was especially true for the central region of the country. In other places, particularly the northern territories, indigenous centers survived in much greater isolation. For this reason, in the North and in some communities in provinces like Oaxaca, Chiapas, and the Yucatán, many elements of the ancient culture have survived up to the present, along with the distinctiveness of native faces: forms of social organization, agricultural methods, traditional medicine, arts, and even religious beliefs and practices of pre-Hispanic origin.

Nonetheless, it must be recognized that in the physiognomy of the maturing country, the Spanish-indigenous ethnic and cultural fusion continued to hold primary importance. Calculations of New Spain's population toward the end of the eighteenth century demonstrate that of approximately six million inhabitants, nearly a third were mestizo. The two principal cultural legacies, even though frequently in conflict, now without a doubt formed the roots of a national being that would very shortly experience new processes of transformation. In terms of the indigenous communities, possessors in many ways of a unique ethnic identity and bearers at the same time of an old cultural trauma, it must be acknowledged that if their present was somber, their fate continued to be uncertain.

THE INDIANS IN INDEPENDENT MEXICO

Numerous Indians participated as the rank and file in the army as well as in the guerrilla bands captained by the leaders of independence, who were, for the most part, of mestizo or Criollo origin. In this sense, the Indians—now not only in terms of their contribution to the mestizo culture, but also through their deeds on behalf of the fathers of

Mexican independence, Hidalgo, Morelos, and Guerrero—implicitly acquired the character of cofounders of the new nation.

Nonetheless, while independence was gained, Mexico was far from having won what for some constituted the ideal: a certain kind of cultural and social unification. In fact, on all levels, the contrasts and discrepancies were obvious. While the mestizo population continued to grow, giving rise to an incipient middle class, there were many other groups like the one of European ancestry and the many communities that, to varying degrees, maintained their indigenous sense of identity.

The new dominant society consisted of members of the upper class of Spanish origin and, to a lesser degree, of people of mestizo extraction. However, by then there was greater aperture in terms of social mobility than what had prevailed during the colonial period. Thus, while the well-off families continued to have indigenous servants and the hacienda owners and ranchers still availed themselves of the labor of many native commoners, new legislation in an egalitarian vein recognized that any person, regardless of origin, could occupy any important position in the life of the country. And even if the proclaimed equality of rights was largely utopic, decades later there were isolated cases of Indians who came to fulfill crucial roles in various spheres of activity. By way of example, there are figures such as the famous writer and politician Ignacio Altamirano, the conservative general Tomás Mejía, and even some prominent members of the ecclesiastic hierarchy.

Benito Juárez was and continues to be a symbol in this context. In the indigenous consciousness and in that of the entire Mexican population—and beyond—he will always be remembered in terms of the historical transcendence of a native of a Zapotec community who came to be the country's president, guarding national freedom by fighting against the French intervention, defeating Maximilian, restoring the Republic and making positive transformations possible in the social and cultural reality of Mexico.

Nonetheless, the country's prevailing conditions did not lend themselves to concentrating on the urgent demands of indigenous communities and other large sectors of the population who shared precarious forms of existence. Instead of improving, their condition continued to deteriorate. With the rise of Porfirio Díaz, a long period of stability was certainly consolidated; without a doubt, one of Díaz's attributes was to make his dictatorship the foundation for an efficient administration. Guided by the goal of converting Mexico into a progressive nation, in line with the liberal and positivist ideals in vogue at the time, Díaz, nonetheless managed to evade in his projects of modernization the wounding problematic of the Indian, and that of the peasant masses in general.

The precursors to independence had already focused on the problem of landownership. Far from receiving an adequate answer, the problem was further exacerbated when, while confiscating religious properties, the indigenous communities were also affected. "Dead hands" were then replaced by the fervor of new owners, the great landholders, or *latifundistas*. During Díaz's tenure, peasants, primarily indigenous with the exception of those who lived in isolated regions, continued to swell the ranks of the haciendas' peons. Ultimately, their situation was probably worse than that of their ancestors on the *encomiendas* of colonial times.

In 1910, while there were approximately 4,860 haciendas in Mexico, many of them of enormous acreage, and more than 48,000 smaller ranches, almost 95 percent of the rural heads of household had no land. Approximately three million people worked for the great landholders. In general, they treated the indigenes, whose social function was to serve, as cheap manual labor in conditions very similar to those of slavery.

FROM THE REVOLUTION OF 1910

The social Revolution of 1910 at last included among its objectives the changes so long required by millions of Indians and mestizos. It should be remembered that, among others, Emiliano Zapata had great indigenous contingents in his forces, with whom—according to surviving testimonies—he spoke in Náhuatl.[15] His proclamations and denunciations, similar in some respects to those made by Father Las Casas, rekindled the consciousness of centuries of injustice.

The series of processes that have developed since the triumph of the Revolution to the present can be described as a patchwork of light and shadow. The entire nation has been the object of profound transformations. With respect to the indigenous communities, certainly many were returned their dispossessed lands. "Indianism," as an official policy of support and exaltation of native values, soon made its effects felt. To the initial postulates of this attitude—sometimes courting romanticism—were added perspectives developed in light of the social sciences, especially anthropology. Special mention should be given here to Manuel Gamio and his approach to the question. In the eyes of Gamio, Mexico continued as a country in which many different peoples and cultures lived on. To him, cultural heterogeneity was a reality in Mexico, the source of many problems on the one hand, but also the origin of its great richness.

The responsibility lay with the federal government to devise and carry out plans of action that would lead to national unity, while respecting the plurality of cultures. According to Gamio, the necessary first step was to identify, through multidisciplinary research, the cultural differences prevalent in the various regions of the country. A second step would be to foster the socioeconomic development of the various culturally distinct groups, so that they would be better able to participate in the economic and political life of the country. Such participation should be attained while respecting the cultural identities of the various ethnic groups. Furthermore, these groups should be assisted to free themselves from the burdens that, for centuries, have been the obstacles to their own development.

With these ideas in mind, in 1917 Gamio succeeded in obtaining the official support to organize a Department of

Anthropology (Dirección de Antropología), the first in the Americas developed to conduct research and act in accordance with the goals outlined above. One very important program Gamio carried out was the multidisciplinary research in the Valley of Teotihuacán. The valley, where the classic metropolis had flourished since the beginnings of the Christian era and whose surroundings had supported many different peoples, presented an excellent opportunity for diachronic research. Gamio had chosen the Valley of Teotihuacán as the first area where different local forms of culture could be identified. Though he lacked support to proceed with the research he had in mind in other regions of Mexico, his work in Teotihuacán was published in three large volumes, *La población del Valle de Teotihuacán,* [16] which was very well received not only in Mexico but also by many distinguished scholars of the United States, Germany, and other countries. It offered, for the first time, a substantial scholarly contribution in which, with the added depth of time, various ethnic groups who lived in proximity to one another were the subject of a multidisciplinary study aimed at the identification of their cultures. Its aim was not merely academic, as the results of the research were to provide the foundation to initiate appropriate projects that would free the native groups from obstacles that stood in the way of their own development and, fostering their cultural identities, make possible their participation in the social, economic, and political life of the country. Gamio's conceptual framework became a milestone in the field of Indianism.

In a different context, Mexican nationalism continued to explore the depths of its cultural heritage in its indigenous roots. Archaeological investigations and studies of pre-Columbian literature, especially of the Mayan- and Náhuatl-speaking peoples, also contributed to this process. The great muralists, Rivera, Orozco, and Siqueiros, focused on the country's indigenous past and also served to reaffirm the cultural capacities of contemporary native groups. New monuments were erected to commemorate the character and accomplishments of indigenous heroes like

Cuauhtémoc, Nezahualcóyotl, Cuitláhuac, Xicoténcatl, and, of course, Benito Juárez. In addition, on all educational levels courses on pre-Hispanic history were broadened, and new ones were introduced that taught the ancient literatures and arts as essential elements in the cultural legacy of the country. This clearly contributed to the fostering of an awareness and pride in their "indigenous cultural roots" among the great majority of the Mexican people.

Keeping all of this in mind, a question persists: Does the nationalist stance of exaltation of everything indigenous always translate into forms of action truly appropriate to the problematic situation of the aboriginal communities still living in Mexico today? It is an unavoidable fact that the living conditions of many native groups continue to be extremely precarious. To some foreigners who visit the country, as well as to Mexicans conscious of socioeconomic and cultural realities, the official stance of admiration for indigenous values certainly does not seem reconcilable with the widespread condition of many native groups whose poverty and marginality are plain to see.

For many years the official policy in Mexico, in terms of the so-called Indian problem essentially supported the belief that it was necessary to "incorporate the natives into the national culture." Thus, though perhaps without very clear intentions, the dominant mestizo- and European-origin society adopted approaches and forms of action not very different from those that had been prevalent during the colonial period in an attempt to change the indigenous ways of life. In other words, a policy of cultural imposition prevailed. Only during the last decades have new forms of approach more respectful of indigenous values been developed. Their aim was to put into play programs for the "integration" of native communities into the Mexican socioeconomic context. With this idea, the Instituto Nacional Indigenista was created in 1948 under the direction of a well-known archaeologist and social anthropologist, Doctor Alfonso Caso. This organization began to take action in different regions through what were designated as "indigenous coordinating centers." With support in social and anthropological research, the purpose of these centers was to initiate programs of "induced acculturation" to propitiate changes considered to be desirable and positive for the aboriginal groups. Their efforts included the introduction of better technology for agriculture, poultry, and livestock; the improvement of sanitary conditions; the establishment of bilingual schools; the opening of roads into outlying areas; and, in a word, long-lasting attention to the most urgent necessities of the community.

It is undeniable that the existence of coordinating centers—many more of which have been organized in recent years—in the indigenous zones in the states of México, Guerrero, Puebla, Hidalgo, Veracruz, Michoacán, Nayarit, Chihuahua, Oaxaca, Chiapas, Yucatán, Quintana Roo, Durango, San Luis Potosí, Sonora, and Baja California—has brought about positive changes in many respects. Among other things, the programs carried out through these centers have, as a common approach, a great respect for traditional indigenous institutions and values. It is also true that these organizations have prepared members of the communities to act as "cultural promoters," with the idea that they should act as a type of bridge between the native group and the functionaries and anthropologists who plan and apply the processes of "induced acculturation."[17]

Nonetheless, unavoidable questions persist that have to do precisely with the approaches adopted in such projects of induced acculturation. What sort of role is played in the development of these projects by those who are going to be subjected to its determined forms of change? In the search for economic and social development, are the consequences of such changes always clear, particularly those that are difficult for the indigenous mentality to assimilate and, above all, those that can eventually function to wear down the traditional structures of the community?

As if there were no escape, time and again we encounter a problem already anticipated and even remarked upon. If induced acculturation runs the risk, even under the best of circumstances, of being nothing but a more or less veiled paternalistic posture, what other forms of action are worthy of pursuit?

This crucial question is connected to the necessary self-liberation of the indigenous communities from the deficiencies and adverse factors imposed upon them throughout centuries of domination and exploitation. Among the wrongs that most obviously aggravate their situation, the following play primary roles: their common confinement in impoverished regions, often with little arable land and with more or less uncertain titles of property or possession; their isolated circumstances and the barriers that constrain free expression of their needs and perspectives; their frequent lack of the most elementary public services; the contrived and, therefore, hardly effective character of certain social and political structures that have been imposed upon them, indiscriminately, from the outside. To this list could be added a string of traumas, from the Conquest to the present, whose effects have included—among other things—a loss of confidence in their own abilities; a resistance or diffidence to fighting in defense of their rights; and, in certain cases, a shame of speaking in public in their own language, as if there were further dangers that could come from merely letting their identity be known.

It has sometimes been postulated that through adequate legal arrangements the Indians' situation could be transformed. Historical experience, however, has demonstrated that many such favorable laws, including some of the colonial legislation of the Indies, soon fell on deaf ears. It could also be stated here that in order to escape paternalistic attitudes in any case, the community, and especially its leaders, should count with the means not only to participate in the formulation of such laws but also to fight for their implementation.

It is important to insist here on an idea that is frequently evaded, or at least remains partially forgotten. Participation in development within a broader social complex, whether at

the regional or the national level, is not necessarily antitheti-
cal to the preservation of the cultural identity of a minority
group. There are examples of this in various situations and in
distinct times and places. An extremely eloquent example,
among others that could be cited, is offered by minorities of
the Italian, Romansh, and even French languages who live
together and fully participate in the national development
of Switzerland, whose population is primarily of German
origin.

In the case of Mexico, there have been and continue to be
several communities, concerned with improving their living
conditions, that have in fact been assimilating the culture
of the mestizo majority. Thus they have implicitly entered
into the process of ethnic and cultural fusion that, ultimately, has forged the identity of the Mexican nation.
The crossing of such communities into the context of the
majority culture has not necessarily meant their forced absorption. Their participation in broader arenas has come
about through more or less spontaneous processes of acculturation, which also consolidated and enriched the mestizo
cultural complex.

This seems to have been the case for many neighboring
communities of the principal centers of population, as well
as others where communications media, and the consequent
interchange of cultural elements, led to a more intense ethnic and cultural *mestizaje*. Like the rest of the majority population of the country, the groups that have contributed in
this way to the formation of Mexico's mestizo countenance
participate, with all of the problems that could be expected,
in the common effort to achieve the economic, social, and
political transformations that the entire nation demands.

But in Mexico there are other communities as well where,
along with an awareness of their own problems, their determination to preserve their own traditions, values, and, in a
word, indigenous cultural identity survives in different
ways. Among the cases that could be cited, special mention
should be made of groups such as the Yaquis and Mayos
in Sonora, the Tarahumaras in Chihuahua, the Coras

and Huicholes in Nayarit and Jalisco, the Tepehuanes in Durango, the Zapotecs and many others in Oaxaca, and the Tzeltales and Tzotziles in Chiapas, as well as other large groups of the same Maya family and of Náhuatl (Aztec) culture and language. Strong evidence of these groups' determination to maintain their cultural identity is offered by a resurgence of their voices demanding to be heard, also giving rise to an authentic literary renaissance, mainly in the Náhuatl, Maya, and Zapotec languages.

It is the state's responsibility to make the liberation of such indigenous societies possible—with respect to obstacles and adversities that have marginalized and kept them in conditions of misery—with the aim of winning their free participation in the social, economic, and political realities of the country. But at the same time, this obligation presupposes an absolute respect for the self-determination of the groups whose participation is being encouraged, not acting against their desires to preserve their own cultural personality. Any attempt to absorb minorities interested in maintaining their cultural differences not only ends up by being converted into a form of colonialist imposition, but is an error of tragic consequences. The results of contrived and artificial projects of "incorporation" will be a cultural uprooting with greater traumas, a new obstacle that would impede effective participation—with a distinct personality—in the social and economic life of the country.

The history of independent Mexico itself offers dramatic examples of groups that, when confronted with aggressive projects of incorporation, responded with violence to defend their own cultural legacy, lands, and existence as a distinct group. A case worthy of mention is that of the Yaquis in Sonora, who for many years were in a state of war with the Mexican government until, finally, their rights as a culturally distinct society and claims to their ancestral lands were recognized both politically and from a legal standpoint.[18]

Above other considerations, and recognizing that the situation and the future of the indigenous societies are essentially related to the structures that make up the integral reality of the country and the changes possible in it, it is evident that the responsibility lies with the state, along with the assessment of anthropologists, sociologists, and other specialists, to encourage the participation of the Indians on an equal footing and with absolute respect for their cultural identity. If these ideas have meaning in the sphere of any society or state that respects human rights, they will be even more clearly understood among those nations and peoples that, for centuries, have been subjected to different forms of foreign domination.

In Mexico, which has known colonial subjugation and repeated foreign aggression and whose international politics is based upon the doctrine of self-determination and the recognition of human rights, it should be almost a given to presume the application of the same principles to the reality of its indigenous populations. Determining the most expedient ways to proceed in order to truly permit the effective participation of all groups is an urgent task, concerning both those who want to make the mestizo culture their own and those who, for centuries, have pursued their aim of safeguarding their cultural identity.

6.
Conveying the Amerindian Texts to Others

In several of the chapters that make up this book, mention has been made of the existence of texts written by Mesoamerican peoples. Further, it was noted earlier that in recent times a true literary renaissance has taken place, especially among the speakers of the Náhuatl, Mayan, and Zapotec languages. At this point, before going on to consider some cultural situations beyond the Mesoamerican realm, it is pertinent to reflect upon the significance of these Amerindian literary creations in the eyes of non-Indians. If, to the Mesoamerican and other indigenes, such compositions have been and continue to be of value as expressions of their own feelings, beliefs, thoughts, world view, and historical consciousness, what might they mean to others who find them culturally alien?

True, the question is somewhat rhetorical. Today more and more non-Indians in the Americas, Europe, and elsewhere are recognizing and enjoying the worth of such Amerindian forms of expression, both past and present, some of which are true literary gems. The question proposed above therefore needs to be rephrased. How have non-Indians been introduced to the literary creations of Mesoamerican indigenous peoples? Such a question obviously has to do with the art of introducing and translating texts, making them understandable and enjoyable to those whose language and culture are very different.

My purpose here is not to attempt to trace the complex history of how the Amerindian texts in general have been translated into English, Spanish, French, German, or any other European or non-European language. Rather, I intend to emphasize the fact that Amerindians have enriched the world's cultures in ways beyond the diffusion of their ancestral staple foods, which include maize, chili, tomatoes, beans, potatoes, tobacco, and many other products that became basic ingredients in European diet and pharmacology. They have also contributed through some of their spiritual creations. The value of the Amerindian arts is greatly appreciated. Sculptors like Henry Moore have been inspired by creations such as the recumbent rain god of the Mayas and Toltecs. And many modern painters in North America and Europe, to say nothing of those Mexican masters like Diego Rivera, José Clemente Orozco, David Alfaro Siqueiros, Rufino Tamayo, and Francisco Toledo, have also experienced the impact of indigenous works of art.

In terms of literature, it is only partially true that their "rediscovery" has just recently taken place. In the early sixteenth century, many European humanists, gaining a limited access to these literary works, began to recognize their merit. They did so in full consciousness of the problems posed by the necessary translation of the compositions. Since translation acts as the bridge enabling the majority to enjoy these pieces, it is no wonder that some of these humanists, confronted with the problem, left us their viewpoints on the subject. The native expressions—voices of peoples who are now culturally endangered—have nonetheless been heard. Let us turn first to what many have already written on the task of conveying Amerindian voices from one language and culture to another. Later, I will comment on my own experience in this matter. Nothing is as important for understanding the Indian cultures, threatened for centuries, as approaching their words, both ancient and modern.

THE FRIAR'S EARLY ATTEMPTS AT CONVEYING THE INDIGENOUS LITERARY WORKS TO OTHERS

The discovery of pre-Hispanic compositions—speeches of the elders, historical annals, sacred hymns, songs, poems, etc.—as well as a recognition of their value as testimony to a culture, and sometimes as noble expressions of moral wisdom, began to take place as early as the third decade of the sixteenth century. An eloquent example of this is provided by the Franciscan Andrés de Olmos who, beginning in 1533, had collected this kind of writing, with the idea that "if something of merit were found, it should be noted, just as many other things of other pagans are preserved."[1]

The method he adopted in his search was succinctly described some years later by a member of the Audiencia, or judicial council of Mexico, Doctor Alonso de Zorita. In his *Breve y sumaria relación,* he wrote about the ancient indigenous rulers of this land. Addressing Philip II, he commented:

> In addition to raising their children with the discipline and care already described, Indian parents also took great care in giving them much and very good advice, and today the principal ones among them keep such admonitions in their books of paintings. And a friar who came to Mexico at an early date [Andrés de Olmos] translated this counsel, and he says he brought some of the principal Indians to write it. . . . And they wrote and put them in order in their language, without his being present. And [the Indians] drew everything from their books of paintings, which are like their scriptures, and by these means they understand themselves well. And nothing was changed in what they gave to him, except putting the text in paragraphs.[2]

Zorita, in his communication to the king, adds two more remarks that complement his description of Father Olmos's procedures. One has to do with the friar's aim in rescuing these moral discourses. He was convinced that they should be kept and remembered, "just as many other things of pagans are preserved." And he was also convinced—as were Fray Bartolomé de las Casas and Fray Bernardino de Sahagún, some time later—that these and other similar indigenous moral discourses "would be of greater profit to young boys and girls . . . said in the pulpit, because of the language and style in which they are written (*mutatis mutandis*), than many other sermons."[3]

But in order to employ the ancient moral discourses, even in the pulpit, one had to apply a sort of conceptual translation. Zorita continues in his missive to the king, "He told the principals [those who had drawn the texts from their painted books] that the names of their gods should be suppressed and that, instead, they should put in their place the name of the true God, Our Lord."[4] Except for this precautionary action, the discourses could be accepted in every respect, and even brought to the attention of the king himself: "And so that Your Majesty [Philip II] can see that they [the Indians] are not so deprived of reason as some would have them, the discourses are copied literally. And I humbly ask Your Majesty to pardon me, if it seems I am departing from the purpose of what your majesty wants to know . . . , as I believe your majesty will receive the service due you by this being made known to you."[5]

The texts Zorita sent to his king were "copied literally" from the translation Olmos had done into Spanish from the original Náhuatl. This translation, as we have seen, was based on the text of the indigenous discourses in which "precautionary actions" had already been taken, according to Fray Bartolomé de las Casas, who also had copies of them:

Andrés de Olmos translated them from Mexican into Romance [Spanish] without adding or taking anything of substance, deriving meaning from meaning, and not word for word. Because, at times one Mexican word requires many from our language and one of our words might necessitate many of theirs in order to be understood. And, as these discourses are so notable, I copied them, so that others might see the greatness of the moral doctrine with which the Indians reared their children.[6]

In this manner Zorita and Las Casas describe one of the earliest attempts at conveying to others—including King Philip II—the gems of Náhuatl literature, the *huehuehtlahtolli*, or testimonies of the "ancient word." For his part, Fray Bartolomé, in the same chapter of his *Apologética historia* where he describes Olmos's procedure in translating these texts, does not hesitate to praise them vividly: "What better or more appropriate admonitions, more necessary in guiding human life to virtue could have been written and proclaimed by Plato or Socrates and Pythagoras, or Aristotle after them, than these that the natives used so frequently to instruct their children? What more does Christian law teach, except for that which pertains to the faith and to those things invisible and supernatural?"[7]

The humanist friars had indeed discovered and recognized the value of these noble forms of indigenous expression, conveyers of great moral wisdom. Olmos, Zorita, Las Casas, Sahagún, and others who worked among those who spoke Náhuatl, Maya, Tarascan, Otomí, and other Mesoamerican languages—as well as a few in the lands of the Quechuas from the ancient Incan Empire—realized the great opportunities open to them. To penetrate the soul of the Indian cultures, to adapt the Christian message to them, and to let others know about the native wisdom, indigenous expressions of their ancient world had to be sought. And, even more difficult, those testimonies had to be translated to make sense to the ears of the Spanish and other Europeans. Fully conscious of this fact, some accepted the challenge of conveying to others the feelings, beliefs, and thoughts of these vanquished and endangered peoples.

A NEW WORLD IN WHICH MANY
LANGUAGES WERE, AND ARE, SPOKEN

A great variety of tongues awaited the Europeans in the lands that became to them a New World. There, in a few years, they learned of the existence of hundreds of languages belonging to many different families, but soon they also realized that their New World was not a Babel. In several large areas of the continent a lingua franca prevailed: Náhuatl in most of Mesoamerica; Maya, and other languages closely related to it, in the Yucatán peninsula and adjacent regions of Central America; Quechua in the vast realm of the Andes, and Tupi-Guaraní in Paraguay, parts of Brazil and neighboring regions. The existence of these so-called general languages obviously meant, among other things, that in the New World some persons could communicate in more than one tongue and, when required, could also act as interpreters or translators.

Hernán Cortés had an early experience of the indigenous ability to act as a translator from one lingua franca to another with the well-known Malintzin, who spoke Maya and Náhuatl and soon also learned Spanish. Other testimonies exist of the indigenous capacities to function as interpreters. One, found in the *Codex Matritense,* tells about some Aztec merchants who had also a command of the Maya-Tzotzil language spoken in Chiapas: "Quimomachtiaya in intlahtol" ("They learned the others' language").[8]

The Spaniards took advantage of the existence of a lingua franca in the viceroyalties of Mexico and Peru and for a while they fostered the teaching and diffusion, respectively, of Náhuatl and Quechua. So did the Portuguese with the Tupi general language in Brazil. The missionaries, some of them with a solid humanistic background, not only learned their lingua franca but also acted as spontaneous linguists in the preparation of grammars and vocabularies. Often they did not limit their effort to the lingua franca but tried to embrace as many of the local tongues as possible.

In some parts of this continent, a two-way process of linguistic approach developed in which missionaries and natives took part. On the one hand, besides preparing grammars and vocabularies, the missionaries looked for adequate translations of parts of the Bible and of various religious texts. On the other, they sometimes also became interested in obtaining information about the indigenous beliefs and traditions, even if only to erase them. As we have seen, several texts of the indigenous tradition were thus reduced to written form and, in some cases, translated into Spanish.

Individually or in groups—as in the cases of Sahagún and other Franciscans—the two-way process of linguistic and textual communication began, as had already occurred in Spain when, in the twelfth century, a famous school of translators was established in Toledo to rescue the wisdom preserved in a rich ensemble of documents in Hebrew and Arabic.

It is obvious that the linguistic effort of the friars in the New World was mainly guided by the purpose of implanting the Christian faith. Nonetheless, such an effort also resulted in attainments of prime cultural significance. Never before in the history of the human race had communication been established in so many different languages in less than a century. With all the limitations that could be expected, the alphabet was adapted to represent a gamut of phonemes, traditional grammar was used to frame unpredictable structures, and vocabularies were compiled, which included entries for which the European languages had no correspondence and, naturally, lacked those to convey ideas and doctrines that were completely alien to the Amerindian nations.

Thus, while such an unparalleled effort made available the basic tools for new forms of interlinguistic communication, evidence was also gained about the difficulties inherent in the attempts to convey meanings when there was not any lexical equivalence, due precisely to a complete absence of the corresponding concept or object. A keen perception of these difficulties is manifest in some of the early bilingual vocabularies—some of which were published in the sixteenth century—and in other works written in the indigenous languages, like the sermonaries, manuals for confession, translations of parts of the Bible, and so forth. In a corresponding manner, the native traditions expressed in songs, poems, prayers, discourses, or in various informal kinds of communication, even if carefully analyzed and reduced to written form, presented a large number of obscurities often appearing as insurmountable obstacles to comprehension and taken at times as a sign of the devil's action in the minds of those so-called primitives.[9]

In this manner, in the New World many problems were inevitably encountered that affect the possibility not only of rendering a message into another language, but, above all, of transferring meanings unknown to the listener or reader, for which, of course, no words existed in the recipient's language.

A rich literature is available today on the subject of translation, its possibilities and limitations. In innumerable papers and books, translation has been discussed as an art and science from the points of view of linguistics, philology, literature, the sciences of communication, cultural anthropology, psychology, semiotics, logic, and epistemology. Contributions that have substantially increased the bibliography of translation sport titles like the following: *A Linguistic Theory of Translation* (Catford, 1965), *Transformulation: Structural Translation* (Bolinger, 1966), *Language Structure and Translation* (Nida, 1975), *Semantics and Translation* (Deibler, 1971), to which one could add many works that describe recent achievements in the technology of computerized translation.[10]

The many studies and manuals published in our time to assist those devoted to the translation of the Bible deserve special reference. I will quote only the very comprehensive book by John Beekman and John Callow (1974), *Translating the Word of God,* which deals with questions relative to the forms and functions of the lexical and grammatical structures, the universe of semantics, and the problems of lexical equivalences and of the transferring of meaning across languages.

It is remarkable that, while today there is available this rich literature on the science and art of translation, with the noted emphasis on biblical translation, the Roman and Greek classics, or today's scientific and technological papers and books, little attention has been given to the subject of how to convey into the European languages the expressions, ancient or contemporary, of those, at times, still considered primitive, specifically the indigenous nations of the New World. I will mention at least a valuable paper published in 1980 by Merce López Baralt on some of the problems to be found by those translating the indigenous texts.[11]

I have said already that never before in human history had such an enormous amount of cultural exchange occurred in so many different languages in less than a hundred years as when, in the sixteenth century, the Spaniards and Portuguese subdued to their rule the nuclear areas of high culture in the American continent. But then, and so it is now, the emphasis of communication across so many languages has been primarily put on the European transmission of religious ideas, patterns of behavior and laws that the natives were supposed to accept. It is undeniable that in this process of contact the Europeans also gained knowledge in areas of so basic an interest to them as food resources, pharmacology and the existence of mineral and other riches. But this did not produce a change in the frequent attitude of indifference, not to say hostility at times, to ideas and beliefs pertaining to the spiritual universe of the Amerindians.

Not until recently did this posture begin to experience a change. It was the appreciation, though confined at first to limited circles, of some of the literary masterpieces of India and China that meant a great opening to the expressions of other very different cultures. Modern Europeans or people of basically European culture had not heard of literary expressions of any value by the Amerindians. Only a few nineteenth-century exceptions can be mentioned. One is that of Daniel G. Brinton, who, living in Philadelphia, had the courage and the economic resources to publish in 1890, as authentic literature, twenty Náhuatl sacred hymns. To propitiate the acceptance of his work in terms of the opening described above, he tried to dignify his contribution, entitling it *Rig Veda Americanus,* with the following subtitle: "Sacred Songs of the Ancient Mexicans with a Gloss in Náhuatl."[12]

A century has passed since the publication of Brinton's *Rig Veda Americanus.* Today there are many scholarly contributions related to Náhuatl, Maya, Quechua, Aymara, Guaraní, and other Amerindian productions, ancient and contemporary. Now that this change of attitude is a reality that enables more people to enjoy the message and wisdom of the Amerindian cultures, our approaches to their testimonies deserve more qualified attention. By this I mean that it is already time to concentrate upon the theme of translation vis à vis the indigenous literatures, ancient and modern. To do this we can follow two different procedures. At first we can recall some limited but very valuable experiences from those few who, some years after the Conquest, set about to translate texts of the indigenous tradition. The second procedure will involve considering ideas and experiences derived from the contemporary linguistic and philological concern with the subject of translation.

OTHER VALUABLE SIXTEENTH-CENTURY EXPERIENCES FROM MESOAMERICA AND THE ANDEAN ZONE

In addition to what I have presented in relation to the pioneer work of Fray Andrés de Olmos, I will comment on the work of three humanists who appreciated the value of the indigenous compositions and translated them into Spanish: Bernardino de Sahagún, who dealt with texts in the Náhuatl language: Jerónimo de Alcalá, interpreter of testimonies originally expressed in the Purépecha tongue of the Tarascans of Michoacán, and Cristóbal de Molina of Cuzco, who collected and translated several sacred hymns from the Quechua of the Incas.

The Work of Sahagún

Fray Bernardino de Sahagún, born in 1500 in the village of Sahagún, kingdom of León, Spain, arrived in Mexico in 1529. He devoted most of his long life (he died in 1590) to an inside understanding of the culture of the Náhuatl-speaking Amerindians. On account of his work, he has been awarded the title of father of anthropological research in the New World.[13] Among other things, he collected from the indigenous elders a large amount of firsthand information on practically every aspect of the culture of the ancient Mexicans. In particular, he assembled hundreds of texts in Náhuatl, many of them spontaneous answers to his questionnaires, and others that were the rendering of the sacred hymns or of old traditions like those about Quetzalcóatl, the cultural hero of the Nahuas, and a large number of *huehuehtlahtolli*, testimonies of the "ancient word."

To Fray Bernardino de Sahagún must be credited the creation of a school of scribes, translators, and commentators of Náhuatl literature.[14] He actually registered the names and places of origin of the Amerindian scholars who worked with him. They were the well-known trilingual students (as they spoke Náhuatl, Spanish, and Latin) who had been his disciples at the College of the Holy Cross in Tlatelolco. Let us now pay attention to their joint effort of many years of research.

Fray Bernardino used a triple form of conveying to outsiders the contents of the Náhuatl texts he had collected. In one form, he conceived of the idea of a three-column presentation and discussion of the texts. The first column, on the left side, provides a Spanish version of the Náhuatl text, appearing in the central column. In this one, numbers are inscribed above certain Náhuatl words, those Sahagún considered in need of morphemic or semantic explanation. In the third column, to the right, the Náhuatl words or sentences that were numbered are explained in more detail.

In a second form of textual presentation, the Franciscan distributed his materials by subject into twelve different books. In one of his early transcriptions—that of the manuscripts preserved in Madrid—he included only the text in Náhuatl with some captions and a few glosses in Spanish. In a later copy, known as the *Codex Florentine* because the manuscript is preserved at the Laurentian Library in Florence, the Náhuatl text of each of the twelve books appears in a column to the left, while a rendition into Spanish is offered in a parallel column to the right. The translation no longer includes the numbers above each word, nor any kind of analytical commentary. It can be described simply as a smooth version that conveys the basic meaning and the dynamics of the original. No attempt is made to follow the rhythm of the Náhuatl expression. While some of the Náhuatl metaphors and other figures of speech are preserved in the translation, an effort is constantly made above all to transfer the connotations of Náhuatl terms for which no Spanish equivalents are available. Thus, while often including the Náhuatl term as a loan word, a generic word in Spanish is added, either in a comparative mood or to indicate the form and/or the function of what is meant by the indigenous word. Examples of this procedure are the following: *capolin,* "a cherry of this land," *Huitzilopochtli,* "God of the Mexicans, another Mars," the *teopixqueh,* "priests, guardians of their gods, satraps" (petty despots).

At times, instead of preserving a metaphor, deemed perhaps of difficult comprehension in Spanish, Sahagún simply offers an equivalence from the viewpoint of meaning. For instance, when the Náhuatl sage is described as a pine torch that does not smoke and as the black and red inks with which the native books are painted, Sahagún keeps, in part, the first of these metaphors and gives only the meaning of the second: "El sabio," he says, "es como lumbre o hacha grande . . . y buen dechado para los otros" (The sage is as a light or big pine torch . . . and a model to others).[15]

In some other cases, as in his version of the *huehuehtlah-tolli*, "ancient words," included in the sixth of his books, Fray Bernardino does his best to transfer not only the meaning but also the metaphors and other symbols. Examples of this can be found in the form in which he translates the traditional expressions employed by the members of the nobility while speaking to others of their own family or to the different dignitaries. He not only tries to convey the idea of the honorific forms of addressing each other but also metaphors such as the following: "little dove" (little girl), "precious green stone, precious feather" (a person of high rank), "eagle, tiger" (a warrior).[16]

A third procedure adopted by Sahagún in his presentation of the Náhuatl texts is found in the twenty sacred hymns he collected, those published with an English version by Brinton. Extremely conscious of the esoterism and other complexities inherent in these religious compositions, rather than trying a translation of them, he preferred to analyze them, offering a linguistic and cultural elucidation of many of their terms and forms of expression. He thus opened an entrance for others to penetrate, centuries later, into the meaning of the sacred hymns. Two scholars, Eduard Seler and Angel María Garibay, profited from the linguistic and cultural elucidations offered by Fray Bernardino.[17]

One last consideration about his work is that in his *Historia general de las cosas de Nueva España*, he did not translate the texts in Náhuatl, but preferred to elaborate a sort of interpretation of them. Thus sometimes he condensed his materials and, at other times, he went into lengthy explanations, having always in mind, as his main purpose, the transferring of information about a different culture. And he expressly added that he wanted to preserve his texts in their Náhuatl original to be at the disposal of the descendants of the ancient Mexicans for their enjoyment as reading material.[18] A guess can also be made that, appreciating the literary value of many of the compositions, he might have also conceived the idea that his elucidations and linguistic references could help others in the future to better understand and translate such texts.

A Tarascan Testimony

Let us attend now to a different case related no longer to the Náhuatl-speaking people of the central plateau, but to the Tarascans, or Purepecha, of Michoacán. An extremely valuable sixteenth-century manuscript exists that contains firsthand testimonies about the ancient culture of the Tarascans. The document, known as the *Relación de Michoacán,* has been attributed to Fray Jerónimo de Alcalá, a Franciscan who, only a few years after the Conquest, was active among the Tarascans. The Franciscan chronicler of Michoacán, Father Diego Muñoz, says about Fray Jerónimo that he was "the first who wrote and knew the language of Michoacán."[19]

Apparently commissioned by Viceroy Antonio de Mendoza, he spent some time collecting testimonies in the Tarascan language from some indigenous elders whom he names. Although, unfortunately, we know nothing about the whereabouts of the text in the native tongue, we have at least a significant indication expressed by the Franciscan, describing the use he had made of the Tarascan testimonies. His words depict with precision the method he adopted in his translation from the Tarascan. Addressing this commentary to the viceroy, he states:

> This scripture and account present to your Lordship the old people of this town of Michoacán, and me also in their name, not as an author but as their interpreter. In this account your Lordship will see that the sentences follow their style of expression, and I think I will be criticized on account of this, but as a faithful interpreter, I have not wanted to alter their form of speaking, nor to do damage to their own sentences. And I have proceeded thus in all this interpretation, with the exception only of some sentences, and those very few, that would be unintelligible and diminished if I did not

add something to them. And other sentences are explained so that the readers will understand them better, as in this form of expression: *No euche hepu hucari xaca,* which literally means in our language, "We do not have our heads with us." And they do not take it literally as we would do, but mean by it that they were afflicted or thought they would be made captives by their enemies and that these would cut off their heads and would put them on the palisade of the sacrificed prisoners. As if thinking that their heads had been cut off, they would say, "We do not have our heads with us."

And in the manner of composition of their sentences it is important to note that they do not employ as many equivocal words as we do in our language.

In this sense, I mean that I act as interpreter of these ancient men and I consider that they are speaking and giving to your illustrious Lordship and to the readers an account of their life and ceremonies and form of government and land.[20]

To summarize, the method adopted by this Franciscan in translating from the Tarascan language is based on the two following criteria: first, he structures the Spanish version so that "the sentences will follow their style of expression," that is, he tries to imitate the Tarascan form of expression, and this he does even if he feels he "will be criticized on account of this"; second, only when it is indispensable for the sake of clarity, he adds a kind of explanation, as in the case of the sentence, "We do not have our heads with us." The reading of the *Relación of Michoacán* demonstrates that Father Jerónimo de Alcalá acted, indeed, as he puts it, "not as author but as a faithful interpreter of these ancient men."

Cristóbal de Molina's Translation of Eleven Quechua Prayers

A secular priest, born around 1529 in Baeza, province of Jaén, in Andalucía, Spain, Cristóbal de Molina, arrived in Peru before 1556, when he was already working in Cuzco.[21]

According to various sources, he learned the Quechua language to perfection. While in charge of the parish of Los Remedios in Cuzco, he was commissioned by Bishop Lartaun to write a history of the Incas. To prepare it, he did ample research, consulting the surviving *quipucamayos,* those who counted and interpreted the knotted-string records, and obtained from them and other *amauta,* or sages, firsthand information not only about the most important events of their past but also about their beliefs, rites, and calendar.

Although his *Historia de los Incas* is now lost, in compensation, another of his works, entitled *Fábulas y ritos de los Incas* (Fables and Rites of the Incas) has come down to us.[22] In it, he includes among other things a transcription in Quechua of eleven prayers or sacred hymns whose text he had obtained from some old indigenous sages. From the viewpoint of our interest here, we will consider the criteria he adopted in the translations into Spanish that accompany the Quechua texts. To do this, I will mainly take into account the valuable contributions of several Quechuists and, in particular, those of John Howland Rowe.

He rightly acknowledges the formal character of these prayers or hymns that belonged to "the official round of ceremonies which Pachakuti had devised."[23] Actually, the eleven prayers pertained to the purification rituals of the feast of *Zithuwa,* which took place in the period of *Coyaraymi* and corresponded at least in part to the month of August.[24]

In his study of these texts, aimed at the preparation of a new English translation of them, Rowe discusses a number of linguistic problems derived mainly from the fact that only defective copies of the original manuscript are available. Noting that "three of the prayers occur twice in the report and that the copyist had made different mistakes in the second rendering from those he had made in the first,"[25] he establishes a comparative analysis of them and of the two corresponding versions in Spanish prepared by Father Cristóbal de Molina. A conclusion Rowe drew is that

"Molina's Spanish translations represent faithfully the meaning of the original, allowing only for differences in style between the two languages."[26] And he adds something that may surprise us: "In a number of cases, I was able to work out a particularly obscure case only by retranslating Molina's Spanish into Classic Inca."[27]

On the basis of what Rowe has told us, and comparing his own translations, including the "comments" he adds to each of them, with Molina's original Spanish renditions, the following can be said about the method adopted by the famous sixteenth-century chronicler and Quechuist. In general his translations literally follow the Quechua text, keeping most of the metaphors and following in a way the rhythm of Quechua expression. Only a different form of rendering an ancient religious concept introduces a slight variation between Rowe's very elaborated English version of the first and second prayers and Molina's. Just as in the method adopted by Father Jerónimo de Alcalá in his translations from the Tarascan language, we also find that Molina at times adds information he deems necessary. One instance is the interpolation he makes about the *huacas* in his version of the third prayer. Except for this, and for the sporadic use of words, such as *Hacedor* (Creator), to render difficult concepts like the one meant by the word *Wirakocha*, Cristóbal de Molina can be cited as a translator who succeeded not only in being faithful to an original that conveyed religious concepts alien to those of Christianity, in a language as different from Spanish as Quechua is, but also in producing a version that could be understood by many of his contemporaries. Let us compare, at least, Molina's version of the last part of the first prayer with Rowe's linguistically elaborated English translation:

A dónde estás? En lo alto del cielo? O abajo en los truenos? O en los nublados de las tempestades? Oyeme, respóndeme y concede conmigo, y dadnos perpetua vida; para siempre tenednos de tu mano y esta ofrenda recíbela a do quiera que estuvieres, oh Hacedor![28]

Where are thou? Without? Within? In the clouds? In the
shadows? Hear me, respond and consent. For ever and
ever give me life, take me in thine arms, lead me by the
hand, receive this my offering wherever thou art, oh
Lord. [Rowe's translation]

A more ample and deeper analysis and discussion of the
translating procedures of Cristóbal de Molina, Jerónimo de
Alcalá, Bernardino de Sahagún, and of several others who,
for different reasons, became deeply interested in the religious or literary expressions of the Amerindians will be
greatly rewarding. There are lessons to be learned from
those who, still close to the ancient cultures, rescued the
texts and did their best to interpret them. At this point,
keeping in mind our goal—conveying to others the literary
achievements of the ancestors of a currently endangered
people and culture—let us turn our attention to some key
concepts derived from contemporary linguistics and philology and also from my own experience as a translator of
Amerindian literatures.

LINGUISTIC CONCERNS AND THE EXPERIENCE
OF TRANSLATING AMERINDIAN TEXTS

I have already referred to the large number of contemporary linguistic and philological contributions specifically
related to the subject of translation. As Eugene A. Nida has
put it: "The actual process of translating can be described
as a complex use of language; but the scientific study of
translating can and should be regarded as a branch of comparative linguistics, with a dynamic dimension and a focus
upon semantics."[29] Following on from Nida's statement, I
think we can be even more explicit in describing the process of translating. There is a complex use of language in any
translation precisely because in such cases its use is conditioned by the many differences—phonological, structural,
lexical, and semantic—of the tongue from which the transferring is being made. Now, to perceive the differences and
to look for the equivalences, adopting a gamut of possible

procedures, imply the examination and bringing together of at least a part of the connotative resources of two languages. To Nida this is the reason why "the scientific study of translating can and should be regarded as a branch of comparative linguistics."

I believe something else in Nida's statement can be made more explicit. It has to do with his reference to "a dynamic dimension and a focus upon semantics." Often, as is the case in any translation from the Amerindian tongues, one has to deal with expressions that convey meanings denoting cultural institutions and objects for which no words with a semantic correspondence exist in the receptor language. In fact, in such cases the complexities and problems exceed the mere limits of linguistics and have to be considered as pertaining also to the fields of cultural anthropology and history. Indeed, the purpose in this kind of translation is not only to transfer a message from one language to another but also information about something—an institution, idea, or object—that is totally unknown to those speaking the receptor language.

To translate from languages spoken by people of a basically different culture—as in the case of the Amerindians— involves two questions that have to be considered separately: one is how to cope with the structural differences of the source and the receptor languages; the other has to do with the diverse semantic attributes of their corresponding lexicons and with the many dissimilar realities—natural and cultural—about which one wants to convey information. I will attend briefly to both questions, the first mainly linguistic in character, the second more closely related to culture and history.

The Structural Differences

From the viewpoint of structure, one has to attend at first to the phonological diversities, that is, the kinds of sound units or phonemes, their arrangements, tones, pitches, accents, intonations, and so forth, as they are uttered in the source language and then in the tongue into which the translation is made. The other basic aspect of linguistic structure is that of the morphemic and syntactic arrangements of all the words or parts of them that, in different forms, function as carriers of meaning.

As far as the phonologic structures are concerned, one has to recognize that it is simply impossible to transfer the phonemes, accents, and tones of one language into another. Nevertheless, one can add that some translations exist in poetry in which attempts are made at preserving the rhythm with a similarly patterned arrangement of the syllables in an equal number of verses, and even with an equivalent rhyme or recurrence of corresponding sounds at the ends of the lines or stanzas. Although some scholars have questioned the acceptability of this procedure, which might oblige the translator to distort the original meaning for the sake of preserving rhythm or rhyme, it is undeniable that, at least in the case of languages not so different, the possibility of such translation cannot be dismissed out of hand.

I would mention here, as an outstanding example, the translations into Spanish of some Latin classics, Virgil and Catullus, prepared by the great Mexican poet Rubén Bonifaz Nuño. In his work as translator he has faithfully transferred not only the meaning, but also the arrangement of the expressions in an equal number of verses, preserving the meter and rhythm, while being as close as possible to the original.[30]

Although it is clear that no Amerindian language can be compared to Latin from the viewpoint of its relation to Spanish or even English, the door remains open to look at least for some phonological parallels, taking also into account both the phonemic and the morphemic and syntactic structures of the source and the receptor languages. This introduces us to the second element we want to discuss.

As the lexical and semantic aspects will be considered in their close relation to the cultural and historical differences that exist between two languages, we assume now that, from the perspective of the structure, two extreme procedures can be adopted in translating. One has been described as literal, that is, that which tries to reproduce the original text word by word. The other has been labelled "free translation," since the interpreter above all looks for a natural equivalence of the conveyed message, feeling free not only to rearrange the structure of the original expression, but even to introduce other symbols or similes more easily understood by those in possession of the receptor language.

These two extreme procedures have been adopted at times in some of the existing translations from the Amerindian languages. Several early Spanish chroniclers who included in their works some testimonies of the indigenous tradition exemplify the procedure of free translation. Turning our attention now to the results obtained by modern translators of Náhuatl literature, some differences can be noted. Let us consider a few examples taken from the versions into English of the words preserved in the *Codex Florentine*,[31] which the Aztec midwife addresses to the woman who is about to give birth. I will transcribe the Náhuatl text accompanied by a literal translation. I will then compare it with two other renditions, one by Arthur J. O. Anderson and Charles E. Dibble,[32] and the other by Thelma D. Sullivan.[33]

1.	*Nochpuchtzin, ca moyáuh.*
Lit.	My little daughter, indeed yours is the battle.
A.D.	My beloved daughter, exert thyself!
Sul.	My daughter, the battle is yours.

2.	*Quen timitztochihuilizqueh?*
Lit.	How will we do our action for you?
A.D.	How shall we deal with thee?
Sul.	What are we to do for you?

3.	*A iz onequeh in monantzitzinhuan,*
Lit.	Here are your revered mothers,
A.D.	Here are thy mothers,
Sul.	Here are your mothers,

4.	*ca moneixcahuiltzin*
Lit.	indeed, yours is the task,
A.D.	it is thine own affair,
Sul.	yours alone is the task,

5.	. . . *ca ticuauhcíhuatl, xicnamiqui.*
Lit.	Indeed you, eagle woman, go to the encounter.
A.D.	Be thou a brave woman, face it.
Sul.	You are Quaucihuatl, work with her!

The main differences to be noted are the following: Anderson and Dibble alter the structure of the text in lines 1, 2, 4, and 5. In the first line, they render the incisive metaphor, *ca moyáuh*, "indeed, yours is the battle," for the simplified equivalence of "exert thyself." In the second, the complex Náhuatl verb *[quen] timitztochihuilizqueh*, "how will we do our action for you?" (i.e., the action corresponding to the midwife) is translated by "How shall we deal with thee?" In the fourth line, the word *affair* is employed, instead of "task," which more closely corresponds to *moneixcahuiltzin*, a term implying the idea of an effort or of something that has to be done. Finally, in the fifth line, *ticuauhcíhuatl*, "you, eagle woman," a title of the mother goddess, is changed into an imperative expression (absent in the Náhuatl original): "Be thou a brave woman."

Sullivan evidently follows the structure and symbols of the source text more closely. An exception occurs in line 5, where she translates the verb *xicnamiqui*, "go to the encounter," by "work with her," as if the midwife were telling the pregnant woman that she should act together with the mother goddess. In reality, the girl is described as being an eagle woman: *ticuauhcíhuatl*, "you, eagle woman," and the command points to a sort of encounter, engagement in battle for the courageous woman, the eagle woman goddess.

My personal preference goes with the translation that follows the structural arrangement of the original as closely as possible, thus keeping its linguistic taste, but without doing offense to the genius of the receptor language. Several translations of Amerindian texts prove that this is possible. Rereading the literal translation of the words of the Náhuatl midwife with minor modifications will, I hope, show that it does not offend the nature of the English language.

> My little daughter, yours is the battle!
> How shall we act for you?
> Here are your revered mothers,
> But indeed yours is the task . . .
> You are the Eagle Woman,
> Go to the encounter!

The idea of respecting the style of expression of the source language as much as possible is far from new. We have noted that the translator of the *Relación de Michoacán,* Father Jerónimo de Alcalá, already followed this same criterion: "Your Lordship will see that the sentences follow their style of expression, and I think I will be criticized on account of this, but as a faithful interpreter, I have not wanted to alter their form of speaking, nor to do damage to their own sentences."[34]

What Father Alcalá says immediately afterwards with respect to "some sentences [in the Tarascan language] that would be unintelligible and diminished if I did not add something to them"[35] can be taken as an introduction to the other aspect we have to consider. I am not referring so much to the linguistic arrangement of the words and sentences as to meaning itself and, therefore, the lexical connotations, semantics, and cultural differences.

Semantics and Cultural Diversities

Mention has been made of the problems faced by the translator who has to convey meanings for which there are no lexical equivalences in the receptor language, precisely because of the absence of the corresponding objects or concepts in the cultural environment of those who speak it. This is, of course, one of the main problems that awaits translators from tongues belonging to peoples of a basically different culture.

Before discussing this problem, let us mention other difficulties that also exist in conveying meaning in translation. Some of the most notable are the existence of a
diversity of connotations attached to words that, at first
sight, seem to be lexical equivalents in two different languages, but actually encompass unequal semantic domains;
the absence in one of the languages involved, not so much
of true lexical equivalences as of several or all of the corresponding referential markers—particles, affixes, or a determined word order—that indicate to which class a word
belongs and the role it plays in a given expression; the
numerous questions that have to do with the most frequently occurring stylistic procedures, such as metaphors,
similes, parallelisms, difrasisms, and, in sum, whatever constitutes a linguistic element that illuminates the semantic
field and helps to better organize the referential content of
a message.

Answers to these and other questions cannot be offered as
a universal remedy to the problems of a translator. Nevertheless, we can learn something from our own experience,
and from that of others. Let us consider the first question,
that is, the lack of lexical equivalents because of the absence
of the corresponding object or concept. This question refers
also to that of the shiftings of meaning in translating ancient
Amerindian texts.

One form of coping with the problem—practiced since
the sixteenth century—has been to employ the indigenous
word as a loan in the receptor language, accompanying it
with an explanatory expression. The nature of these expressions can be multiple. One can employ, for instance, a
kind of comparison, such as *copal:* "the incense of this land";
patolli: "a game played by this people similar to back-
gammon."[36] In a simpler manner, one can also attach to the
indigenous word a general statement such as *tlacochcálcatl:*
"one of their captains"; *Tlaxochimaco:* "one of their principal
feasts." The use of footnotes has been criticized at times,
and even rejected, as in the case of translating poetry.
We may remember at this point the use of glosses, marginal

notes or other explanatory devices adopted by the great
Bernardino de Sahagún when he presented the twenty sacred hymns of the Nahuas.

In translating ancient Náhuatl texts, I accept that I have
been ambivalent at times. Thus, I have followed some of the
described procedures in some cases, while in others I have
looked for a literal rendition of the indigenous word, whose
ultimate meaning I thought could be understood in function of the context. An example of this is provided by the
word *neyolmelahualiztli,* which literally means "the action of
straightening up the heart." The person in charge of this
ritual was the *tonalpouhqui,* "the one who tells or elucidates
the destinies," a priest to whom persons went to manifest
their transgressions, in particular those of a sexual nature.
Sahagún, trying to communicate to his sixteenth-century
countrymen the meaning of this practice, compared it to the
Christian confession. The modern translators of the *Codex
Florentine* into English have also equated the complex connotations of this indigenous practice with what a Christian
understands by following the same procedure and using as a
correspondence the term "confession."[37]

It is true that sometimes the literal version of a complex
or compound word meaning a ceremony or institution unknown to the speakers of the receptor language will sound
strange to them. Nevertheless, strangeness—taken not by
itself but within the context of the translation—will probably permit us to convey much more of the original meaning
than the artificial comparison or semi-identification with a
practice, object, or institution that can be considered akin
only superficially. One has to realize that, behind the differences, diverse cultures stand out. If the intention is to
convey to readers concepts and feelings alien to those of
their own culture, one is forced to try various procedures in
order to understand "the other."

This takes us to another of the questions that have been
raised in describing the problems deriving from the semantic and cultural diversities inherent in the different
languages. The diverse lexical units of each language carry

with them complex and unequal universes of potential connotations. The great scholar Angel María Garibay referred to this by comparing the lexical units to goblets,
wineglasses, cups, or vases of different shapes, some with
the same capacity and others with a different capacity.
Thus, for instance, the lexical units of the source language
can "contain" a larger or smaller universe of connotations
and carry it with their own determined shapes.[38] The receptor language, although in possession of lexical units
that apparently render what one wants to convey, most
often carry utterly diverse potentialities of meaning and
correlation. Its goblets, wineglasses, cups, and vases have
different shapes and capacities.

In the case of texts dealing with the ancient Mesoamerican
world view, many words are included with connotations
about which whole treatises can be written. Think of words
of so basic a cultural importance as the following: *tonatiuh*
(the sun), *yóllotl* (the heart), *ixtli* (the face), *yaóyotl* (war),
miquiztli (death), *tonalpohualli* (count of the days and destinies), *calpulli* (a group of kinsmen and also their residential
quarter), *tlatoani* (a ruler), *teotl* (god), *cuauhtli, ocelotl* (eagle,
ocelot), and many more. To cope with the problems that
these lexical units present—eventual subjects of a scholarly
dissertation—one great help can be to employ specific devices to delimit in each case the connotative potentials of the
corresponding word. This can be done by means of an adequate syntactic structuring within which the connotations of
the linguistic unit can be clarified. Another possibility is
opened by what is described as "the semotactic structure,"[39]
that is, the organization that results from the use of markers
to identify various classes of lexical units.

Let us consider a few examples. The first is from the translation of the *Popol Vuh* prepared by Munro S. Edmonson:

> . . . they declared to the Sun priests,
> and then indeed was the throwing,
> their divining,
> that they cast with corn.[40]

To delimit the connotations of the expression "the Sun priests" (the *ah Qu'in* literally in Quiché-Maya "the one of the Sun"), one has to attend to the whole structure of the context. "The Sun priests" were not those particularly concerned with worshiping the sun god. They were those "throwing . . . cast[ing] with corn," those who thus performed "their divining," who knew the destinies attached to the various periods of time (*kin*, "sun, day, time"). Connotative potentials of the lexical units "Sun priests" are delimited by the syntactical context in which they play a role.

Another example, taken from Náhuatl poetry, demonstrates how the connotative potentials of words like flowers and hearts are also delimited:

> There, where the darts are dyed,
> where the shields are painted,
> are the perfumed white flowers;
> flowers of the heart,
> the flowers of the Giver of Life
> open their blossoms.
> Their perfume is sought by the lords,
> this is Mexico-Tenochtitlan.[41]

Flowers and hearts are here closely related: they constitute that sacred object that strengthens the Giver of Life, whose perfume is the glory of the warriors who take it from those defeated in the flowery battles fought by the Aztec eagles and tigers.

Metaphors and symbolism in general, including the references to an ample gamut of colors, connoting tangible or invisible realities, are a recurrent ingredient in Amerindian literatures. To transfer into another language such a universe of similes and of imagination, which appears at intervals, deals with a concept smoothly and employs parallel expressions and other stylistic procedures, is by no means an easy task. Nevertheless, many examples can be quoted of translations from Náhuatl, Maya, and other indigenous languages that demonstrate that the universe of symbols can actually be conveyed. Father Sahagún in the sixteenth century, conscious of this, elaborated a special treatise to analyze what he described as "Some figures of speech called metaphors; difficult phrases accompanied by their explanations and interpretations."[42]

From the many Náhuatl similes and expressions he analyzes and explains, let us take the following examples:

Ca nauh, ca notláqual.
It is my food, my drink.
This means, he explains, "These are my lands, these
   are my tools,
these are my means of livelihood."

Téhuatl, tlachinolli.
Divine water, fire.
This was said, he comments, when a great war or a
   great pestilence
occurred.

Cuitlapilli, atlapalli.
The tail, the wing.
This means the common people. For this reason the
   subjects are
called tails and wings, and the ruler, the lord of the
   tails and wings.

Zícoti, pipiyolti.
Horneting, bumblebeeing.
This is said of those who eat and drink at the expense
   of the nobles
of the city. They either ask for sustenance or are
   simply given it.

Instead of diminishing the semantic and cultural importance of the metaphors in Náhuatl—found also in other Amerindian literatures—Sahagún facilitated the approach to them of those desiring to know and enjoy the indigenous forms of expression. The attitude of this sixteenth-century humanist contrasts with the procedures adopted by some modern translators whose renditions of the Amerindian texts are nothing else but cemeteries of the symbols. To act in this manner is once again to injure a cultural legacy, which belongs above all to the living descendants of the creators of such admirable expressions. Therefore, it is utterly offensive to the peoples we have described as "those of endangered cultures."

In Father Sahagún's work, particularly in the *History of the Things of New Spain,* where he introduces the Spanish-speaking reader to the wealth of Náhuatl testimonies he had collected, there is another very valuable lesson for the contemporary translator. Realizing how difficult it is to convey information from a different language, which is the means of expression of a different realm of culture, Sahagún paid particular attention to previously preparing his readers so as to acquaint them with the distinctive semantic attributes and the structural variations of the testimonies to be transmitted. That is why Sahagún himself, to introduce his readers to the cultural world of the Nahuas and other Mesoamericans, prepared special sections in his work to elucidate themes, like the one dealing with "the metaphors and other difficult phrases," or the pertinent glosses he added to his transcriptions of the twenty sacred hymns of the Aztecs.

The perception of the need of cultural preparation to better understand and enjoy—even in translation—what is being transferred from a separate culture is extremely important. Only when readers of ancient or contemporary Amerindian literatures have become, little by little, informed about the social realities, the world view and the symbolic universe of the corresponding culture, will they be able to perceive the meaning of the message or information that is being offered to them.

It is not enough to have a translator with a command of the source and receptor languages deeply informed of what he or she has to transmit. One has also to rely on the receptive capacities—mainly the cultural preparation—of the person to whom the translation is being brought. To take this into account is to understand the ultimate meaning of the art and science of translation: the rendering of a testimony or a message from a living individual who belongs or has belonged to a specific living culture, to another living person who belongs to the same or to a different living culture. Being a process of communication, a true translation can only be achieved when a convergence of feelings, knowledge, and spiritual sympathies occurs between the one who originally expressed the message, the one who carefully transferred it into a different language, and the one who has become prepared to receive and enjoy it.

In this summary presentation of the extremely complex theme of translation, with a specific emphasis on the Amerindian literatures, I have considered at first the experiences of three sixteenth-century interpreters of the indigenous mind and culture: Sahagún with the Nahuas, Alcalá with the Tarascans, and Molina concerned with the Quechuas. Valuable lessons can be derived from their achievements. Later I have paid attention to some basic principles, for the most part developed by modern linguistics. Relevant structural, semantic, and cultural differences that often exist between the source and receptor languages have been discussed and illustrated. And although the emphasis has been put on the ancient or classical Amerindian literatures of the great civilizations of Mesoamerica and the Andean region, I want to say that very similar analyses and considerations can be formulated in relation to the many contemporary manifestations of indigenous literary creativity. I firmly believe that the word of the descendants of the most ancient Americans will never vanish. The art of translating the Amerindian literatures has to improve its methods and enlarge the field of its interest.

Our contemporary world, so much concerned with the perils that threaten its own existence, will learn words of peace and hope from the Amerindian voices, ancient and modern. And since it is impossible to receive the messages of all these voices in their respective languages, recourse to translation will be a necessity and will also be the means to enrich us, adding pages of great spiritual wealth to a literature truly universal, the legacy of humankind.

Interpreting was and still is frequently practiced by a good number of Amerindians in several areas of this continent. I have mentioned the case of the Nahua merchants. The idea of interpreting as decoding from one set of symbols into another was familiar to the Mesoamerican sages, experts in the calendar's multiple connotations or in the reading of the glyphs in their books. The *quipuicamayos,* in the Andean region, were expert in the art of interpreting their knotted-string records.

A magnificent poem has come down to us, composed by the fifteenth-century sage Nezahualcóyotl, in which he attempts to interpret the mysteries that surround human existence on the earth. To do so, he imagines that everything that comes into being exists only in a book of hieroglyphs and paintings. This book that he has to translate so as to understand is a book painted and written by the supreme Giver of Life. He does his work of creator with flowers and songs, symbols and art. The sage Nezahualcóyotl, feeling he can interpret the book, dares to say:

> With flowers you write,
> Giver of Life,
> with songs you give color,
> with songs you shade
> those who will live on the earth.
> Later you will erase eagles and tigers,
> we exist only in your book
> while we are here on the earth.[43]

The Amerindian sages and artists, like the Giver of Life, invent and compose, with flowers and songs. To approach their message, ancient or modern, one has to try, with respect and sincerity, to be as faithful a translator as possible. This is a difficult task but greatly rewarding. In translating the Amerindian literatures one is a guide who leads others toward the beauty, mystery, and truth of the ancient word and the modern testimony of those whose languages were the first to be spoken and chanted in the New World. To better understand and respect the cultural identities of those who have chosen to maintain their differences, a more fitting approach would be to take into account their ancient and modern literary creations. Through them, their grandeur, suffering, and hopes will come to light.

7.
Beyond Mesoamerica: *Norteño* Cultural Pluralism in the Pre-Hispanic and Colonial Periods

Mesoamerica—the area where high culture developed since at least the end of the second millennium B.C.—has been the scene of many types of cultural confrontation. Even before the Spanish invasion, conflicts among different Mesoamerican peoples and other kinds of internal disturbances put some native cultures in danger. The arrival of the Spanish caused profound physical and spiritual wounds for all Mesoamerican peoples. Many of them remained *nepantla,* "in the middle," deprived of what had given their world its foundation, and many remained unwilling to accept the impositions that, whether of a religious or secular nature, disturbed their traditional forms of behavior. From that moment on, Mesoamericans, millions of whom are still very much alive in contemporary Mexico and the other Central American countries, although they have managed to survive, bear the deep imprint of an enduring trauma on their souls.

In the faces and spirits of modern Mexico there are many easily discernible traits of Mesoamerican origin. Nevertheless, the predominantly mestizo nation sometimes minimizes the reality and worth of the more than ten million Mexicans who still speak Mesoamerican vernacular languages and maintain cultural identities distinct from that of the country's majority. Mesoamerica, as a living cultural entity, continues to pose a challenge. Here, as in many other parts of

155

the Americas, there are dramatic cases of peoples whose cultures survive, but are in imminent danger.

The north of Mexico, in many ways, has a different history and experiences distinct demographic, ecological, socioeconomic, and cultural conditions. Geographically, Northern Mexico encompasses about half of the nation's territory, from Sinaloa, Durango, and southern Tamaulipas to the present-day international border, the long U.S.-Mexican frontier.

As a term applied to human groups, their forms of culture, and a vast geographic area of the country, *"norteño"* (northern) has had various meanings in Mexico. Nevertheless, beyond the differences, there are a series of constant traits that emerge from the numerous appraisals of what the North truly is. In Mexico, the North has consistently been thought of as a physical and cultural frontier, an area where the development of human life is far from easy, despite the possibilities for great wealth. Thus, beyond the relative character of what has been understood by "North" throughout different periods, these and other consistent traits are mentioned repeatedly when reference is made to the northlands.

THE NORTH, FRONTIER REGION

In pre-Hispanic times the Nahua peoples of advanced culture believed that the North, the frontier of their civilization, was a country of "broad plains and rocky lands."[1] In the North lived the Chichimecs, people of the bow and arrow, who perpetually threatened the Mesoamerican world; but also to the North were found Chicomóztoc, "the place of the seven caves," and Aztatlan, "the place of the herons," mythical regions that had given origin to their ancestors. Though many wonders had taken place in those areas to the north, life there was difficult in the extreme, which is why only the Chichimecs—or barbarians—remained. During certain periods, the limits of Mesoamerica had been extended toward the north, but in others, pressure from the Chichimecs forced them to contract. This is further evidence of the hostility attributed to both these regions and their inhabitants, groups described as having rudimentary cultures.

During colonial times, since shortly after the Conquest, the North, without ever losing its character as a physical and cultural frontier, was seen as an open field for new forms of expansion. However, penetration was always difficult. In the North it was not a simple matter to obtain cheap labor to work in the mines or to cultivate land, as it had been in Central and Southern Mexico. Nonetheless, the belated echo of medieval myths, strangely parallel to some with a pre-Hispanic origin, declared that lands of incredible riches were situated to the north, where seven marvelous cities, instead of the seven caves of the indigenous tradition, were said to exist. With far greater success than pre-Hispanic Mesoamericans, the expansionist force of conquerors, missionary friars, and all types of people desirous of profit and adventure, penetrated the North and broadened the area of domination, pushing back the border again and again.

In the years that followed the conquest of the Aztec capital, penetration was begun by way of Michoacán and Colima in what is known today as Western Mexico, until founding Guadalajara in New Galicia (Jalisco) and later continuing through Sinaloa and the south of Sonora. Further, in the central regions of the country, in Chichimec lands, settlements and mining towns were established as far as Zacatecas. Still during the sixteenth century, the expansion reached Durango and with one bound began to explore New Mexico. By the seventeenth century, there were already missions, Spanish towns, and forts, or presidios, in what was called Nueva Vizcaya, in Sinaloa, Sonora, and New Mexico. The California peninsula, the site of numerous projects, was not host to a series of missions until the end of the seventeenth century. In the final hundred years of the colonial period, the advances toward the northwest meant the establishment of missions in Upper California, with a series of subsequent explorations into territory where the Russians and the English had already appeared. In the northeast of New Spain the colony of Nuevo Santander, known today as Tamaulipas, was founded in the eighteenth century—an act that, combined with the expansion in Coahuila and in New Mexico, strengthened the Spanish foundations in Texas.

Reflections on the difficulties that had to be overcome during many of these efforts became the titles of classic works written at the time of the northern expansion and settlements. From the mid-seventeenth century there is the *Historia de los triunfos de Nuestra Santa Fe entre gentes las más bárbaras y fieras del Nuevo Orbe* (History of the Triumphs of Our Holy Faith among the Most Barbaric and Wild Peoples of the New Orb), written by the Jesuit Andrés Pérez de Rivas, a missionary for several years in Sonora and Sinaloa.[2] And from the era of Father Eusebio Francisco Kino comes the story titled *Luz de tierras incógnitas en la América septentrional y diario de las exploraciones en Sonora* (Light Shed on Unknown Lands in Northern America and Diary of the Explorations in Sonora), by Captain Juan Matheo Mange.[3]

As a result of the triumphs achieved during the colonial period in lands hitherto unknown, at the time of independence the northern frontiers consisted of territory far removed from the center of Mexico. But by then the vast expanse, colonized to differing degrees by the viceroyalty of New Spain—with its new cities and towns, mining camps, large haciendas, and missions and forts to contain the so-called barbarous Indians—had been extended to such a degree that it reached an unforeseen neighbor, that of the new Anglo-Saxon country known as the United States of America. In 1819, two years before Mexico gained independence, Spain was compelled to sign a border treaty with this young American nation whose expansionist drive had already brought it into contact with the northernmost settlements of New Spain.

The 1819 "Transcontinental Treaty," also known as the Onís Treaty after the Spanish ambassador to Washington, was ratified by Mexico and the United States in 1832. In it, the northern border of Mexico was set in the following manner: from the mouth of the Sabine River at the Gulf of Mexico, following its course to the thirty-second parallel;

from there, in a straight line north to the degree where the Rojo or Natchitoches River enters and then, following its course until the point where the hundredth degree of longitude west of London crosses it; from there, in a straight line north to the source of the Arkansas River at the forty-second parallel. From this spot the northern border of Upper California was established, on this parallel, in another straight line toward the Pacific.[4]

By virtue of this treaty, the North gained a new kind of border, both physical and cultural, that was internationally recognized and no longer open to subsequent penetrations. The boundaries were established in the face of an Anglo-American state of powerful vitality rivaling the former expansionist drive of Spain. In contrast, in the decades following independence, Mexico found itself immersed in frequent insurrections that left little hope of attaining any form of political stability. Under the circumstances, it could not afford to pay much attention to its northern provinces or states.

Soon different kinds of infiltrations by people from the United States began to make themselves felt in the northern territories. In 1836, only four years after the ratification of the border treaty, the Anglo-Saxon colonists of Texas declared their independence, an act that culminated in the territory's annexation to the United States in April of 1845. This event, along with the North American drive—described as "manifest destiny"—to appropriate, even through the force of arms, the territories of New Mexico and Upper California, gave rise first to the war with Mexico and later, in 1848, to the establishment of a new border.

As a consequence, both the idea and the reality of Mexico's northern lands were altered in a profound way. For Mexico, the rapid North American colonization of Upper California, the territories of Arizona and New Mexico, and the earlier takeover of Texas resulted in the much closer presence of a physical and cultural border with a powerful country whose desire for even greater expansion and other forms of penetration was justifiably feared. In this context, it is worth recalling the United States's acquisition of the Mesilla territory (the Gadsden purchase of 1853), as well as repeated attempts aimed at obtaining Lower California and parts of Sonora and Chihuahua.[5]

The brief summary above confirms that throughout Mexican history, above and beyond numerous differences in the appraisal of the significance of the North, there have been certain features that remain constant. One such feature is the recognition of its great geographical expanse, which has been considered a possible source of great wealth. At the same time, the idea that such riches are not easily come by has persisted, since in the North, cultural development must overcome obstacles unknown in other places. Further, it is believed that there always exists a hostile frontier beyond what has been colonized, both physically and culturally speaking. Thus to the Mesoamerican peoples the frontier was composed of inhospitable lands, under the dominion of the Chichimecs. In the days of New Spain, garrisons shielded the frontier against the so-called barbarous tribes. In independent Mexico the presence of Anglo-Saxons created a new kind of frontier where a different culture and the threat of expansionism were perceived as constant dangers. These traits, discussed here in an introductory fashion, help to clarify why it was precisely in the north of Mexico that very different cultural processes developed from those that have characterized history within the limits of ancient Mesoamerica.

THE PRE-HISPANIC PERIOD

As a first step, it is necessary to specify the limits of the present study. Though the theme is northern cultural pluralism, for reasons of methodology and space the focus will be on describing and analyzing the conditions and processes of contact within a determinate area, itself quite extensive. This area is the Mexican Northwest, or the territory that includes the present-day states of Sinaloa, Sonora, North and South Baja California, and parts of the adjacent regions of Durango and Chihuahua.

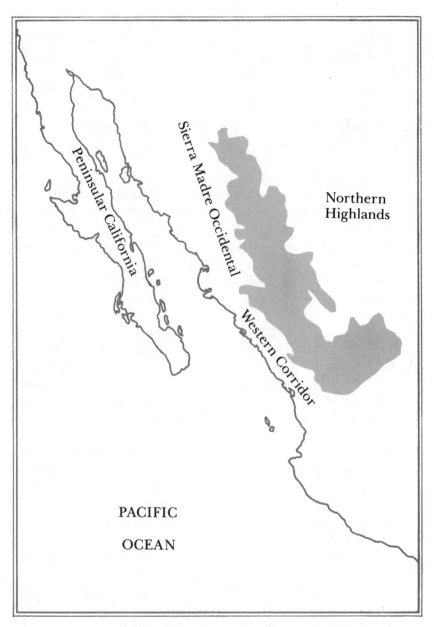

Physiographic Provinces in the Northwest

It was precisely in the direction of the Northwest that, early on, the Spanish penetration began. Further, until the days of independence, Mexico's greatest geographic expansion took place in the Northwest. This region, following the establishment of towns, missions, and forts in northern Sonora and Baja California, was witness to advances and later settlement in places as distant as San Francisco in Upper California. Of all of the great Northwest, which until 1848 embraced an area six times the size of France, our attention will focus here on the cultural history of the fraction that Mexico was able to save from foreign avarice.

The territory in which a distinct pluricultural evolution developed can be seen as an ensemble of diverse "physiographic provinces"—that is, geographic areas with distinct and well-defined characteristics.[6] Thus, the cultures of the ancient indigenous inhabitants of these natural provinces must be considered first.[7]

The West Coast Corridor

The region that Herbert Eugene Bolton designated as "the West Coast corridor"[8] is delimited on the east by the Western Sierra Madre and on the west by the coasts of Nayarit, Sinaloa, and Sonora. It includes the subtropical lowlands to the south, the semidesert plains with fertile valleys in the low basins of several rivers, and the region known as the Sonoran desert. In pre-Hispanic times this physiographic province was home to the ancestors of many indigenous groups who survive today. In terms of the title of "the West Coast corridor," since pre-Conquest times the region served functions that already justified this name: archaeological evidence has shown diffusion of Mesoamerican-origin cultural elements by way of the "corridor." This explains precisely how, in certain historical periods, the high cultures of Mesoamerica came to expand through Nayarit and then Sinaloa, until reaching as a northern boundary the river that bears the same name of Sinaloa. Thus despite their many cultural differences, the natives that inhabited the various regions of this area at the time of the Conquest—

with the exception of the Seri and Yuman Indians—had important cultural affinities.

The Upper and Lower Pimas, the Opatas, and the members of the Cahita group, such as the Yaquis and Mayos, all spoke languages that pertain to the Uto-Aztecan linguistic family, which also includes Náhuatl from Central Mexico. In the same vein, these groups were among the most developed of the area, surpassed only by the Pueblo Indians of New Mexico and northern Chihuahua. All of them practiced agriculture and manufactured ceramics.

Many common traits can be found, again despite great diversity, in their settlement patterns as well. The Pimas lived in relatively compact communities, but they maintained a certain mobility, especially in the North, descending from the mountains to the valleys during winter to cultivate corn, beans, and squash. To the south, the Opatas, Yaquis, and Mayos had their *rancherías,* some already-nascent towns, in the river valleys. These were found both on the upper course of the rivers (in the case of the Opatas), and downstream in the coastal area (among the Yaquis and Mayos). The social organization of these groups was sufficiently complex to allow not only for the presence of shamans and sorcerers, but also an incipient priesthood. These groups received various forms of Mesoamerican cultural influences from the coastal region of Nayarit.

In sum, this physiographic province of the "West Coast corridor" was home to the most highly developed indigenous populations of the Mexican Northwest. The two exceptions mentioned above, the Yumans, who lived in the valley of the Colorado River, around its mouth, and the Seris of Tiburon Island and the area along the Sonora coast, belonged from a linguistic point of view to a completely different family, known as Hokan. The culture of the Yumans, though less advanced than that of the Pimas, maintained certain similarities with it; the Seris, on the other hand, were the region's only example of considerable primitivism. Grouped in bands or families of hunters, gatherers, and fishers, they practiced no agriculture and led a very precarious existence. Their cultural level can only be compared with that of the Baja California Cochimíes or peninsular Yumans, groups with whom, at least linguistically, they had a certain connection. In any case, the enclave of the Seris is a noteworthy exception in this physiographic province of the West Coast corridor.

Just as a Mesoamerican influence was felt to differing degrees through the corridor in pre-Hispanic times, a similar process would later take place during the colonial period. Thus, from the first half of the sixteenth century, the earliest form of Spanish penetration into the Mexican Northwest would be by way of the West Coast corridor.

The Western Sierra Madre

Another physiographic province, entirely different from the one just described, is the neighboring region of the most important mountain range in all of Mexico, the Western Sierra Madre. In its northernmost reaches lived the Tarahumaras and the Conchos and, farther south, the Tepehuanes, Acaxees, Xiximíes, Coras, and Huicholes.

All of these groups, like the great majority of those along the West Coast corridor, spoke languages of the Uto-Aztecan linguistic family. Their ways of life included *ranchería* settlements, although in general they were much more dispersed than their neighbors to the west. To differing degrees, they all practiced agriculture. The Tarahumaras and Conchos, for example, cultivated small cornfields in the little valleys and on the mountain slopes, descending to the plains during winter or taking refuge in caves. Like the Tepehuanes, Coras, and Huicholes, they supplemented their diet by hunting and gathering. As a whole, these Uto-Aztecan groups of the Sierra Madre kept themselves highly isolated and, in the case of the Coras and Huicholes, maintained a protracted resistance to the penetration of the Spaniards and any contact with them during the colonial period.

Ethnohistorical research done on the Tarahumaras and the Tepehuanes reveals certain forms of contact during the

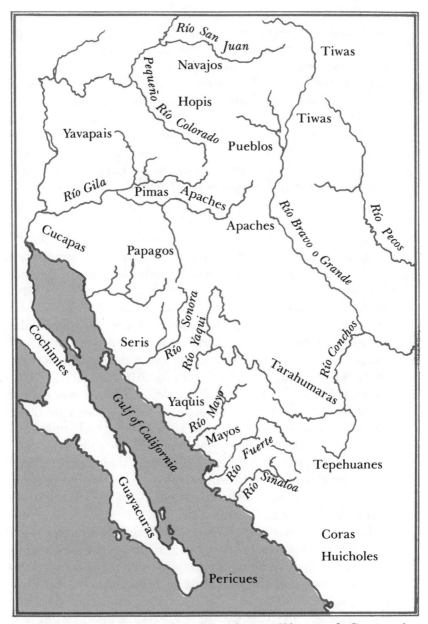

Indigenous Groups of the Northwest (Sixteenth Century)

pre-Hispanic period between these groups and the somewhat more advanced inhabitants of the western slope of the same Sierra Madre. As a consequence, it is possible that they received certain cultural elements from the peoples who lived in the regions of the West Coast corridor. Nonetheless, it is clear that the inhabitants of the Sierra Madre and, to a certain extent, also those of the plains of the Northern Plateau in places like southern Durango, while they may have felt some Mesoamerican influence, maintained ways of life in the sixteenth century that were indicative of their remoteness from the centers of advanced culture.

The Northern Plains

The third physiographic province, only partially included within the area of the Mexican Northwest, is composed of the plains region now known as the Northern Plateau. Specifically, this refers to the territory situated on both sides of the lower Rio Grande. Within the borders of the area belonging to Mexico lies the northwestern zone of the state of Chihuahua, where indigenous groups very different from those of the Sierra Madre or West Coast corridor lived. They spoke languages from the Athabascan family, to which the Apache, Lipanes, Mezcaleros, Navajo, and others pertain. The presence of some of these groups in these lands was relatively brief, since they had recently migrated from the Northwest. They had no fixed places of residence in the region they inhabited. Yet despite their seminomadic life, they already practiced agriculture to a limited degree, though their diet consisted primarily of foods obtained through hunting and gathering.

The various Apache groups, who were able to make raids over great distances because of their high degree of mobility, were considered true barbarians during the colonial period, the source of all kinds of dangers and misfortune. Thus it was undoubtedly surprising for the Spanish to discover that these northern regions were also home to other Indians, the Pueblos, who, in contrast to the Apache, were the bearers of the most highly developed culture in all the northern territories. It is enough to say that there are clear signs from the archaeological evidence and comparative ethnohistorical research to confirm that the Pueblos had several forms of contact or exchange with groups that possessed, to differing degrees, Mesoamerican cultural elements.

The Peninsula of California

Mexican California is a territory with a well-defined geographic profile, due to its peninsular nature. With a longitude from north to south of approximately eight hundred miles, its mean width is only about one hundred miles. Its Pacific and Sea of Cortez seaboards, due to numerous geographic accidents and a good number of nearby islands, total about seventeen hundred miles. Along this peninsula, which itself constitutes a particular physiographic province, runs a mountain range, the continuation of the Sierra Nevada of Upper California.

Three major ecological areas or zones can be distinguished in the peninsula: the extreme South, the great central desert, and the North. Though almost all of Baja California suffers from a scarcity of rain and offers a semidesert landscape, in the southern zone the prevailing ecology is somewhat more benign. There the natural flora is relatively richer, including some forests of oak and conifers in the area known as Sierra de la Laguna. In contrast, the central region is extremely inhospitable; it is situated between the twenty-seventh and thirtieth north parallels and includes the Vizcaíno desert in its western lands. In the northern zone, where the Baja Californian mountain range reaches its greatest heights, there are similarities in climate and flora to the south of Upper California. In contrast, along the eastern slope of the Sierra, the climatic characteristics of the valley of the lower Colorado River and its outlet are related to those of the south of Arizona and the border areas of Sonora.

Traits characteristic of the peninsula are its semidesert climate, its lack of flowing water, with the exception of the lower Colorado River, and its isolation, linked to the continent only by way of the north, and connected to what is today the state of Sonora through the Altar desert. These facts—especially the isolation and hostile environment—help in part to explain why the great majority of the indigenous populations that penetrated the peninsula never managed to advance beyond extremely precarious cultural forms.

To the extreme north, in the region neighboring the mouth of the Colorado River, there were Yuman-related groups like the Cucapas, small communities of whom survive today. These are the only groups in all of the peninsula who practiced agriculture and made ceramics, reflecting the influence of peoples with a more complex culture, like the Pimas. In the rest of the northern portion of the peninsula and in the central area, reaching almost to the twenty-sixth parallel, were the so-called Cochimíes, also described as peninsular Yumans. Many groups, ethnically and linguistically related, were included under this designation. Given their seminomadic lives, they subsisted by gathering fruit and seeds, hunting, and fishing in the coastal areas.

The social organization of these groups went no farther than kinship ties among a certain number of families. Such groupings were later designated by the missionaries with the name of *rancherías*. On the whole, the number of individuals who made up a *ranchería* fluctuated between 100 and 250 persons. The term "*ranchería*" did not imply, in the peninsular case, the existence of villages with huts or some other form of permanent dwellings; for refuge the Indians simply used caves or built small stone corrals. Their mode of habitation as much as the diet, technology, and clothing of the Cochimíes, typified an extreme case of the absence of cultural development.

Though they shared a similar cultural level, the Indians of Southern Baja California differed from one another linguistically and sometimes also somatically. Those who pertained to the Guaycura linguistic family lived from the south of Loreto to the region bordering another missionary settlement, Santiago. Among the best-known divisions or factions among the Guaycuras were the Aripes, Callejúes, Huchitíes, and, of course, the Guaycura namesake.

The extreme South, from Cabo San Lucas to about the twenty-fourth parallel, including some of the islands in the Sea of Cortez, was territory occupied by the Pericú nation, linguistically and somatically different from the Guaycuras as well as from the rest of the inhabitants of California. Preserved human remains demonstrate that the Pericús constituted an ethnic group that was pronouncedly doli-chocephalic, or long-headed. Information about their lan-guage demonstrates that it was not related to any other in California, or within the American territory. Other fea-tures attributed to the Pericús were their warlike inclination and sense of independence, their talent for navigation on rafts, and their more widespread acceptance of polygamy. Otherwise, their culture, also extremely precarious, was similar to that of their northern neighbors, the Guaycuras.

As a whole, the indigenous population of the peninsula, probably as a result of a lengthy process of adaptation to the environment, had reached approximately forty thousand in-dividuals at the time of the entrance of the Jesuit missionar-ies toward the end of the seventeenth century. What has been mentioned about the scant cultural development of the California Indians will help to better understand what it meant for them to be subjected to the processes of accultur-ation that accompanied the introduction of missionary rule in the area.

This summary description of the cultural levels of the indigenous groups of the Northwest leads to several consid-erations. The substratum of the indigenous world, both as an antecedent and because of its continued presence during the colonial period and, in some cases, through the era of independence up to the present, cannot be ignored in the search for understanding the pluricultural physiognomy of the Northwest. The Indians who lived there in the past and today continue to reside in this vast region, far less numer-ous and also much less culturally evolved than the peoples of the Mesoamerican area, demonstrate along with some common characteristics obvious differences among them. The ways of life of those who were established in villages and dedicated themselves primarily to agriculture contrast sharply with the tribes with precarious settlements who derived their subsistence primarily from hunting, gathering, or fishing. It is also important to underline the absence of a lingua franca in these regions, as opposed to the role that Náhuatl (Aztec) fulfilled in the central area of Mesoamerica.

All of this conditioned the processes of contact and exchange, first among the tribes themselves and then between them and the Spanish conquerors, colonists, and missionaries. These and other factors can help in evaluating the forms that the colonial settlements took, and the types of enterprises the Spaniards entered into to take advantage of natural resources. In any case, it is clear that the specific forms of indigenous presence in the Northwest have been and continue to be an important element within the cultural peculiarity of that vast area situated on the outskirts of Mesoamerica.

THE COLONIAL PERIOD

In contrast to what had unfolded in the Chichimec lands immediately to the north of the ancient Aztec domains, the indigenous populations of the Northwest, with some exceptions, far from disappearing, survived the Spanish penetration. For the conquerors, expansion into the North was a radically different experience from the subjugation of the chiefdoms with an advanced culture in the central region of Mexico. Hernán Cortés needed little more than two years to conquer the Aztec capital and destroy the hegemony it had exercised over vast territories. And despite the Indians' resistance to accepting Spanish forms of government and institutions, the new order of things began to establish itself in Central Mexico with relative efficacy and speed. The existence of a true civilization in Mesoamerica made it possible, within the process of change, to take advantage of certain existing elements of the ancient social, political, and economic structures.

With respect to the North, the Spaniards knew from the outset that it was inhabited by peoples devoid of cultural refinement. In spite of this, soon after the Conquest rumors began to circulate about the existence, in regions farther north, of other kingdoms with towns and cities at least as rich as that of the Aztecs. Such fables, and the fact that years later mines of precious metals were discovered in the North, awoke the interest of the conquerors and of a great number of explorers and adventurers.

The First Expeditions

As early as 1522 Cortés sent one of his captains, Cristóbal de Olid, to Michoacán. Shortly thereafter, Gonzalo de Sandoval ventured in the direction of Colima. In 1529, Nuño de Guzmán, already famous for his abuses as president of the first Audencia, or judiciary council, and for the atrocities he committed in the region of Pánuco, entered through Michoacán and, in a short time, was established in what was to be called New Galicia. So rapid was his advance up the West Coast corridor that, in 1531, only ten years after the Conquest of Mexico, the village of San Miguel of Culiacán was founded in Sinaloa.[9] Some of his men advanced even farther, though only on exploratory treks, to the Yaqui River in Sonora.

Despite the rugged terrain of these territories and the manifest hostility of the tribes who lived there, their attraction grew with the passage of time. Hernán Cortés, with the royal licenses he held for his discoveries in the "Southern Sea," began in 1532 to dispatch maritime expeditions that, touching on land in New Galicia, ended in the discovery of the peninsula of California. And though he did not discover the riches he sought, like so many others he refused to abandon his projects in these regions. The first viceroy of New Spain, Antonio de Mendoza, highly encouraged by news brought by Fray Marcos de Niza, sent out new expeditions to the Northwest. By sea, in 1540 Hernando de Alarcón sailed up the mouth of the Colorado River. By land, Francisco Vásquez de Coronado set out and crossed Sinaloa and Sonora, reaching beyond Arizona and New Mexico. Despite their efforts, neither the scouts of Cortés nor those of Mendoza found the fabled towns and cities of fabulous riches.[10] Instead, what they discovered was that in these enormous and sometimes arid expanses lived aggressive tribes whose ways of life could not be compared with those of the Indians of Central and Southern Mexico. Violent encounters with native groups had already taken place in Nueva Galicia. A particularly serious example is the one known as the Mixtón rebellion of 1541, which had to be personally put down by Viceroy Mendoza.[11]

These first attempts at expanding the ancient borders of Mesoamerica through the West Coast corridor and also by sea toward California did not achieve their purpose. A more fruitful advance followed the triumph over the Mixtón rebellion of 1541, which permitted penetration from Nueva Galicia in the direction of Zacatecas. There, in 1546, the first justification for the interest in pushing northward was finally obtained as great mines of precious metals were uncovered. Zacatecas became a great center of attraction as well as the point of departure for undertaking new conquests.[12] Thus was established what would later be known as the "Road of Silver." To ensure communication between Zacatecas and Mexico City, new towns, missions, and forts were founded. Soon deposits were discovered where other mining centers were established, in Guanajuato in 1555, and Mazapil in 1568. The frequent assaults and rebellions of the Chichimecs, though repelled time and again, made constant precaution and defense necessary.[13] Nonetheless, the desire to exploit the gold and silver kept the settlers from abandoning what territory had been gained and further compelled them to attempt new advances.

The history of the myriad processes that, over centuries of colonial rule, led to the ultimate conquest of the various northern provinces is a lengthy one.[14] What is fundamentally of interest here are the characteristics of this penetration, which serve as a necessary ingredient in appreciating the culture that developed in the different types of settlements founded throughout the conquered regions. Many of the characteristics that typify the cultural physiognomy of the Mexican North have their roots precisely in what took place during this formative stage of the colonial period. A point of departure in a better-organized process of expansion was the opening, around 1550, of permanent communications between Mexico City, Guadalajara, and Zacatecas.

More Permanent Settlements

Since the founding of Zacatecas in 1546, the North had attracted an increasingly large number of people from different social backgrounds. First there were the original conquerors or their descendants and men recently arrived in New Spain, desirous of emulating the exploits of the past and especially committed to becoming rich. Following them were others more or less familiar with mining, adventurers of all stripes, and soldiers of fortune. Also headed northward were groups of Indians, former Tlaxcaltecan allies of the Spaniards, almost always forced into the role of servants and auxiliary troops.

When mining camps and forts were established to defend them from the "barbarous" Indians, some of these Spaniards and allied natives began to dedicate themselves to agricultural and ranching work, enterprises necessary to provide a nearby source of supplies to those who worked in the extraction of metals. Thus the first northern ranches and haciendas were born, as well as some towns that would come to rival the mining centers. Special mention should be given to those men who, sometimes from the start, participated in the different expeditions and settlements in the North—the missionaries, who in these vast territories were Franciscans and Jesuits. To the former is owed, among other things, the creation of numerous missions, beginning in Zacatecas and then expanding into New Mexico; and to the Jesuits is due the spiritual conquest of a large part of Sinaloa, Sonora, southern Arizona, and Baja California.[15]

Around 1563, the famous Francisco de Ibarra advanced from Zacatecas and once again broadened the boundaries of the frontier, founding Durango and Nombre de Dios. Ibarra then crossed the Sierra Madre in the direction of Topia and headed down to Sinaloa, uniting for the first time the West Coast corridor with the regions of the "Road of Silver."[16] With the actions of Francisco de Ibarra, Nueva Vizcaya was born. Later expansion into areas of modern-day Chihuahua made possible the definitive penetration into New Mexico and other regions, Sinaloa and Sonora in the Northwest and Saltillo and Coahuila in the Northeast. The ways of life that began to settle more deeply into these vast territories, inhabited earlier only by tribes of a limited cultural level, would consolidate and expand in the coming centuries.

There was considerable diversity in the motives and behaviors of those who penetrated toward the North, people so different among themselves as missionaries, royal officials, captains and soldiers, miners, and *hacendados* with their peons, Indian servants, and black slaves. But despite their differences, in their own ways they all had to face the realities that characterized the northern lands. These vast expanses were frontier country. To create any kind of settlement in this terrain was always difficult in the extreme. The lack of means of communication, especially in the beginning, meant almost total isolation. One way or the other, contact with the so-called barbarous tribes of the various regions seemed at once dangerous and necessary. Within this context, throughout the colonial period much of the cultural distinctiveness of the Mexican Northwest was forged.

Characteristic features of the majority of the recent arrivals were their determination, courage in the face of danger, and will to work. All of this assumed physical strength. In fact, perhaps due to a process of natural selection, given the difficulty of survival in the region, even the indigenous natives of the area appeared endowed with similar qualities.

Among such people, whether settlers or Indians, confrontations were inevitable. As a frontier land, the Northwest was witness to all sorts of violence on the part of those who entered the area, as well as rebellions among the Indians; but it was equally the scene of profound, though gradual, transformations. These were brought about through the introduction of Spanish institutions, adapted—for better or worse—to their new circumstances. This introduction, in turn, was accomplished primarily by the creation of the mining camps, forts, towns, haciendas, ranches, and missions.[17] A brief description of these types of settlements will focus our study on the distinct cultural situation that developed in these lands.

The Lure of the Mines

The chief incentive for northern penetration was to exploit the mines of gold and silver discovered there. However, from the moment of entrance into Zacatecas, alongside the soldiers and adventurers were the Franciscan missionaries, determined to broaden their field of action. The Franciscan chronicler José Arlegui concisely describes this development: "The captain Don Juan de Tolosa, having word of the mines of silver that there were in Zacatecas and in its environs, the land possessed by the barbarous pagans, he entered with men of war, accompanied by four religious. . . . And on the eighth day of the month of September of 1546, he established his camp on the side of a high hill, which is today called La Bufa, where the Indians of the Zacatecan nation had their fortress."[18] There, while some began work in the mining camp, the friars dedicated themselves to converting the natives. Arlegui, who was interested above all in missionary work, insists on the importance of the mining camps that were then founded in Durango, in the Sierra Madre, and in southern Chihuahua, as foci of attraction and culture contact. From this perspective his *Crónica* could almost be considered an introduction to the development of cultural processes as a consequence of mining in northern Mexico: "In this time"—he tells us—

"with the news of the opulence of the mining center, many Spaniards gathered there, attracted by the secret virtues of silver, as effective in stirring men's wills as magnets are in attracting steel."[19] And speaking of the mines in Sombrerete, Parral, and Santa Bárbara, he reiterates that the creation of the centers came to be a reason for still more people to arrive as silver offered new opportunities for work:

> It is the case that of all the rich minerals that are discovered, then a multitude of people flock to the vibrant echo of the silver, from so many places as there are in America, and as the region where the mines are discovered is unproductive of the necessary sustenance, the farmers and the stock raisers of the area sell from their grain and animals, and since they alone cannot give enough supply to the people gathered, others are needed, whether by necessity or greed, to discover new arable fields and populate stocks of animals even in the lands in most danger of the barbarians, God disposing in this way that, though the mines may fail, the surrounding lands remain with the new arable fields and well-stocked animals and with enough trade between the inhabitants.[20]

This occurred from Zacatecas to Topia, Chihuahua, and Alamos in Sonora. The settlements of Spaniards and mestizos were expanding and their ranks swelled with the allied Indians of Central Mexico and black and mulatto slaves. At the same time, the missionary enterprises, first those of the Franciscans and later also of the Jesuits, grew and served to increase contacts with the indigenous groups.

An experience that contrasted sharply with what had taken place in Mesoamerica was the need first to pacify the northern Indian groups, and only then to initiate their gradual transformation. The Spanish authorities were soon forced to discard the idea of organizing *corregimientos* (forms of local civil government) and *encomiendas* in the North as they had done in the rest of New Spain. Such institutions had functioned in Mesoamerica, but there the cultural antecedents of those who had lived in towns or cities since ancient times meant that the inhabitants were already familiar with forms of communal work, domestic services, and the forced pay of tribute. Such a manner of subjugation among the northern groups was unfeasible. Thus, the processes of acculturation among Indians and Spaniards would follow a different course in the North. On the one hand, some royal officials, as well as many miners, *hacendados,* and ranchers, continued to push with all the means at their disposal to have the natives with whom they had established contact subjugated for their own benefit. On the other hand, the missionaries seized the opportunity to isolate the communities in separate missionary centers, making possible their Christianization free from the violence and servitude that otherwise loomed as permanent threats over them.

THE MISSIONARY ACCULTURATION

The old ideals of re-creating ways of life among the Indians similar to those of the ancient Christian communities reappeared and guided the course of Franciscan as well as Jesuit activity in the northern lands. From the beginning of the penetration, the Franciscans, who had joined the march alongside the commanders and founders of mining centers, towns, and haciendas, were committed to safeguarding the Indians through their "reduction," or concentration in areas seemingly most adequate for the establishment of missions. They followed this course of action from the first entrance toward Zacatecas, and later in regions of Durango, Chihuahua, and New Mexico, the field of their proselytizing task. The Jesuits, who later expanded their missionary work in the North, diverged from the Franciscan approach to introduce methods worthy of special consideration.

In the Northwest, the area of Jesuit activity included the regions of Chínipas, Tarahumara in the Sierra of Chihuahua, part of Durango, Sinaloa, Sonora, southern Arizona, and Baja California. Fully aware that to Christianize the Indians, the first and most fundamental step was to block their immediate destruction, they insisted on the necessity of organizing the missions as institutions totally detached from the new Spanish centers. Predictably, it was rarely easy for them to establish their first contacts with the Indians. Sometimes through friendly invitations and gifts, other times availing themselves of the assistance of small but efficient military forces, their primary objective was to put an end to what they saw as the seminomadic or vagrant life of many of the Indians with whom they established contact.

In each missionary center they built the church, the priests' house, the school, the storehouses, and the generally scattered dwellings for the Indians. Their concern then turned to seeking the best ways to provide for the upkeep of the Indians and the economy of the mission. The necessary means of support would be gained through agriculture, stock raising, and also limited forms of trade and craft production. The missionary system of government placed authority in the hands of the priest, who in turn obeyed his superiors in the religious hierarchy and maintained contact with royal officials. It was left to the head of the mission to choose the governors, mayors, judges, fiscal officers, teachers, and catechists from among the Indians. In the most developed missions it was not uncommon to find a florescence of arts and trades like carpentry, weaving, iron working, pottery, and brickmaking.

Miners, *hacendados,* ranchers and some public administration officials frequently decried the missionary system. Their acute need for labor led them to seek control of the Indians to work in the mines or the fields of the haciendas. Toward this end they acted with deceit and subterfuge, at times culminating in overt demonstrations of force. Their attempts resulted not only in violent confrontations with the missionaries opposed to their designs, but also in numerous outbreaks of rebellion that, in some cases, were transformed into well-organized Indian uprisings.

To comprehend the significance to the northern indigenous groups of their subjection to the missionary process of change, one need only consider the suggestive testimony of a Jesuit missionary who worked with a community of Cochimí Indians in the California peninsula. As discussed earlier, the Chochimíes were not distinguished by a significant cultural development, as their seminomadic existence was dedicated to gathering, hunting, and fishing. In contrast, the Jesuit Nicolás Tamaral describes in detail the distribution of time to which the Indians were subjected in the California mission of La Purísima:

The usual distribution of time is this: at daybreak, the bell rings announcing the time to say the Ave Marías; then the entire domestic family comes to church; they pray and greet the Very Holy Virgin, they sing the Alabado [the Eulogy], first the men, then the women, then the two choirs, men and women; and, in this and in all the distributions of gatherings of men and women, the men are always apart, together, and in a separate place the women, together . . .

Afterwards, those who then have an occupation go to their trade, as do those of the kitchen and they who also make breakfast for the workers, for the sick, old, orphaned, etcetera.

Those who have no occupation come to help at the mass that is said every day and, when the mass is over, they pray and sing in chorus the Alabado, as has been said. Afterwards the father gives out breakfast, which is *atole* [a thin gruel made of cornmeal]. When this is done, each one does what they are charged with: the men, to work in the field or in the building of the church . . . the women, some to spin cotton and wool, others to knit, others to their weaving. . . .

At ten in the morning the bell rings and they come to the church . . . and, separated one from another, they pray the whole doctrine and, once finished, they sing in chorus the Alabado with a decent unhurriedness. At midday, the bell rings and, on their knees, they all greet the Very Holy Virgin and sing the Eulogy once. Afterwards they share the meal, which is, for the workers,

pozole [a stew made of hominy grits]; and the old men
and women, the boys and girls, *atole* and some *pozole*.

After eating they rest until two and then each one
continues with the work that they have undertaken. At
five in the afternoon the bell rings and they come to the
church to pray all the prayers and doctrine. . . .
At sunset, they say their Ave Marías and on their knees
they greet the Very Holy Virgin; afterwards they share
their supper, as at midday. After eating, they all go to
church and with the father they pray in chorus the
rosary, litanies, and sing the Alabado. . . . Afterwards
they all leave and, in completely separate places, they
pray the doctrine and they gather together. The young
people and singles have a space apart, where they sleep;
the married ones have their little houses, because it is
the custom that, when marrying one of the family,
a little house is made so that they live and sleep with
decency.[21]

This lengthy description of how time was divided in the
mission of La Purísima and, presumably, similarly so in
the others, brings to mind a series of questions: To the
northern Indians, almost all of whom were accustomed to
a life of liberty without worry of doing this or that, what
could it have meant to be subjected upon the ringing of a
bell to devoting themselves to specific activities, prayers,
and devotions, fixed hours of eating, clearly defined work
roles and then more prayers and devotions, always at the
sound of the bell? Even granting the best of intentions on
the part of the missionaries, is there not good reason to
suppose that this new rhythm of life imposed upon the
Indians provoked within them a profound cultural
trauma?
History reveals that, while not amid the California
Cochimíes, among other indigenous groups of the peninsula
like the Pericúes and Guaycuras, initial submission was later
transformed into a stance of resistance, finally sparking the
violent rebellion of 1734 and 1735. Another fact worthy of

note is that during this rebellion two Jesuit missionaries lost their lives at the hands of the Indians.

The northern missionary experience, resulting from noble intentions to allow for the Christianization and cultural transformation of the Indians through isolation, bears elements worthy of analysis and evaluation in light of the approaches developed not only in ethnology but also in some contemporary currents of social anthropology. Some pertinent issues that come to mind are the problematics that arise in the mutual understanding of different mentalities, the often unforeseen consequences of culture contact, and the so-called induced acculturations, especially in the form of "spiritual conquests" as carried out by the Franciscans and Jesuits in the Northwest of Mexico. It should be added, however, in an attempt to understand the missionary perspective, that it is to these same priests that we owe the survival of indigenous populations like the Yaquis, Tarahumaras, Mayos, and Tepehuanes amid this world of conflicting interests and frequent violence.

OTHER FACTORS IN THE CULTURAL EVOLUTION OF NEW SPAIN'S NORTHWEST

Diverse forms of unrest and alarm were often experienced in the various northern regions. To the more or less sporadic rebellions of indigenous groups already subjected to the missionary processes of acculturation were added frequent sieges by so-called barbarian Indians, usually the Apache. As a consequence, permanent garrisons were established in the centers of population, paralleled by the creation of forts or presidios situated in strategic areas as military outposts. The presidios, in fact, marked lines of defense that were moved increasingly toward the North throughout the colonial period.

Working the mines meant, in periods of bonanza, amassing considerable wealth, especially for the benefit of the large merchants and the royal treasury. With affluence came the transformation of many mining centers into towns and cities made of sumptuous buildings—churches, government palaces, shops, warehouses, and luxurious houses for the most prosperous townspeople. But frequently the veins dried up, and the decadence of these centers became apparent. In this case, as Father Arlegui noted earlier, the situation of the *hacendados* and ranchers was much luckier, for in their boundless expanses of land they raised thousands of head of cattle, and far-from-worthless harvests. An early example of this from the end of the sixteenth century are the vast possessions of Diego de Ibarra, whose haciendas at Trujillo and Valparaíso, in the modern-day state of Durango, produced more than 130,000 head of cattle.

The historian François Chevalier, by studying similar cases, has demonstrated in detail how the economy of the North was consolidated with the introduction of livestock-and cattle raising on a large scale.[22] On the other hand, the propagation of horses and livestock in general also deeply influenced the ways of life of the northern colonists. Herding and the art of horseriding came to be everyday occupations. In festivals, the highest prestige was given to those with skill as horsemen and to demonstrations of the artistry of the cowboy, or *vaquero*. A mastery of horseriding was also crucial for *hacendados*, ranchers, majordomos, and even laborers when they found themselves in situations of danger, such as in the attacks of the "barbarous Indians." In fact, many of the latter—the Apache, Navajo, and Comanche—also became excellent equestrians who used horses in their assaults on towns and other establishments of northern New Spain. The introduction of cattle raising in the North came to be so influential that several modern historians have referred to this "horse and beef culture" as peculiar to northern Mexico, while acting as a forebear to the way of life that later prevailed in what was to become the southwest of the United States.

Thus, the cultural distinctiveness of the Mexican North was forged in terms of these institutions—the mining camps, new centers of population, missions, presidios, and great haciendas and ranches. Nonetheless, the number of people settled in the region had not reached great heights. Calculations based on reports and accounts of the time demonstrate that around the year 1760, slightly more than two centuries after the beginning of the colonial penetration, the number of inhabitants reached only about 230,000 individuals, excluding the "barbarian Indians."[23]

The New Spanish establishments were still like islands, whether along the West Coast corridor, on the so-called Road of Silver, in the foothills of the Sierra, or throughout the isolated environment of the California peninsula. Despite the fact that provinces already had been sectioned off through the implantation of Spanish forms of government and administration in the northern territories, the colonists living there continued to suffer from great isolation. Aside from elementary schools, established in monasteries or on the mission grounds, there were no institutions of formal education. Nor was the cultural refinement of the majority of those who dedicated themselves to mining, agricultural work, or commerce highly notable. The quest for power, mixed with unleashed greed and the presence of unsubdued Indian tribes, made for frequent violence. All of this influenced the way of being, the life and culture, of those who called the North their home.

The decades preceding the independence of Mexico were, for the Northwest, a period of final expansion and also an era of ambitious projects only partially realized, like those of the inspector José de Gálvez. Missions were built throughout Upper California, but in Sonora, Chihuahua, and New Mexico, the situation became increasingly difficult. The Seri Indians of Sonora rebelled repeatedly during these years, and those considered the biggest threat of all, the Apache, were more visible than ever in numerous assaults.

Nonetheless, New Spain exercised effective control from Zacatecas to what could be described as the enclave of New Mexico, primarily along the Rio Grande. Viceregal power also reigned in Sinaloa and Sonora, to the area surrounding the Gila River, in what is today Arizona, and also in the small missionary centers of Baja California and in those most recently established through the western area of Upper or New California.

The social and economic physiognomy of the Mexican Northwest was forged within this context, in terms of the institutions already described and as a consequence of the culture contact and changes that developed within them. The indigenous groups of the area, rather than being subject, as in the Mesoamerican case, to municipal authorities and *encomiendas,* experienced a very different process of change through their gradual concentration in the missions, whenever possible in isolation from the centers of Spanish colonization. These, in turn, were settlements constructed entirely on the Spanish model, since in the Northwest there had not been earlier pre-Conquest cities or towns per se, as there had in the center and south of Mexico. Thus, in the Northwest the New Spanish centers of population responded more fully to the specific needs and interests of the colonists. This helps to explain how several of these new establishments prospered through extensive mineral, agricultural, and livestock exploitation.

Frequently, in the considerable isolation of the New Spanish centers of population, ethnically and culturally heterogeneous groups lived side by side: miners, royal officials, captains and soldiers, cattlemen and agriculturalists of Spanish, Criollo, and mestizo origin, a number of black slaves and also, at times, the descendants of allied Indians, primarily Tlaxcaltecas and in general of Nahua or Mexican origin, brought from the central region of Mexico. The Northwest continued to maintain its character as a frontier land. Adventurers were the most common of those who lived in the different parts of this region, audacious people dedicated to making their way in the face of danger and considerable hard work. This appraisal is also valid, to a degree, with regard to many missionaries who, with total dedication, labored to incorporate ever-increasing areas inhabited by indigenous tribes that had to be converted.

Worthy of mention in this regard are, among others, Eusebio Francisco Kino, Juan María de Salvatierra, and Junípero Serra.

Toward the end of the eighteenth century, and particularly at the beginning of the next, other factors increased in their importance to the area. Without the full awareness of the residents of the Northwest, opposing interests were developing, including the greed of a foreign entity that had fixed its gaze upon these rich and sparsely inhabited provinces. Meanwhile, in the first decade of the nineteenth century the Spanish motherland, in evident decline, was incapable of lending any support to the New Spanish expansion into regions so distant from the center of the viceroyalty of Mexico. All of this, as it came to influence the whole of the overseas kingdoms and provinces in a similar manner, had serious consequences—at first hardly perceptible though in the end definitive—throughout the frontier territories of New Spain. Very soon the region would begin to experience the impact of another, even more decisive, factor: the political changes brought forth by Mexico's independence.

8.
The Northwest since Mexican Independence

The processes of contact and transformation that took place in the Northwest over centuries of Spanish domination irrevocably molded the physiognomy of this vast part of the country. From that time on, what can be described as a special *norteño* variety began to develop within Mexican culture. What follows is an attempt to evaluate how, and to what extent, the changes wrought through independence and the subsequent national development up to the modern day have strengthened certain aspects—and perhaps weakened others—of the cultural identity considered to be characteristic of the Northwest.

Mexico's independence was much more than the mere rupture of a submissive stance with respect to the Spanish motherland. The country, having gained its liberty, faced the necessity of developing forms of political and social organization better suited to its own current circumstances. Principles derived from the French Revolution, as well as the example of its northern neighbor, the United States, were powerful influences against conservative groups committed to preserving old Spanish institutions like the monarchy and the union of church and state. The series of struggles resulting from these antagonisms made any form of political stability impossible for a protracted period of time.

THE NATIONAL QUESTION: KEY TO
UNDERSTANDING THE PREVAILING
SITUATION IN THE NORTH

It was during the war of independence that the two radically opposed perspectives first appeared. Father Miguel Hidalgo, who initiated the struggle on September 16, 1810, was a man of progressive ideas who soon brought upon himself the open condemnation of his ecclesiastic superiors. In addition to the separation from Spain, Hidalgo sought to establish new forms of local government that would make feasible necessary changes that, he believed, could no longer be delayed. Hidalgo proclaimed the equal rights of Indians and issued a decree condemning slavery. His words found a resounding echo in the legion of peasants and common people who joined his cause. His struggle was, at the core, the first upheaval in Mexico that was not only political, but profoundly social in orientation.

With Hidalgo's death, after falling prisoner to viceregal authorities in the northern territories, the struggle's leadership passed into the hands of another figure who enriched and broadened the ideology of the insurgence. José María Morelos was also a priest who knew from experience the problems of the peasant masses. He formulated the ideals that gave meaning to his campaign with precision: Mexico has the right to constitute itself as a sovereign state and therefore to grant itself the form of government best suited to its needs; its sovereignty emanates from the people themselves, and from no other source; for equality to exist it is necessary to do away with exemptions and privileges; and tributes and duties should be distributed equitably, just as possibilities for work and all that is connected with this, in particular the possession of land.

The ideology expressed by Morelos, enriched with the thought of other insurgents, was written into the first constitution drawn up by a congress in which representatives of the people in struggle participated. The Constitution of Apatzingán, issued in October of 1814, was their first document, a formulation of the principles and aims of those who were persuaded that substantial reforms and changes had to be introduced, referring not so much to Northern Mexico as to the prevailing conditions in the central and southern parts of the country.

Morelos, like Hidalgo and many others, also succumbed in battle. For a brief time it appeared as if the struggle would be stamped out by the viceregal armies. However, just as in Spain, where the rebels remained an implacable form of opposition to the invasion of Napoleon, in Mexico the scattered groups that survived took advantage of similar strategies while waiting for an opportune moment to continue the fight. Soon unforeseen events in Spain would indeed precipitate an outcome, though it was not the one that the rebel followers of the ideologies of Hidalgo and Morelos would have wanted.

As a result of the revolt initiated in Spain in 1820 by General Riego, Ferdinand VII was forced to reestablish the liberal constitution issued years before in Cádiz, with the participation of representatives from the American continent. This constitution, which included some of the same political, social, and economic transformations that the insurgents fought for, provoked a growing uneasiness among conservative groups in Mexico. Leading ecclesiastics and high-ranking military officials, wealthy people dedicated to the preservation of the traditional institutions, began to adopt the cause of independence—but with very different sentiments than it had originally carried. Agustín de Iturbide was the executor of the plans of those who dreaded the possible transformations now originating in Spain itself. With the help of the old insurgents, surprised and confused, Iturbide brought an end to the war, with Mexico's gaining independence in 1821. Along with it, paradoxically, the viewpoint of those who would soon receive the title of "conservatives" also triumphed, for the time being. New Spain retained the monarchy, but the Spanish princes, considered as possible sovereigns, refused the crown and it fell instead to the one who had consummated the struggle. Thus was born the ephemeral experiment of an empire that was to last less than two years.

Those who believed in the need for radical change were soon given reason to act. With the installation of the constitutional congress in 1822, a revolutionary ideology soon materialized among its members. Shortly thereafter the brand-new emperor, who could not govern with an opposing congress, moved toward the dissolution of the assembly. Antagonisms grew, and in early 1823 Iturbide was forced to abdicate the throne.

One year later the first Mexican republic was born, with a constitution that established the federal organization of the country and formulated the liberal rules that would run it. Those who had fought for the transformation achieved the first of their triumphs now, a full three years after gaining independence. The opposition forces—the high clergy, the aristocracy, and parts of the army, especially military personnel of the upper echelons—refused to concede defeat even remotely. The historical direction of Mexico continued on this path, with the struggle enduring for more than half a century. Both sides included distinguished ideologues. Standing out among the conservatives was the cultivated statesman and energetic entrepreneur Lucas Alamán. Deserving of mention in the ranks of the liberals were Lorenzo de Zavala, a politician and historian, Doctor José María Luis Mora, an anticlerical priest who was to become the father of Mexican liberalism, and Valentín Gómez Farías, a lawyer and broad-minded politician who put into practice many of Mora's ideas.

As always in history, there were also many ambivalent figures who changed parties according to their own best interests. The most famous of these is Antonio López de Santa Anna. Due to circumstances and a rare intelligence, he came to power on numerous occasions and was in a position to make decisions of highest import, some of which had to do directly with the destiny of the northern provinces of the country.

THE LONG-FORGOTTEN
NORTHERN MEXICO

Amidst the upheaval caused by frequent uprisings and civil wars, it was impossible to attend to even the most elementary problems inherent in national organization and development. The distant provinces of the North, with their scarce population, remained peripheral to the immediate area of concern. The northern isolation grew with every passing day and, in the case of provinces like Upper and Baja California and New Mexico, the ties to the center of the country appeared no more than symbolic. This explains why, in the North, rulers who were no more than genuine *caciques* thrived, interested only in maintaining their dominant positions. The North's association with a strong government weakened to an extreme, the old systems of defense had also disappeared or were reduced to a minimum, including the presidios that had protected the settlers against the assaults of the so-called barbarous Indians. As a result, insecurity mounted, paralleling the increasing isolation, and both factors influenced the decay of many of the old mining centers and the haciendas dedicated to agriculture and livestock. Business also became shaky, due to the decreased production of former sources of wealth as well as to the total lack of protection on the roads. The missions, though they survived for some years, also began to experience symptoms of deterioration, a foretaste of their upcoming legal, and definitive, suppression.

The situation of northern Mexico was somber indeed during the decades that followed independence. It is only natural that, in their isolation, the *norteños* would clutch tighter to their own cultural tradition, awaiting the arrival of better times. Soon, however, they were to face events that put their very cultural and national identity at risk. In 1835 the restless and ambivalent General Santa Anna, in collusion with the Conservative party, rose up to establish a form of political government that abandoned federalism and shifted Mexico to a centralized republic. This would prove to be the aperture for a series of disgraces that, in the end, prodded the country into a foreign war.

In the province of Texas, where numerous Anglo-Saxon colonists had settled over the years, an open rebellion broke out. In 1836, ironically only four years after the ratification of the Treaty of Onís, which had established Mexico's borders with the United States, the Anglo-Saxon colonists of Texas declared their independence. The ultimate aim of such a resolution was uncovered when, in 1845, Texas was annexed as a new state in the North American Union. This event, immediately preceding the open attitude of "manifest destiny" assumed by the United States, would lead to the unleashing of hostilities in 1846. In May of that year the North Americans, with a pretext of aggression on the part of Mexico, commenced the war. The international confrontation continued until September of 1847; its outcome is well known.

The idea and reality of Northern Mexico was profoundly altered. Mexico was forced to cede to the victor all of what was rather vaguely referred to as Upper California and New Mexico, which included the enormous territories that later became the states of Arizona, Nevada, Utah, and parts of Colorado and Oklahoma. Though Mexico managed to save at least the coveted peninsula of California, approximately eight hundred thousand square miles were lost, home to a Mexican-origin population of approximately eighty thousand.[1] The Treaty of Guadalupe-Hidalgo, in which the new borders were established between the two countries, included several articles designed to protect the Mexican people and properties that were enveloped by the territory acquired by the United States.[2] It should be recognized, however, that the inclusion of such stipulations in the international treaty was far from an effective safeguard for the rights of such groups living, from then on, under a foreign jurisdiction.

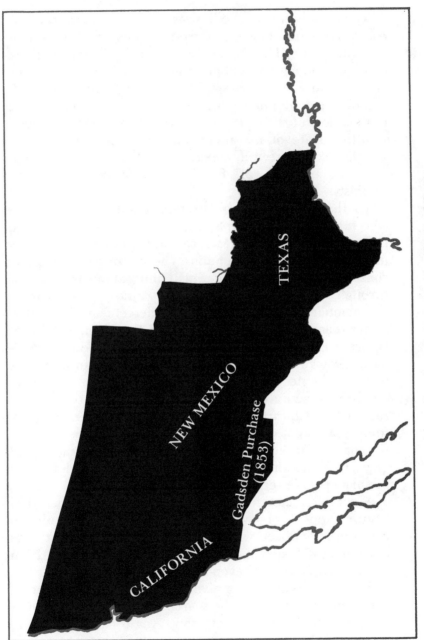

Northern Territories Lost to the United States

As is obvious, the Anglo-Saxons, clearly the masters of the conquered lands, began to introduce their own institutions and ways of life. Thus began for the Mexicans living in these territories a long series of processes of acculturation experienced from a disadvantaged position, and in many cases accompanied by open violence. Among other things, the gradual loss of their property, racial discrimination, and a resulting state of marginality all soon became realities. For the sake of survival, Mexicans were compelled to accept the worst jobs and work for the profit of the Anglo-Saxon colonists.

To these groups of generations-old Mexican *norteños* who remained in United States territory would be added, over time, many other Mexican immigrants. In this way numerous minority communities were formed and grew constantly, through continuing immigration as much as through their own demographic expansion. Around 1910 the number of people of Mexican descent in the United States reached around four hundred thousand; today that figure is calculated to be at least twelve million.[3] The almost always negative socioeconomic and cultural experiences, while necessarily accepted as inevitable, also led to defensive reactions that originally were more or less sporadic. The Chicano movement, which reached its peak some years ago, openly reflected the awareness of those who have suffered discrimination and marginalization and gave rise to a militancy that sought to make the rights of a minority people respected.

A notable characteristic of the Chicano movement has been its appeal, in a variety of ways, to the very cultural roots directly linked with the past of these lands that once belonged to Mexico. Thus what is meant by *"norteño,"* even in the areas situated beyond the present Mexican border, rather than disappearing gives cause for the invocation of traditions and myths in the search for ethnic identity vis à vis the culture of the dominant Anglo society. Among other declarations, Chicanos have argued that it was their ancestors who achieved the original colonization of today's

Southwest United States. They refer not only to the historical fact of New Spain's expansion but, with even greater symbolic force, they proclaim that it was precisely in these regions that the Aztecs' Aztlán, original homeland of their indigenous ancestors, was located.

Certainly, the fate of those Mexicans who remained "on the other side" has been very harsh. Only recently can it be said that, thanks primarily to the Chicanos' militant stance and reaffirmation of their identity, some of their demands have begun to be heard. Influences were also felt in the northern provinces that Mexico managed to save in the war with the United States, as a sudden increase in contacts with this powerful nation with a different culture and language developed. The isolation so characteristic of the Mexican North with respect to the center of the country paradoxically gave way to a surprising form of closeness with the Anglo-Saxon world, which, through its resolute expansionism, continued as more of a threat than ever.

NEW THREATS TO THE INTEGRITY AND CULTURAL PROFILE OF THE NORTHWEST

The mutilation of Mexico's national territory has been a trauma difficult to erase. Perhaps too late, the center of the country began to feel an almost anguished preoccupation with strengthening the ties to the North and, above all, attending to its defense when faced with the risk of renewed hostilities. The idea of establishing a line of forts or presidios, as in the days of the colony, was discussed, but the shortage of federal funds and the prevalent condition of political instability blocked any form of effective action. As a consequence, the North continued for years in isolation from the rest of the country.

In accordance with the Treaty of Guadalupe-Hidalgo (1848), in which new borders between the two countries had been established, the United States was obligated to repel the assaults of so-called barbarous Indians in the lands of the frontier. In practice, however, it was the pressure exerted by the North American colonists that caused bands of

Apache, for whose welfare nothing had been done, to penetrate Mexican territory, establishing centers of operation at
various spots in Chihuahua and Sonora.[4] The traditional
antagonism and fear that the *norteños* felt for the Apache
began to mount exceedingly. Many ranches, haciendas, and
even towns had to be abandoned because of frequent attacks
by the tribes. Numerous stories have been passed down
about how it felt to fight for decades against these groups
that no one succeeded in suppressing. In addition, plentiful
decrees in the legislation of Chihuahua and Sonora demonstrate the hostile attitude of the local governments towards
this problem that seemed to have no solution.[5]

To these sources of insecurity were added other dangers
familiar to the Northwest during the second half of the
nineteenth century. Its continuing isolation, sparse population, and the potential wealth believed to be hidden in these
regions inspired invasions of filibusters from North American territory. Among many such cases is that of William
Walker, who, in 1853, declared the ephemeral Republic of
Baja California and Sonora.[6] Other bands of adventurers,
who had been in Upper California during the gold rush,
also penetrated the state of Sonora. Examples of this last
include Henry Crabb and the Frenchman Gastón Raousset
de Boulbon. But in spite of their extreme lack of resources,
the *norteño* population repeatedly withstood such attempts
at invasion, and several filibusters, among them the two just
mentioned, paid for their greed with their lives. Such events
inflamed the attitude of continual defense among the northern Mexicans. And this, in turn, intensified their feelings of
nationalism, connected in an essential way to the determination to preserve their own culture and the land colonized by
their ancestors.

Accustomed to withstanding Apache assaults, filibuster
raids, and what was considered to be the constant threat of
Anglo-American expansion, the *norteños* once again demonstrated their capacity to resist at the time of the French
intervention. The troops of Napoleon III were repeatedly
repelled from the North, and it was precisely along the

borders of the frontier of Chihuahua that President Benito
Juárez was able to reorganize his government and head the
forces that, ultimately, expelled the French from Mexico
and brought an end to Maximilian's empire. This last war of
intervention gave the North a favorable balance in relation
to Central and Southern Mexico. More than ever since the
days of independence, the distant regions of Chihuahua and
Sonora began to feel stronger ties to the rest of the country.

The years that followed, especially during the long period of Porfirio Díaz's rule, were a bonanza for many of the
old upper-class families in the Northwest. The haciendas
took on new life and were concentrated in the hands of a
few. The northern *latifundios*, the extremely large landed
estates, became famous for their sometimes unbelievably
vast landholdings. In the particular case of the forgotten
peninsula of California, enormous territorial concessions
to foreign companies, with would-be goals of colonization,
gave basis to the fear that an experience similar to what
took place in Texas would come to be repeated.

The mining industry was also rejuvenated, though almost
totally in the hands of foreigners.[7] The regime granted
all kinds of concessions to foreign interests, including the
construction of railways that led to the center of the country
from the border of Chihuahua, and later also from Sonora.
The people working on the great *latifundios* and in the
mines, in contrast, lived under precarious conditions. The
indigenous tribes, whose traditional culture was the object
of continuous scorn, were violently suppressed at the least
sign of rebellion, as if what was sought was their total disappearance. Such was the panorama of events in the Northwest at the beginning of the twentieth century. As in the
rest of the country, what advancement was achieved almost
exclusively favored the upper classes and foreign interests.

THE NORTHWEST AFTER THE REVOLUTION

It is significant that among the various movements that fore-
told the Mexican Revolution, many took place precisely in
the North. The discontent of the lower classes was obvious,

especially among those who worked the mines and on the agricultural and livestock *latifundios*. In 1906 the strike in the mines of Cananea, Sonora, arose as a movement for social justice and was put down with extreme violence. The people of the North, who had repeatedly demonstrated their capacity for struggle, must have been aware of some of the grave problems that engulfed the country as a whole. On the one hand stood the dictatorship of Porfirio Díaz, which blocked any political change; on the other, with every passing day the condition of the popular masses who labored and lived in inhuman conditions became more precarious. While there were individuals in the center of the country who now openly embraced the need for radical changes, it was the men of the North who more forcefully committed themselves to building the movement that, in the end, culminated in revolution. Francisco I. Madero, a native of Coahuila, appears in this context as the apostle of democracy, upon whose implantation a general transformation was expected. A great many *norteños* strongly supported him, particularly in Coahuila, Chihuahua, and Sonora.

Following the assassination of President Madero, when the Revolution became generalized and its intentions more broadly defined, leaders appeared in the Northwest who would decidedly influence the entire state of affairs in Mexico. The names of Francisco Villa, Alvaro Obregón, Plutarco Elías Calles, Abelardo L. Rodríguez, Adolfo de la Huerta, Joaquín Amaro, and Felipe Angeles should be mentioned in this context. They, along with other northern leaders like the former governor of Coahuila, Venustiano Carranza, not only controlled the principal revolutionary forces but also ultimately were the ones to overcome rivalries in order to organize the new government, which was the immediate antecedent to Mexico's contemporary political order.

As Herbert E. Bolton noted in his brief essay on the evolution of the Mexican Northwest,[8] it seems more than mere conjecture to relate the emergence of these revolutionary leaders with the series of processes that, from colonial

times, had molded the cultural physiognomy of their home-
lands. In the Northwest, the hostile environment that made
work so arduous, the isolation, and the necessity of being
prepared to defend oneself, all had given way to the appearance of a particular type of individuals, aware of their rights
and capable of throwing themselves into a struggle over
them whenever necessary.

For the *norteños* the revolution meant a broader awareness
of their problems, now conceived in terms of those that
affected the entire country. For the first time, large numbers of people who made up part of the revolutionary troops
of the northern states were in direct contact with life in the
center and south of Mexico. Among its many other accomplishments, the Revolution certainly created a forum for
gathering together people who customarily lived separately
from one another. Evidence of the traditional and massive
differences that existed lay in the very appearance of the
northern armies when compared with some of the revolutionary groups of the South, such as the Zapatistas. Among
the latter were many Indians, descendants of Mesoamerican
groups, commanded primarily by men of mestizo extraction. In the *norteño* armies, in contrast, it was common to
find the descendants of the Spanish agriculturalists and
miners of colonial times; but only rarely were Indians
present, except in the famous Yaqui battalions, whose appearance and dress were completely distinct from the natives of Central Mexico.

The triumph of the Revolution marked once and for all
a period of *norteño* rapprochement and influence with
Central Mexico. For almost a decade following the rule of
Venustiano Carranza, the nation's presidents were all men
from Sonora: Adolfo de la Huerta, Alvaro Obregón, and
Plutarco Elías Calles. Thus it follows that in their course of
government they took seriously the need to attend to their
native regions and to put an end to the old isolation. From
then on, between 1920 and 1930, they took the first steps
toward these goals. This initial drive, despite all kinds of
limitations, continued under the succeeding revolutionary

governments. A statistical and economic analysis of the
resources of the states of Sonora, Sinaloa, and Nayarit,
published by the Mexican government in 1928, is quite
revealing.[9] The report evaluates the socioeconomic possibilities of these states, identifying as well the primary obstacles standing in the way of their development and
participation in national life.

One of the greatest problems continued to be the North's
sparse population. Sonora, Sinaloa, and Nayarit, with a combined expanse exceeding one hundred thousand square
miles, had something less than six hundred thousand inhabitants around 1921, or fewer than six inhabitants per square
mile. Incentives had to be created to attract more people to
these regions. It was not sufficient simply to divide up the
great *latifundios,* for the means to exploit the land adequately were needed. The mining centers, in a state of
decline after the Revolution and still primarily owned by
foreigners, could not serve as the foundation for such development projects. The indigenous groups that survived in
different parts of the Northwest, including Pápagos, Seris,
Yaquis, Mayos, Tarahumaras, and Tepehuanes, were marginalized, traditionally impoverished, and even more isolated than the rest of the population.

In the California peninsula, until then served only by
maritime routes with few reliable ships, great territorial
concessions to foreign interests still existed, including the
very important Colorado River Land Company, which ex-
ploited great plantations in both the Imperial Valley and
in Mexicali. In close to fifty six thousand square miles of
peninsular land, the total population in 1930 reached only
ninety five thousand, fewer than two persons per square
mile. Of the almost completely extinct ancient indigenous
groups, all that remained were some minuscule *rancherías* of
Chochimí and Cucapa origin in the extreme North, living
under extremely precarious conditions.

In order to attend to the problems presented by the
Northwest, the government's actions were directed essentially to the following issues: the expropriation of *latifundios*

and land redistribution, the construction of a series of large dams that took advantage of the rivers descending from the Sierra Madre and that in turn created centers of agricultural development, encouraging an internal immigration that soon made itself felt. Other measures included the establishment of a broad educational system, which was also supposed to reach the indigenous groups; the nationalization of the already-existent means of communication—that is, the railways—and the launching of construction on the first roads for motor vehicles in these regions. However, it would be overly simplistic to think that these and other programs, at least partially realized, constituted a complete response to the problems and possibilities of this great region of Mexico.

There are, nonetheless, several facts worthy of mention as they reflect some of the changes taking place in the cultural reality of this area. First and foremost is the extraordinary and permanent increase in population in the years that followed the Revolution. This was due only in part to a natural increase shared throughout almost the entire country, especially during the last decades, which has been described as a "demographic explosion." Taking the case of Sonora as an example, there are the following figures: in 1921 it had a population of 257,127; in 1930 it experienced a small increase to bring the number to 316,271; in 1940, the demographic growth was still fairly limited, with 364,176 inhabitants. By 1950, migration from other regions of Mexico had contributed a considerable human contingent to the area. According to data from the Mexican Bureau of Statistics, between 1940 and 1950 those who had migrated to Sonora totaled 62,570. The 1950 census showed considerable growth, with 510,607 individuals. The process of internal migration resulted in the arrival to the same state of another 142,312 persons during the decade of 1950–1960. Its population at the beginning of 1960 amounted to 783,378. In 1970 it surpassed one million inhabitants, and in 1988, the numbers were approaching two million persons.

The other northern states shared this attraction for immigrants from other regions of Mexico. The following table demonstrates this internal migration, based on the number of persons in 1960 not born in their current state of residence:[10]

Northern Baja California	308,322 immigrants
Southern Baja California	11,552 immigrants
Chihuahua	206,022 immigrants
Durango	78,281 immigrants
Nayarit	62,673 immigrants
Sinaloa	76,202 immigrants
Sonora	142,312 immigrants

If immigrants received by the other northern states were added to the above—Coahuila (155,728), Nuevo León (254,521), and Tamaulipas (291,379)—it is clear that around 1960, more than a million and a half Mexicans, primarily from the central area, had come to settle in the border states. This process, obviously not a result of coercion, can only be explained in terms of the great economic attractions that the immigrants perceived in the northern regions. Indeed, if in 1988 the total population of the Mexican border states (Baja California, Sonora, Chihuahua, Coahuila, Nuevo León, and Tamaulipas) far surpassed the number of thirteen million inhabitants, demographic predictions taking into account internal growth and immigration estimate the population in the year 2000 to be close to twenty million.

Among the attractions of the North was the opening up of great expanses of land to cultivation, thanks to numerous works of irrigation. Until recently Northern Mexico was the area most favored with these types of projects. Today it is in the North that, to a considerable extent, forms of modern agricultural technology are found. Another very important lure has been the proximity of the United States. In addition to the hundreds of thousands of Mexicans, mainly from the central area of Mexico, who legally or furtively cross the border to go to work as field hands, there are many other inhabitants of the border cities who work in North America while maintaining their residency on the Mexican side of the dividing line. Furthermore, the development of various industries in the northern states, many with North American capital such as the *maquiladoras,* or border factories— mainly assembly plants—has led to greater possibilities for work. This also helps to explain why in several of the northern states the minimum wage, set officially, reaches higher than average amounts.

Today the traditional isolation of these, Mexico's largest states, is on the verge of disappearing. The North is now connected to the rest of the country by railroads, highways, air flights, and modern sea ferries. It is equally linked to the neighboring states of North America, some with large populations and high rates of growth like California, Arizona, and Texas, which, together with New Mexico, boast the greatest concentration of Mexican descendants who continue to hold on, in large part, to elements of their original culture.

On the other hand, it is necessary to recognize that the changes that have taken place in the North of Mexico during the last few decades, particularly those derived from the increasingly intense North American influence, pose new questions with regard to the theme of the cultural profile of the region. Our study now turns to such questions.

THE ETHOS AND CULTURAL DIFFERENCES OF THE NORTHWEST

It could be argued that the Mexican Northwest is in the process of losing some or many of the traits that, for centuries, have characterized the core of its cultural physiognomy. According to this perspective, improved communications with the rest of Mexico and the immigration of groups from other regions of the country are bringing about a process of national homogenization. For its part, the North American influence undeniably has left its own mark. Thus both the national and the North American influences appear as complex and, in some aspects, opposing forces that would inevitably alter the cultural reality of the Mexican border states.

Another hypothesis would acknowledge that the very personality of the Northwest, composed through the historical process described earlier, has been able consistently to assimilate various outside influences while preserving many of its ancient characteristics. In further support of such a position, it should be added that some of the unique elements and traits of *norteño* culture are precisely those that have survived among the population of Mexican extraction settled in what is today the southwestern United States.

Detailed research is necessary to accept or reject either of these hypotheses. Such research has only partially been carried out. Missing are, essentially, more penetrating studies of a historical character and fieldwork with an anthropological focus, from the perspectives of ethnology as well as other branches of the social sciences. The questions that need further investigation focus around themes like the following: Has the full participation of the Northwest in national life implied a loss of its distinct cultural physiognomy? Has it been seriously affected by the influence of the proximity of North America? What role have the hundreds of thousands of immigrants coming from the central and southern parts of the country played within the context of the regional culture? Has the cultural homogenization of the Northwest with the rest of Mexico been a political objective at the national level?

Without attempting to offer a response to such questions, but rather aiming to evaluate the significance of what has been understood as the "*norteño* variety of Mexican culture," the following considerations are in order. In an effort to identify some key cultural traits that are characteristic of the Northwest, this study incorporates the concept of what has been called the *ethos,* or the general meaning and orientation of a culture. Keeping in mind the historical background of the Northwest, it is important to highlight those elements that most deeply have influenced the formation of this region's particular ethos: the motivations, values, attitudes, and kinds of relations most typical of the population of the area.

A first, almost constant, characteristic in the attitude of those who have settled in the Northwest since colonial times seems to be their determination to confront, head on, all kinds of risks and difficulties for the chance to gain the wealth and advantages that supposedly existed there. It is this determination that motivated the various movements of penetration, thus establishing, from the very beginning, new types of settlements where the inhabitants were forced to work to their maximum potential in order to survive. Such was the case for the mining centers, haciendas, ranches, new towns, and missions.

In the midst of their isolation, the *norteños* found themselves in the presence of indigenous tribes, from whom they expected little gain and much danger. The missions and presidios were the two forms of response to the problem posed by the Indian tribes. The missionaries, particularly the Jesuits, sought the concentration of the Indians, their conversion and better means of subsistence, isolating them as completely as possible from all external contacts. At the same time, the troops stationed at the presidios had the responsibility of repelling tribes not under the missionaries' control, the so-called bands of barbarians. One way or another, the missions and forts operated as institutions that ultimately separated or alienated the natives from the new centers where the Spanish-Mexican population settled.

Thus took shape in the consciousness of the *norteño* a very different attitude from the one that prevailed in the Mesoamerican area after the Conquest. In the North, since it was so difficult to take advantage of the labor of the "barbarous tribes," it seemed best to repel them or to concentrate them in the hands of the missionaries. This approach probably explains why even today, within the area of interest here, a very well defined multicultural reality still exists. Many contemporary groups like the Tarahumaras of Chihuahua, the Pápagos, Yaquis, Seris, and Mayos of Sonora, and the Tepehuanes of Durango, continue to live separately and to preserve much of their ancient culture. Further, keeping in mind that in the nineteenth century, and even in the twentieth, there were uprisings among several of these groups, it is easy to understand why, for the *norteño,* ideologies like Indianism often seem like romantic postures of little practical significance. The response of the indigenous groups, for their part, has been distrust and almost continuous resistance because of the abuses and exploitation to which they have been victim.

The ethos of the *norteños* has been formed, therefore, in their rejection of the indigenous world and willingness to confront danger, devoting themselves to any work that would permit them, if not to gain the riches desired, at least to work for a better way of life. Their very isolation and accentuated need for protection produced a strong family cohesion and an enduring preservation of kinship ties. To date, in many of the northwestern states the institution of the family shows greater stability than in other regions of Central and Southern Mexico.[11] In fact, both in colonial times and more recently, when other migrations have taken shape, those who arrived in the North were frequently accompanied by their wives and children.

The ethnic configuration of the *norteño* population also presents certain characteristics worthy of special consideration. As has already been noted, *mestizaje* with the different indigenous tribes that lived in the area was very limited. A good number of the early colonists were of Spanish extraction, many were Criollos born in Mexico, and still others were mestizos of a predominantly Spanish culture. Only the Indians from Central Mexico, primarily of Nahua-Tlaxcalteca origin, who had gone to the North as companions and servants, actually mixed with the Spanish or Hispanicized colonists. In any case, the result was the introduction of New Spain's culture, still in the making. At present, despite the recent waves of immigration, cultural habits and elements with ancient roots survive in the Northwest. Thus, in the Spanish spoken in the North many archaic expressions have been preserved, and even phonetically

what is known as the "*norteño* accent" can be clearly perceived. There are also differences in the diet of the region.
An interesting example is the existence of wheat tortillas,
demonstrating a Mesoamerican influence that has been assimilated by people of predominantly Spanish extraction.
Currently, the consumption of meat and vegetables continues to be higher in the Northwest than in other areas of the
country. These examples only hint at what a systematic investigation could discover in terms of distinctions. In the
same vein, the traditional costume of the *rancheros* could be
studied, a form of dress that came to exert a powerful influence on the famous cowboys of the southwestern United
States.

Some of the most important decisions adopted by the people of the North throughout the life of independent Mexico
can also be explained in terms of their ethos. Although in
general the doors to higher education or any other type of
refinement were not open to the *norteños* until recently, they
developed qualities that enriched them culturally. Among
them was their great capacity to adapt, their attitude of
resistance when faced with any threat of losing what they
considered to be theirs, and along with this, an increasingly
strong sense of "Mexicanism." As already mentioned, proof
of this is found in several historical incidents, such as the
resistance in the war with the United States, the strong
repulsion of the filibusters, or the struggle during the
French intervention. These forms of participation in the
life of the country, meanwhile, themselves engendered a
drive for greater links to the national reality of Mexico.
This might also explain the decisive participation of the
North in the Mexican Revolution, when leaders arose in
many of the border states and effectively opposed the dictatorship, struggling to put an end to the alienation inherent
to the great *latifundios,* mines, and other concessions in the
hands of foreigners. In more recent times, what has been
described as the stagnation of the ideals of the Mexican
Revolution and the severe economic crisis prevailing in
Mexico have moved large numbers of *norteños* to look for

political alternatives. Denouncing Mexico's traditional cen-
tralism, many people in the North have opposed what has
been until recently the almighty official party (PRI) and
have given their support mainly to the National Action
party (PAN).

The discussion of particularly significant events, from
pre-Hispanic times to the present, confirms the distinctiveness of the trajectory of Northern Mexico. Despite today's
stronger ties between these regions and the center of the
country, and beyond the undeniable North American influence, the Mexican North preserves traits and values that
continue to form its characteristic personality, its own ethos
within the broader context of Mexico's national culture.

The complex reality of the North, as already stated, is in
need of more penetrating forms of research. The archaeological investigations related to the region's multicultural
indigenous past, for instance, should be expanded. Of equal
importance is the inquiry into the likely pre-Hispanic contacts and exchanges between *norteño* groups and the Mesoamerican zone of high culture. With regard to the Spanish
penetration and colonization in the Northwest, while some
valuable studies exist, much still remains to be done. The
political and socioeconomic development of the northern
states since Mexican independence is a subject that requires
more attention, particularly in terms of interdisciplinary
investigations.

Attempts at understanding the surviving indigenous cultural identities, as well as the methods and motives adopted
by government agencies and religious missions that continue
to work among the native communities, have also been
scarce. Nor has there been enough research on the characteristics and consequences of immigration, demographic
growth, and the whole of the socioeconomic realities prevalent in the Mexican North. Another issue of obvious interest
is the processes of acculturation with respect to the powerful
Anglo-American society sharing a border of many hundreds
of miles with Mexico. It is clear that the North American
culture exercises decisive forms of influence throughout the

world, especially in the realm of Latin America, and thus it is crucial to analyze its consequences in the area closest to the United States, the one true intercultural border on our continent. A further subject for research is the interaction between groups of Mexican descendants in the southwestern United States and the border population of the Mexican North, particularly as it has developed since the Chicano liberation movement. In many ways, the *norteño* ethos may be perceived in the survival of values and other cultural traits among the Mexican Americans of the U.S. Southwest.

In any light, the Northwest, at least as much as the rest of Mexico's borderlands, is an area with great possibilities for development. It includes vast expanses of land with natural resources that have been only partially tapped. Its population, though experiencing an accelerated growth, is still proportionately small compared with that of the center and south of the country. Finally, if there is an ethos or distinct meaning and orientation of a *norteño* variety within Mexico's own culture, among the questions that should not be overlooked are the following: Will the whole of cultural values, traits, and elements that historically have made up the profile of the old *norteño* majority survive? What importance should be given, in the process of the integration of this vast portion of the country, to the loss or preservation of what has specifically constituted the foundation of its own sense of identity? On the other hand, should the complete homogenization of the Northwest with respect to the national culture be seen as something inevitable and even desirable?

The Mexican North is a vast area wide open to the study of situations of culture contact and exchange. The purpose of this chapter has been to reflect upon some of the available information, underlining the promise and importance of the theme and, at the same time, the gamut of subjects that still remain to be investigated.

9.
Beyond the Present-Day Mexican Border: The Navajo Cultural Experience

This case differs in many respects from those discussed earlier. The Navajo are today the largest indigenous group of the United States, numbering close to 160,000 people. The reservation on which they live is made up of the northeastern portion of the state of Arizona and other areas that flank neighboring New Mexico and Utah. Together, the lands constitute an expanse close to twenty-five thousand square miles, approximately the same as the combined territories of Austria and Belgium.

In this chapter I will take into account published work and testimonies, as well as my personal experience from several stays on the Navajo reservation. My most recent visit to the Navajo Nation took place in 1972. In that year, the president of the Navajo Tribal Council, Mr. Peter Mac-Donald, along with other officials from the Navajo Department of Education, invited me to give a series of lectures at the Navajo Community College. By way of explanation it should be noted that this college, established in 1968, is distinguished, among other things, by two significant factors. First, in the courses and subjects offered, special emphasis is given to those dealing with the cultural heritage of the Navajo people. Second, both administratively and academically, the institution is totally run by members of the indigenous community.

The lectures I gave there focused precisely on the topic of endangered cultures and situations of possible loss or strengthening of ethnic identity. While the teachers, students, and other people in attendance, all Navajo, showed considerable interest in the subjects discussed, I also learned a great deal listening to their points of view and the accounts of their own experiences.

In recent years the Navajo have been forced to confront numerous pressures that, due to their threatening nature, have prompted their leaders to make truly pivotal decisions. The Navajo are, more than ever, committed to substantial improvements in their living conditions. Specifically, the Navajo leaders firmly believe that it is high time the Navajo themselves, with an awareness of their own cultural reality, plan and put into effect the most conducive methods for achieving overall socioeconomic development. Within this context it has been necessary repeatedly to raise the topic of preserving cultural identity. The main issue has been to find a way to adapt to changes caused by outside influences or encouraged from within while avoiding absorption by the overwhelming force of the predominant Anglo-American culture. Thus, the discussions that took place under the general title of "Cultural Identity versus Assimilation into the Mainstream" were of vital interest to them.[1]

While dealing with the topics of other cultural experiences and processes—especially in Mexico and the Latin American indigenous world—attention almost always returned to the history and current situation of the Navajo Nation. It is well known that within the broader context of the United States's indigenous population, the Navajo's past and present have been tightly linked to the events that shaped the physiognomy of the vast territory of the U.S. Southwest. In this setting, the cultural history of the Navajo has included repeated contacts with peoples very different from themselves.

Archaeology, ethnology, and history, as well as the traditions that the Navajo maintain today, underline three salient forms of contact with peoples of different cultures. These include processes of contact and exchange with other Indians, especially the Pueblos; with various groups

of Spanish-Mexican origin; and, finally, with those described in a generic way as "Anglos," or members of the
United States's majority society. As an aid to reflecting upon
the significance and consequences that these contacts have
had for the Navajo, there are many written sources and the
especially valuable testimonies of the Indians themselves.

THE PLURALITY OF CULTURAL
CONTACTS FOR THE NAVAJO NATION

As do other indigenous groups, the Navajo preserve ancient
stories concerning their cosmic and divine origins and
about the community itself. According to their traditions, in
many ways parallel to those of pre-Hispanic Mesoamerican
thought, there were four ages or times in which the world
existed. The first was the black world, where the people of
mist lived, without the defined shapes of men and women
today. The second world was that of the color blue. In this
time human beings had to struggle against enormous
animals, now extinct. The coyote, a benevolent deity, saved
a few of the humans and allowed them to pass to the order of
the third world. This age had yellow as its color. The threat
of ferocious beasts endured and in addition, various kinds
of transgressions also endangered the survival of Man on
Earth. Ultimately, water put an end to the world of yellow
color. A fourth age began anew, described as the time of
heat and light. Some traditions proclaim that it was during a
fifth duration that the ancestors of the Navajo appeared
in the world. In any case, the Navajo myth, paralleling the
cultural traditions of Mesoamerica, also signals the succession of the cosmic cycles.

According to the ancient word, carefully preserved
by the chiefs and medicine men—the ones professionally
dedicated to the knowledge and practice of ancient medical
wisdom—the tribes had journeyed from distant places before arriving at what is now considered to be their sacred
land. As one of their stories relates: "For long years I have
kept this beauty within me, it has been my life. It is sacred."[2]
As a symbol of the definitive settlement of the Navajo in

what is today their land, the traditions recall the erection of the first hogan, destined for ceremonial purposes. The hogan's hexagonal wall construction had an enduring strength, and thus the people's dwellings had to be built along these lines.

Archaeological research, linguistics, and other historical accounts confirm that the Navajo have not long been residents of the southwestern United States, where their sacred ground is now located. Their language, as well as that of their neighbors, the Apache, is related to the Athabascan linguistic family, to which the languages of other groups still living in northwestern Canada also belong.[3] The date of the Navajo's entry into the Southwest is not known, though it probably took place between the thirteenth and fifteenth centuries A.D. From the time of their arrival in the region, they initiated contact with other peoples long ago established there. Despite the rife hostilities, for the Navajo these contacts ultimately meant the acquisition of valuable cultural elements. While defensive against seeing themselves culturally or politically absorbed by the Pueblo Indians, it is from them that the Navajo learned agriculture and, among other things, the arts of weaving cotton and sand painting for ceremonial purposes. The Pueblo religious world view, in which traces of Mesoamerican influence can be detected, left a deep imprint on the soul of the Navajo. Though they borrowed selectively those traits best suited to their own culture, certain of these acquisitions, such as the practice of agriculture, nonetheless marked a radical transformation in the Navajo way of life. No longer would they subsist only, as before, on the spoils of gathering and hunting.

Centuries later contacts with explorers, conquerors, missionaries, and Spanish colonists followed. The first testimonies in Spanish about the Navajo, dating from the beginnings of the seventeenth century, are limited. It was not until more than a hundred years later that the Spanish presence was to be felt in full force. Numerous attempts were made to subjugate the Navajo, but overall they resulted

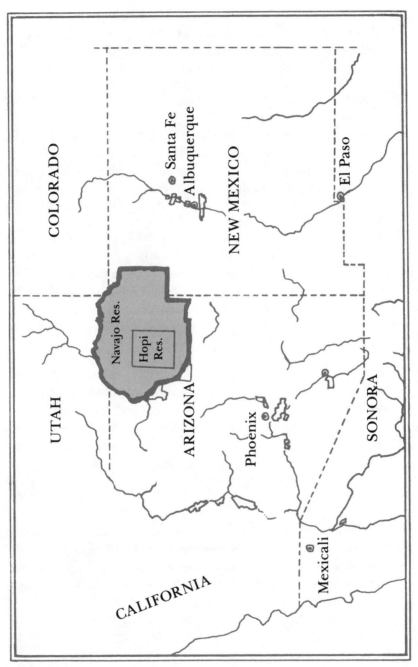

The Navajo Reservation

in failure. While the Pueblo Indians remained subject to
Spanish domination, the Navajo once again wisely took advantage of the opportunity to take on additional cultural
elements. Appropriating horses and as many sheep and
goats as were within their reach, they began a new transition in their way of life. With the horse, they were better
able to repel the Spanish attempts to penetrate their territory. At the same time, the life of the Navajo started to take
on the character of a pastoral society. Though they never
abandoned agriculture, their wealth began to be measured
in terms of the number of horses and head of livestock
possessed by each family. Assimilating those elements that
were desirable to them while violently rejecting any attempt
at conquest, the Navajo resisted the acceptance of Christian
religious beliefs or practices that a few Franciscan missionaries, working among the Pueblo Indians of New Mexico,
tried to preach to them. Thus, while the Navajo took advantage of the proximity of the Spaniards, it did not alter their
world view, their system of values and beliefs, or, in a word,
their cultural identity.

The Navajo also maintained some contact and exchange
with a people of a culture somewhat related to that of
the Spanish, but who were seen as considerably different.
The people in question were precisely Mexicans, of mestizo
extraction. For the Navajo there was such a distinction
between the Spaniards and mestizo Mexicans that they
soon began to apply a specific title to the latter. Using a
highly expressive word from their own language, they
christened Mexicans with the name "Nakai," which means
"wanderers," or "they who move around here."

The presence of Mexicans, especially amid the Pueblo
Indians and to a lesser degree among the Navajo, was probably felt by the middle of the seventeenth century, increasing steadily throughout the colonial period. Much later,
while for nearly three decades the present-day American
Southwest formed part of independent Mexico, the contacts between the Navajo and the Mexicans continued to be
frequent.

An initial consequence of this interaction is visible in the cases of Navajo-Mexican *mestizaje*. Thus, today a prominent clan among the Navajo still sports the name of Nakai, originally given to the Mexicans.[4] Another result of these contacts was the enrichment of Navajo culture with the art of silversmithing. The Navajo, now famous for this art, only then began to make necklaces, bracelets, and other objects in silver with turquoise inlay. Once again, however, the assimilation of this technology was far from mere cultural mimicry. The creations of Navajo silversmiths are testimony to their native inspiration, as is equally the case with their textiles and rugs, which include elements of ancient Navajo symbology, closely related to their traditions and world view.

THE PRESENCE OF ANGLO-AMERICANS
IN NAVAJO COUNTRY

Finally the "Anglos" entered the scene. They proclaimed that their manifest destiny was to expand and conquer the vast territories of the Southwest. No doubt the Navajo were acutely interested in the events, beginning in 1846, that took place in New Mexico and other neighboring regions. The people of Spanish origin and the Mexican mestizos living there soon would become subject to representatives of a much more powerful people. In effect, since 1848 the Southwest, which included the Navajo Nation, came to form part of the United States of America.

It is significant to note that from the time of the Anglo-American occupation of New Mexico, the declarations of General Kearny vowed that the government of the United States would defend whoever lived there against possible attacks by barbarous Indians, who, of course, included the Navajo. Little time passed before the Navajo saw themselves compelled to face and enter into treaties with the Anglo-Americans, especially members of the United States Army. From the beginning, the Anglos, in contrast to the Spaniards and Mexicans, wanted to control the situation through treaties or agreements with the Navajo. In fact, their goal was to obtain the Indians' clear recognition of the authority they represented as soldiers of the country now in control of the conquered territories. The American forces had proceeded thusly several times in the past, when establishing contacts with other indigenous groups.

Soon thereafter, however, misunderstandings took place. The American military men, unfamiliar with Navajo social structure, dealt with leaders of certain clans and believed—or wanted to believe—that the agreements they constructed had been accepted universally on behalf of a supposed supreme tribal government, which was in fact nonexistent among the Navajo. When certain groups, perhaps belonging to other clans, acted without adhering to the treaties, confrontations escalated. To the Anglos such behavior confirmed that, as in the case of other Indians, the Navajo's word could not be trusted.

The overall situation deteriorated in 1862, when American forces located in this part of the Southwest diverted their attention to events closely related to the Civil War between the states of the North and the South. The Navajo, aggravated by the pressures the military detachments exercised over them, took an offensive stance and increased their raids into American settlements. The consequences were drastic. In 1863 Colonel Kit Carson received orders to initiate a campaign against the Navajo. Less than a year later, the victories achieved by Carson allowed the American authorities to adopt radical measures that would deeply affect the Navajo Nation. These measures consisted of concentrating as many members of the tribes as possible in order to facilitate their en masse deportation.

On March 6, 1864, the exodus began, an event still known as the "Long Walk" in evocation of the deep trauma that such an experience left within the Navajo consciousness. Several thousands of Indians, including children, women, and the elderly, were taken by Kit Carson's forces to a point situated almost three hundred miles away, at Fort Sumner, New Mexico. According to the information available, nearly eight thousand Navajo suffered this fate, since only isolated groups were able to remain hidden in parts of what had been, until then, their ancestral land. The tragic confinement of the Navajo in Fort Sumner lasted four years. As American anthropologists Clyde Kluckhohn and Dorothea Cross Leighton, diligent scholars of the Navajo culture, described it:

> Fort Sumner was a major calamity to The People; its full effects upon their imagination can hardly be conveyed to white readers. Even today it seems impossible for any Navaho of the older generation to talk for more than a few minutes on any subject without speaking of Fort Sumner. Those who were not there themselves heard so many poignant tales from their parents that they speak as if they themselves had experienced all the horror of the "Long Walk," the illness, the hunger, the homesickness, the final return to their desolated land. One can no more understand Navaho attitudes— particularly toward white people—without knowing of Fort Sumner than he can comprehend Southern attitudes without knowing of the Civil War.[5]

When the Navajo were finally allowed to return to their homeland, their situation was truly desperate. Everything they owned had been destroyed or had disappeared: their cultivated fields, horses, livestock, and hogans. More than ever, in order to survive they had to muster all of their energy and skill. Fully aware of their own identity, a sentiment only heightened through suffering, they who had been deprived of all of their material goods were compelled to grasp more tightly to the traditions, beliefs, and values that for centuries had oriented their existence on earth.

LATER PROCESSES OF ACCULTURATION

The Navajo developed other forms of contact with the Anglo, but one way or another it was always tied to the memory of past suffering. As in other indigenous regions of North America, merchants opened trading posts, or centers of exchange, within the Navajo reservation. Although the Navajo rarely received fair treatment in such establishments, they were able more easily to obtain materials and products they urgently needed: agricultural tools, seeds, livestock, medicine, food, clothes, and many other items.

From this point on their relations with the dominant society became forcedly peaceful. To the whites the most important issue at hand was to "civilize" the Indians. This implied, above all, that they be settled in more compact centers of population, accompanied by the introduction of a school system so that Navajo children would assimilate Anglo-American culture, and the encouragement of missionaries from various Christian denominations to convert the Indians while eradicating their ancient rites and beliefs. In sum, their aim was radically to transform the ways of life of a people considered to be restless and "primitive," and thus incapable of behaving themselves as citizens of a country destined to be an international power.

Any analysis, however superficial, of the influences to which the Navajo were subjected demonstrates that the ultimate purpose was to eliminate, in the end, everything that had made up the soul and roots of their cultural orientation throughout their existence as a people. But once again, as had occurred in other situations of both free or forced contact, the Navajo only selectively accepted from the dominant culture what seemed to them to be worthy and adaptable to their own way of being. Thus they entered into new negotiations and treaties to obtain legal recognition with respect to the territory they considered to be their own. At first they recovered only a fraction of their sacred lands, but later their persistence resulted in about seven million hectares for the reservation, in what are today the states of Arizona, New Mexico, and Utah. The land possessed by the Navajo, a territory larger than some European nations, thus came to be the most extensive indigenous reservation in the United States.

The Navajo not only accepted but actively sought out certain elements of Anglo material culture. For example, they adopted all kinds of metal instruments and utensils, wagons for transport, and new materials for building their homes while preserving, at least for ceremonial needs, their traditional hogans. In more recent times the appropriation of elements from the dominant culture includes sewing machines, radios, cars and trucks, movie theaters, television sets, modern supermarkets, sanitary assistance and the construction of hospitals, and new kinds of food and dress.

Another significant innovation within Navajo social and political structures was the creation of a supreme Tribal Council in the decade of the 1920s. The new political institution was originally a result of the Anglos' desire to facilitate economic transactions with the Navajo. For some time the officials and authorities of this Tribal Council were in effect "straw men," almost always inclined to approve the programs of the federal government's Bureau of Indian Affairs, the controlling body on the reservation. Nonetheless, the Navajo, with undeniable foresight, gradually transformed the institution of the Tribal Council into an effective body of autonomous government. At present, the council is a political organism fully responsive to the interests of the community. Its freely elected members are now the ones responsible for the decisions that have to be made on behalf of the Navajo Nation.

In fact, a considerable percentage of the functions executed in the past by the Bureau of Indian Affairs have passed to the direct and exclusive jurisdiction of the Tribal Council. This includes not only concessions and contracts with outside institutions that have established themselves on the reservation, but also projects or programs directly linked with the social and economic development of the community. As the legal administrator of a budget that is increased every year, the council now lays claim to considerable resources that, as the communal property of the tribes, are meant to be used honorably and wisely for their benefit.

It would be naïve to deny that constant contact with the Anglo-American culture has brought about numerous changes in the way of life of the Navajo. But at the same time, as highlighted above, it should be acknowledged that this nation has demonstrated a surprising ability to make foreign elements and even institutions its own while maintaining its resistance to being absorbed by any larger or more powerful society. Thus, beyond all of the changes, the Navajo sense of cultural identity survives to the present.

However, recently, perhaps more than ever before, other more subtle and powerful forces threaten this oft-defended cultural integrity. First, there is the constant desire, even if not always conscious, of the dominant American society to impose upon the rest of the population its own forms of life, customs, and values almost as cultural ideals. Added to this are the resources that this dominant sector has at its disposal in order to diffuse, within North America and throughout most of the world, its ideas, trends, and, in short, its seemingly unchallenged world view, including all of the attractions of the consumer society of the most rich and powerful country on earth.

Within such a context, will it be possible for a marginal group like the Navajo to achieve technical and economic development without seeing themselves, ultimately, impaired by the irresistible influence of the predominant culture? Moreover, it is necessary to question the meaning of insisting on the preservation of identity when its disappearance could be interpreted—at least from the point of view of the dominant majorities—as the culmination of a homogenizing process that offers equal opportunity to all people in the country. In light of these ideas, the case of the Navajo takes on important significance as an experience that should be evaluated within a broad historical and anthropological perspective.

REAFFIRMATION OR LOSS OF CULTURAL IDENTITY

Rather than turning now to theoretical reflections on the possible consequences of the loss or reaffirmation of cultural identity, it is pertinent to analyze what it has meant for the Navajo to have maintained their consciousness as a nation and a people with a distinct personality up to the present time. When Navajo are asked to name the ethnic community to which they belong, their answer is eloquent. They say that their nation is made up of the men and women who constitute the Diné, or "The People." To belong to the Diné also indicates an active participation in the ancient legacy, preserved and enriched by determined efforts that they carried out together. As one of their ancient "songs of the night" soundly declares:

This covers it all,
The Earth and the Most High Power [Spirit] Whose
    Ways are Beautiful.
All is beautiful before me,
All is beautiful behind me,
All is beautiful below me,
All is beautiful above me,
All is beautiful all around me.
This covers it all,
The Skies and the Most High Power Whose Ways Are
    Beautiful.
All is Beautiful . . .
This covers it all,
The Mountains, the Water
The Darkness, the Dawn,
All is beautiful,
The White Corn and the Yellow Corn.
The Ways of the Most High Power
Are Beautiful,
All is Beautiful,
This cover it all.[6]

The ancient traditions that speak of the legacy that "covers it all"—including, of course, the origin of the Diné—are in no way dead. Navajo rites and beliefs continue to give root to a living universe of symbols, legends, medical practices, ceremonies, and artistic creations. To give an example, sand painting and ritual dances maintain their complex character as expressions of art, knowledge about how to cure the sick, entreaties to the divinity and, in a word, the ancestral cosmic vision. For those who make up the Diné, their ancestral values and other cultural traits have been enriched with foreign elements that they have adopted as their own. Their cultural identity has also been strengthened by a consciousness stemming from more recent experiences. Thus a series of legends speak of the acquisition of the horse, while recollections of the traumatic "Long Walk" constitute a central theme of the epic poetry that unifies and distinguishes the community.

The ancient concepts of time and space, the primordial cosmic ages and the four quadrants of the universe, so rich in symbolism, retain their profound meaning even today. They help in understanding the attachment that every member of the Diné feels to the sacred universe in which they live, the ancestral land of the Navajo.

Language is another link that continues to unite the majority of the Navajo people. As a vehicle of their thought and traditions, it enables them to preserve their world of symbols. Though a high percentage of the community is actually bilingual, able to speak both English and their own language, the later is always used when sharing intimate sentiments and ideas. And while it is true that various Christian denominations have managed to gain a number of followers, the great majority of the Navajo—including some of those who have been baptized or converted—retain their spiritual roots in the ancient beliefs and practices, whose irreplaceable means of expression continues to be the Navajo language.

Members of the Diné, "The People," clearly possess a rich cultural inheritance that includes a world view, religious beliefs and ceremonies, a complex theory of sickness and health, a system of values, historical traditions, language, symbols, distinctive forms of artistic creation, and also a sacred and long-defended land. This sense of bearing an ancient cultural heritage sustains and gives vigor to the Navajo's sense of identity.

More can be said with regard to the sphere of social relations among members of the community. First, there is the functioning survival of the ancient clan system, which continues to play the role of a powerful cohesive force and, at the same time, of an element of social control. People respect and consult the clan headmen. Similar attitudes are evident in the treatment of those who know traditional medicine, whose services are frequently sought after and highly esteemed. Another example of the culture's vitality is offered by the confidence that many Navajo feel in a relatively new institution, the Tribal Council. Originally, the council was imposed from the outside, designed by officials of the federal government. However, as mentioned above, when it was transformed into an institution under Navajo control, they found it was a powerful instrument to shore up a political structure that needed to be more in keeping with contemporary reality. Thanks to the fact that the Tribal Council became a genuine Navajo institution, it was able to satisfy the anticipated necessity of counting with an independent government that was also a symbol of Diné sovereignty and authority.

Today the Tribal Council, with the dedicated support of considerable sectors of the Diné, "The People," has attempted to put into practice a variety of programs that actually respond to the native needs as well as the character of the collectivity. A continuous problem, worsening over recent years, has been a scarcity of job opportunities on the reservation. As the active and brilliant Navajo teacher Ruth Roessel, director of the Program of Navajo Studies in the Community College, points out:

In 1970 the Navajo tribe and other interested parties carried out research on the human potential for work on the reservation. From a workforce of 32,350 persons, more than 20,000 had no paid occupation. This means that unemployment during that year reached 63%. Other extremely revealing data from this research showed that 70% of the total workforce declared that they did not wish to abandon the reservation to seek employment.

From this it appears that the greatest efforts to achieve the development of the Navajo economy should be directed toward those that effectively offer job opportunities to the natives on their own lands. . . .

An example of the lack of understanding of some people with respect to the interests and aspirations of the Navajo and other Indians is an article by Benjamin Taylor, from the State University of Arizona, published in the December, 1970, issue of the *Arizona Business Bulletin*, under the title of "The indigenous reservation and the prevailing trends of its economic life." In it Taylor states that the policy of supporting the economic development of the reservations makes no sense. In his opinion all government subsidies should be suspended so that the Indians would be forced to abandon the reservations and finally adapt themselves to the ways of life of the American majority society. In an interview given by Taylor to the newspaper *The Arizona Republic*, he agreed that in his study he had not considered it pertinent to take into account ideas such as ethnic identity or the value of preserving a culture with distinct characteristics. . . .

Basically, the question once again at hand is whether "experts" like Taylor should be the ones who dictate or direct the policies that Indians should adopt. This was the prevailing attitude in the past, with the well-known results of true chaos and disintegration. Today, it is to be hoped that the Navajo and all Indians can finally exercise, if necessary, the right that the majority of Americans take for granted: the right to make mistakes, but acting freely and for themselves.[7]

It is enough to add that thanks to the actions of the Tribal Council, which has persistently presented its case to the corresponding federal authorities, as well as taking it before the states of Arizona, New Mexico, and Utah, a jobs program was launched to offer new work opportunities and, in addition, to exploit the reservation's natural resources on behalf of the indigenous community. In this way the Navajo themselves have created, among other things, the Navajo Forest Products Industry, the Navajo Arts and Crafts Corporation, the Tribal Stores, the Navajo Tourist Agency, the Navajo Hotel System, and the Ranches of New Mexico, as well as their own press, which puts out publications like the newspaper *Navajo Times*. It is also interesting to note that, currently, Navajo participation is widening in management positions at hospital centers, in the schools, and in the various administrative offices of the reservation. It is now the exclusive right of the Tribal Council to name the officials and all of the personnel who make up the Navajo Police Department.

THE NAVAJO COMMUNITY COLLEGE AND THE THEME OF CULTURAL IDENTITY

The educational system on the reservation deserves special attention. The position of the Tribal Council has remained firm on this point: the education of the Navajo should be in the hands of the natives themselves. In the past, all the schools had been controlled by the Bureau of Indian Affairs, by the respective education departments of the states of Arizona, New Mexico, and Utah, or by the missionaries of various denominations. In 1966 an experiment was put into operation at what is called the Rough Rock Demonstration School. There, Navajo teachers, under a Navajo director, applied a new program of study in which the subjects of Navajo culture and language were included as essential elements in all of the courses offered. Some time later, the results achieved by the Rough Rock School led to the conception of a more ambitious plan. In addition to elementary schools, middle and secondary education should be organized around similar principles.

A step of even greater importance was aimed toward the establishment of an institution of higher learning, organized and governed by the Navajo themselves. After overcoming a series of difficulties, in 1968 the founding of the Navajo Community College became a reality. Provisionally situated in high school buildings located in the town of

Many Farms, Arizona, the allocation of an adequate budget allowed for the construction of new and more convenient buildings on a university-style campus, near beautiful Tsaile Lake, Arizona. Today the large complex of buildings, including some, like the Navajo Culture Center, in the shape of great hogans, creates a truly propitious atmosphere where the possibility of a superior education conceived in terms of the Navajo culture and administered by members of the Navajo Nation has been brought to fruition.

The extraordinary significance of this center of higher learning, still unique within the context of the American indigenous world, justifies listing the names of at least some of the principal Navajo leaders who have made its operation possible. Among them is Raymond Nakai, former president of the Tribal Council; Dillon Platero, from the Rough Rock School; Dr. Ned A. Hatathli, president of the college until his death in 1972; Guy Gorman, president of the Board of Regents of the college; Ruth Roessel, director of the Program of Navajo Studies; and Peter MacDonald, president of the Tribal Council.

When the college opened its doors in January of 1969, 301 students entered. Today their number is in the thousands, primarily Navajo youth and, to a lesser degree, members of other tribes, as well as some Anglos and others of Latin American or Mexican descent who have a serious interest in the curriculum offered there. In order to assess what can be expected from this institution of higher learning, it is important to return to the philosophy that gave birth to the college. Thus, cited below are several paragraphs of the official statement included in the college catalog for academic year 1972–1973. What is expressed there clearly responds to the Navajo's position of making their development a reality by assimilating from the majority culture what is useful to them, preserving at the same time their own ethnic values and identity.

After many decades of waiting, the dream has become a reality. Once the Navajo Tribal Council supported the idea in 1968, classes began on January 20, 1969. . . .

The Navajo Community College is directed and guided by the following principles:

For any community or society to grow and prosper, it must have its own means for educating its citizens. And it is essential that these educational systems be directed and controlled by the society they are intended to serve.

If a community or society is to continue to grow and prosper, each member of that society must be provided with an opportunity to acquire a positive self-image and a clear sense of identity. This can be achieved only when each individual's capacities are developed and used to the fullest possible extent. It is absolutely necessary for every individual to respect and understand his culture and heritage; he must have faith in the future of his society.

Members of different cultures must develop their abilities to operate effectively, not only in their own immediate societies, but also in the complex of varied cultures that makes up the larger society of man.[8]

As one might expect, the specific objectives of the college are in full agreement with the declaration of purpose. Essentially, it is the aim of the college to offer, through its curriculum, academic training in and knowledge of various fields while concentrating on the cultural heritage and the socioeconomic requirements of the Navajo Nation. For some, the studies completed at the college will constitute the necessary base to continue their career at a university center. For others, the college offers special training in technical specialties such as automobile mechanics, plumbing, accounting, veterinary technology, and secretarial skills.

Those who complete a brief scholastic training, as well as those who seek preparation for later professional goals through the sciences or humanities, follow a curriculum that includes Navajo culture studies. The Program of Navajo Studies, whether as a specialization or as complementary to any curriculum, includes the following fields: (1) Navajo history and culture; (2) Navajo language and literature; (3) arts and industries; (4) seminars on the problems of the Native Americans; (5) various courses with emphases in anthropological, historical, sociological, economic, and psychological studies aimed toward analyzing specific situations, traits, and elements of the indigenous cultures of the New World.

In close relation to the ideas and goals that gave origin to the college, its operation constitutes new proof of the Navajo consciousness of their own identity. Far from weakening, such a consciousness has brought the Navajo to create a functioning institution dedicated to the understanding, preservation, and enrichment of their own heritage. Clearly, the Navajo people recognize that, if it is a necessary condition to be able to develop as a community, it is equally important to have a definite self-image and sense of identity, deepened by the study of themselves and their historical past, a state of awareness achieved through the preserving efforts of people who belonged precisely to the same cultural context.

The crucial question—the idea of whether an indigenous group, until the present day totally marginalized in many respects, can itself establish the necessary means to achieve its own development—has thus received an original and valuable answer in the creation of the college, a modern center of culture, founded and administered by Navajo leaders. There, the goals pursued include the preparation of the youth who will be the future officials of an autonomous government, or who will have under their direction businesses and programs benefiting the community. And at the same time, the courses offered at the college examine, in a humanist vein, the heritage that individualizes and enriches the Navajo self, and in terms of which all projects should be conceived in the future.

Thus, subjects such as the foreseeable consequences of the absorption of any minority group by a majority society are

discussed in complete freedom. Historical and anthropological analyses are directed toward reviving among the Navajo
an awareness of what it means to be dispossessed of all that
is the foundation and strength for self-determination; the
significance of remaining trapped by a foreign and hostile
world until ending in genuine nepantlism, "being caught in
the middle," with no hope other than that of swelling the
ranks of the most impoverished sectors of a society that has
exercised discrimination and domination.

Through higher education, more effective forms of development and participation are sought, even at the national
level, while keeping in mind the strength of a cultural profile that is itself considered to have its own being and destiny. Such are the unwavering ideals and aims that the
Navajo have expressed by founding and advocating an educational system that is both made up of them and there to
serve them.

The dynamic preservation of Navajo identity—open, as it
is, to all positive exchange of cultural values—presents itself
as a challenge endowed with profound human meaning. In
the final analysis, the future of the Navajo, beyond any form
of determinism, will depend on the wisdom and courage
with which they act, and on the understanding that the government and other members of the dominant society choose
to demonstrate. Will the latter be able to forever free themselves from the old danger of confusing cultural homogeneity with national unity? The sum of the cultural values of the
Diné, the wealth of a people with a distinct physiognomy,
certainly offers ample possibilities of contributing to the
good of the nation. Indeed, the United States of America's
official motto, "E pluribus unum," is itself a recognition of a
plurality of peoples and cultures, out of which a great country has been formed.

10.
History
from Within
and from Without

Because of its relation to the themes discussed in this book, and as a final consideration, I include this essay on what I have described as forms of historical research *from within* and *from without*. Of course, the problems of endangered cultures should not be studied only in the light of history. As evident in the cases already considered, the complexity of the issue demands diverse modes of approach and action. Nonetheless, it is undeniable that history, as the search for roots and antecedents to one's own orientation, is fundamentally linked with an awareness of cultural identity and its defense. If a sense of cultural identity stems, above all, from perceiving oneself as a member of a group or society that considers itself to be different from others, an indispensable element in the preservation and enrichment of this sentiment is the consciousness *from within* of the experiences of that community, its historical past. Deprived of its memory, cultural identity dissolves.

These ideas concerning history *from within* and *from without* were presented at the Fourth Meeting of Mexican and North American Historians, held at Santa Monica, California, in October of 1973. Representatives from minority groups also participated in the conference, especially Indians and Chicanos. The commentaries and discussion provoked by my reflections confirmed that the subject is closely tied to the themes discussed earlier. Therefore, as a personal testimony, I offer the text of my presentation at that multicultural meeting with colleagues who practice either one of these historical approaches, the subject of this analysis.

TWO FORMS OF HISTORICAL RESEARCH

History, and the philosophy of history, can be pursued in many ways. There are great differences between the impressive lucubrations of men like Saint Thomas Aquinas, Hegel, or Marx, and the more modest considerations on problems of historical endeavors in light of the corresponding cultural background. The following reflections are of the latter type. They deal with a theme that—in a meeting where historians of diverse backgrounds participated— seemed to fit like a hand in a glove.

Those who declare a professional interest in the study of the historical reality of Mexico, or of any other country, come from all over the world. In this case, some of those present were Mexicans, others were North Americans, and still others from the Old World, but all were carrying out research on the history of Mexico. Despite this common endeavor, our varied cultural backgrounds made for inevitable differences in perspective. The Mexicans, studying the history of their own country, do so while inheriting and participating in that very cultural context. Independently of their abilities, they genuinely are, and feel, linked to the object of their investigations. Thus, they are carrying out research *from within*. The foreigners, on the other hand, whether North American, European, or of any other extraction, no matter how familiar with all things Mexican and however greatly their sympathy might lie with the country, must necessarily see it as a reality with roots and features different from those of their own culture. In this way, they approach their subject *from without*.

My reflections deal with the distinction just proposed. The aim here is to consider what it might mean to write history, taking into account the diverse origins of those who do the research. To avoid misunderstandings, an anticipatory explanation is in order. When speaking of doing history *from within* and *from without,* it should not be assumed that the first of the two forms of historical approximation—carried out by native researchers on their own country—necessarily implies the better of the possible approaches. In actuality, the native researcher, as well as the foreigner, can certainly produce historical scholarship of greater or lesser value. But even thinking of the best possible scholarly productions, are there any historians from without or within who can honestly claim such an identification with the past as to declare that they have come to know it as if they had lived it?

Thus it is not in terms of professionalism or historical critique that the outlined distinction is proposed. Instead, my aim is to analyze, in light of this concept, certain aspects that may stem from the simple fact that those who are investigating what took place in a determined time and place are either nationals or foreigners.

It is clear that the problems this distinction raises have to do not only with the historical being of Mexico or any other particular country, but instead demonstrate a much broader significance. The question could be related, for example, to research being carried out on the history of a nation that is different from, but at the same time linked in a myriad of possible ways to, the past of the historian's own country. Instances of this include cases such as the Latin American who studies the history of Spain or another Ibero-American country. In addition, many historians are committed to the study of an alien cultural past in order to unveil the possible influences it has exerted, even during remote periods, on the development of their own nation.

Among the implications perceived in the light of the proposed distinction are some that appear self-evident. Historical research from within, which is to say, done by natives interested in the past of their own country, is something that appears to be a natural and obvious undertaking. In fact, all of the peoples of the world, first through oral tradition and later in writing, have attempted to preserve their memories of the past. Thus, in various ways, they have done and continue to do history from within.

The other type of historiography, directed toward investigating the cultural reality of a people or nation to which one does not belong, certainly has not flourished equally everywhere nor with the same degree of intensity. This last type of concern more frequently arises in richer or developed countries, where there are both abundant reasons to want to know about another's cultural past and material resources to support the endeavor. Thus, for example, since the Europeans' discovery, conquest, and colonization of different parts of the world, works have proliferated describing the customs and past of peoples often considered to be of a lesser culture. At other times, travelers and adventurers from prosperous countries were the first to come to know and report on the customs and history of peoples previously ignored. Currently, it is almost impossible to absorb the increasingly abundant works of historiography prepared by scholars from countries that are economically developed, concerning those nations that are not. Numerous examples could also be presented of such an approach taken by people from highly developed countries about the history of other, equally rich and powerful, nations. This would be another case of works from without, such as those by the British about the United States or by North Americans on France.

In contrast, the attempts by members of societies that have limited economic resources—or are even culturally endangered—to do history from without on the events and institutions of more powerful states are extremely scarce. Thus, just as it has been said that the victors write the history, the historical approach from without also tends to be an enterprise of the powerful.

HISTORY FROM WITHIN AS A
CULTURAL NECESSITY

A need to know about their own past has taken shape in those societies and nations described as part of the underdeveloped world. An uneasiness has risen within them concerning the fact that what might prevail as their historical image could well be one constructed by others. Thus an old adage takes on new life as it compassionately proclaims: "Poor are they whose history is written by others." Perhaps this explains why the rise of modern nationalism and sentiments of identity has been accompanied by the proliferation, increasingly forceful and greatly as a reaction, of new efforts to do history from within, by people who belong to the group wishing to move beyond its underdeveloped state. An example of this is the *General History of Africa*, eight volumes currently in press (1980–   ), written in large part by African historians, sponsored by UNESCO and enthusiastically supported by its former director general, Amadou-Mahtar M'Bow, a native of Senegal. In the same vein are numerous ethnohistorical investigations done from within, meant to better focus the present state of the nation in light of the roots of its cultural heritage.

As instances of history from without, the kind that might cause alarm for the weaker party, there are numerous writings by historians of obviously powerful countries. One example is what has often been stated about the actions of Spain in the Americas. While Spain was a world power for some time, its dramatic decline made it an easy target for historical criticism from the outside, as former rivals vied to let the world know about the innumerable atrocities perpetrated by the conquistadors and those who followed. History from without thus became an interpretation of events made into a black legend. A specific instance of this, referring to the situation of Mexico, is cited below. These are the final words from the conclusion of a book of considerable merit. While I refrain from mentioning its author, I will merely say that it is a work whose theme centers on changes introduced by the Spaniards in the aboriginal society of colonial Mexico:

> The [Aztec] civilization became infused with Hispanic traits at many points, but it retained an essential

Indian character, partly through the conviction of its members, partly because it was depressed to a social status so low that it was given no opportunities for change. One of the earliest and most persistent individual responses was drink. If our sources may be believed, few peoples in the whole of history were more prone to drunkenness than the Indians of the Spanish colony.

Is this an accurate or overly simplistic conclusion in a book of otherwise considerable historical value? Is it not a bold generalization—made from without—that runs the risk of assigning to the Mexican mestizo's ancestors despotism on the Spanish side, and evasion and a tendency toward drunkenness on the indigenous side? Faced with conclusions such as these, it is understandable that not all is applause on the part of those who are having their history told like this.

A good example of the contemporary stance of self-affirmation, in the case of ethnic and cultural minorities, is offered by several indigenous groups such as the Navajo, who, as we have seen in the case of their recently established Community College, have organized a department for the study of their own history. Added to this is the recent proliferation in many universities of Chicano studies centers, where Mexican American scholars attempt to elucidate, from within, the roots of their cultural heritage.

The relationship between a history from without as an enterprise of the powerful and from within as a growing interest of the disadvantaged is easily elucidated. This does not imply that all history done from without always carries with it a burden of imposition or arrogance. Members of powerful states have also written history from without on the events and institutions of other powerful countries. Further, all historians attempting to write world history are inevitably confronted with the fact that they will have to deal with the past of other peoples, as well as the links of their own country with other cultures and nations.

DIFFERENCES IN
HISTORIOGRAPHIC CONCERNS

Let us put aside the sometimes thorny issue involving the powerful's very special relationship to history done from the outside. The distinction proposed here should also be viewed from other, very different, angles. Among them are the purposes of doing history from within or from without, the different problems of objectivity in these two kinds of approaches, and the often-varied consequences or reverberations that one or another form of historiography may have. As an illustration of this, let us turn our attention to what different viewpoints of nationals or foreigners have meant, or could mean, in the inquiry into a particular period in Mexican history.

The Mexican Revolution of 1910 is a subject that continues to attract a great deal of attention from scholars—from its antecedents in the regime of Profirio Díaz, to its current consequences. Both natives and outsiders have written amply on this theme. Because it deals with such a recent period in the life of Mexico, it could be suggested from the beginning that those who do history from without might enjoy a certain advantage in terms of objectivity. The Mexicans, due to their proximity to events of such concern to them, may be more open to the suspicion that their interpretations merely reflect their own political ideology or stance.

Even the ultimate goal of both types of historians, the Mexican and the other, may be openly divergent. Mexicans may still feel an urgent need to deepen the significance of this period, among other reasons in order to better understand their present reality and its future potential. For foreigners, studying the 1910 Revolution could reflect other, possibly broader, objectives that should not necessarily be considered a priori as biased. To approach one of the truly pivotal revolutions of the twentieth century, taken for its own sake or in relation to other similar movements of a social, economic, or political nature, can be a subject of great interest for those who study it from without and even in terms of world history.

It is true that the study of the Mexican Revolution can present particular problems to foreign researchers. Just like their Mexican colleagues, they will have to dig through documentary sources, the majority written in a language not native to them and including twists and nuances that make them far from crystal clear, as in the case of proclamations, manifestos, and battle plans. In addition, foreign investigators will have to endeavor to gain a preliminary and coherent understanding of a different cultural context, without which their interpretations may suffer from various kinds of distortion.

There is another aspect that should not be overlooked. Natives who write about the history of their own country, such as on the Mexican Revolution, even while they may suffer from a lack of economic support, are nonetheless encouraged by the expectation that within their own country there is an audience interested in the subject of their future contribution. On the contrary, as foreigners dig deeper into a specific event from a history other than that of their homeland, they run the risk that the results from their research will interest few of their countrymen, while they may be criticized and even disdained as an imposition of the powerful by those whose past they wished to study with objectivity.

Thus, without intending to, we return to the difficult and in many ways unfortunate issue that it is most often the powerful who do history from without. On the other hand, there is something to be said in favor of this perspective. After all, sometimes, when judging contributions from the outside, is it not the case that the nationalism of the disadvantaged threatens to become chauvinism? Is it not an indication of greater maturity to also be interested in knowing what others think of one's own historical being?

As an example, there are issues that could be called "taboo subjects" in a historical context like that of Mexico. Are there not some historical figures who, from within, have been presented as impeccable and practically canonized while others have been inexorably cast into damnation through the influences of partisan currents of official or politicized history? In such cases, the view from without, distanced from such pressures, can take on tremendous importance. To the professional historians of a Third World country, the contributions made from without can constitute a kind of catalyst or incentive for new modes of confrontation in the search for objectivity.

To underline the significance that history from without has often had for Mexico, a simple reference to research on the pre-Hispanic past is illuminating. It would be ridiculous to consider the great majority of works by an outstanding list of scholars of German, French, British, Spanish, North American, and many other nationalities to be an imposition of those more powerful. The inverse is also true: with regard to those studies done by Mexicans, it would be naïve to assert that merely because of the scholars' nationality, their worth is guaranteed. In the final analysis, it could be argued that, despite the fact that native investigators live in the very lands where the ancient cultures flourished, they, too, are forced to do history from without, since after all, they cannot consider themselves to be an Aztec, Mixtec, or Maya living and thinking in complete isolation from European culture.

Doing history from within or from without is indeed two different and, at times, complementary forms of approaching the events and institutions of the past. Would it not be highly significant for the most powerful nations to have researchers from less-developed countries emerge from isolation and write, with professionalism, various kinds of history from without? In the case of the ancient Mexicans, there are texts in the Náhuatl language in which the indigenes offer their image of the other, including those that depict the behavior of the Spanish at the time of the Conquest. Would it not be of consequence for historians from modern Mexico and Latin America in general, and from Africa and Asia, to offer their own images of others, that is, of the developed peoples and nations of the First World?

It should be recognized that such an enterprise presents problems difficult to overcome. Assuming there are Third World people with sufficient training, the chief stumbling block stems from the conditions of underdevelopment itself, as varied resources are lacking for such an endeavor, not least among them economic. It is possible that to overcome these obstacles, Third World historians could appeal to the wealthy in order to construct their historical image in the eyes of the poor. But clearly, this would open the door to doubts about the objectivity of the project, as such attempts could be considered portraits paid for by the powerful.

Beyond these difficulties it is imperative, for the benefit of both the wealthy and those who feel culturally endangered, that genuine historical research from the outside be fostered, including that done by the disadvantaged with respect to the powerful. It is especially important to find ways to encourage this last form of historiography, so rare until now. When this becomes a reality, the orchestration of the world of history will be better tuned, as other tones and notes make themselves heard. Old differences and antagonisms, their roots brought to light, will facilitate catharsis, recognition of past sins, and new forms of mutual understanding. It is time that we all, fully aware of our different origins but no longer believing that our respective homeland is the *omphalos mundi,* or center of the world, open the door to genuine forms of understanding. There are unlimited possibilities and a whole gamut of perspectives for history, art, and science, whose doing and redoing never end— whether from within, from without, or from both sides—in a shared endeavor to comprehend and deal evenhandedly with the distinct faces and hearts of the many peoples and cultures of the world.

Glossary

Acculturation. The process of, or reciprocal consequences derived from, the coming together or contact of groups bearing different cultures.

Alcalde. Mayor, chief administrative official of a town or municipality.

Alcalde mayor. Spanish magistrate or official in charge of a district.

Audiencia. Court and governing body in legal affairs, or the area of its jurisdiction.

Cabildo. Municipal or town council.

Cacique. Indian chief or local political ruler.

Corregimiento. Jurisdiction or province under the charge of a Spanish officer.

Encomendero. Master of the *encomienda.*

Encomienda. A grant or concession of Indians put into service as workers and/or tribute payers; or the granted geographic area where the Indians live.

Fiscal. Treasury official or prosecutor.

Hacendado. Master of the hacienda.

Hacienda. Large ranch or properties.

Indigenismo. Indianism; Latin American ideological movement in favor of Indians and their culture.

Latifundio. Large landed estate.

Mestizaje. Cultural and/or biological mixture, mainly between Spaniard and Indian.

Mestizo.   A person of mixed Indian and European parentage.

Nepantlism.   To remain in the middle, especially with regard to culture.

Norteño.   Northern; a person from the North.

Presidio.   Fort, stronghold, garrison.

Ranchería.   Settlement, camp; a band of Indians.

Rancho.   Ranch, or small hamlet.

Spiritual Conquest.   The attempt to impose the Christian religion upon the Indians.

Notes

1. Conceptual Framework and Case Identification

1. See Richard H. Robbins, "Identity, Culture, and Behavior," pp. 1199–1222.

2. Ibid., pp. 1208–1218.

3. About the concept of acculturation, understood as "the consequences and changes effected in a culture upon entering in contact with another," see R. Redfield, R. Linton, and M. J. Herskovits, "Memorandum on the Study of Acculturation," pp. 149–152. Consult also Gonzalo Aguirre Beltrán, *El proceso de aculturación*, pp. 9–16.

4. Aguirre Beltrán, *El proceso*, pp. 43–48, 193–199.

5. Diego Durán, *Historia de las Indias de Nueva España y Islas de Tierra Firme*, vol. I, p. 268.

6. Fray Bernardino de Sahagún, "Coloquios y doctrina christiana," cited in M. León-Portilla, *La filosofía náhuatl estudiada en sus fuentes*, pp. 130–133.

7. Thucydides, *History of the Peloponnesian War*, Book V, pp. 4, 11. With regard to this theme, in the sense given it here, see M. León-Portilla, "Aculturación y écosis," pp. 131–136, and idem, "Acculturation and Ecosis, a Proposed Term to Express an Anthropological Concept," p. 479.

8. See Alfonso Villa Rojas, "La responsabilidad de los científicos sociales. En torno a la nueva tendencia ideológica de antropólogos e indigenistas," pp. 787–804.

9. Edward H. Spicer, *Cycles of Conquest: The Impact of Spain, Mexico, and the United States on the Indians of the Southwest, 1533–1960*, pp. 576–580.

10. See, for example, the work of Richard Nostrand, "'Mexican American' and 'Chicano': Emerging Terms for a People Coming of Age," pp. 389–406.

11. Georges Balandier, "The Colonial Situation," pp. 36–57.

2. Transformation without Loss of Identity:
The Acculturation of Xólotl's Chichimecs
(A.D. 1300–1400)

1. Charles E. Dibble, *Códice Xólotl.*

2. These editions are E. T. Hamy, "Codex Tlotzin et Codex Quinatzin." There are commentaries as well in J. M. Aubin, *Memoire sur la peinture didactique et de la escriture figuratif de anciens mexicains.*

3. See note 2 and also *Anales del Museo Nacional de Arqueología, Historia y Etnografía,* pp. 345–368.

4. See the reproduction of the *Mapa de Tepechpan,* edited by Xavier Nóguez, with ample commentary.

5. Fernando de Alva Ixtlilxóchitl, *Obras completas.*

6. See, for example, the section concerning the ethnic groups, in which are described the various types of Chichimecs and the manner in which they came to establish themselves, in Francisco del Paso y Troncoso, ed., *Códice Matritense de la Real Academia de la Historia,* fol. 117r. and following.

7. Informants of Sahagún, Paso y Troncoso, *Códice Matritense,* fol. 173r. and passim.

8. *Anales de Cuauhtitlán,* fol.5.

9. Tacitus, *Dialogus, Agricola, Germania,* book I, pp. 283–287.

10. Alva Ixtlilxóchitl, *Obras completas,* II, p. 35.

11. The Náhuatl text whose translation we have used is found in the right upper middle of the *Códice Tlotzin.*

12. Alva Ixtlilxóchitl, *Obras completas,* II, p. 47.

13. Ibid., p. 57.

14. Ibid., p. 65.

15. Ibid., p. 51.

16. Ibid., p. 70.

17. Fray Juan de Torquemeda, *Monarquía indiana,* I, p. 73.

18. Chimalpahin Cuauhtlehuanitzin, *Troisième relation,* fol. 77 v. to the margin.

19. Alva Ixtlilxóchitl, *Obras completas,* II, p. 73.

20. Ibid., p. 74.

21. Ibid., p. 73.

22. Paso y Troncoso, *Códice Matritense,* fol. 180 r. and v.

23. Ibid.

24. Alva Ixtlilxóchitl, *Obras completas,* I, p. 137.

25. *Cantares mexicanos,* fol. 7 r.

26. Angel M. Garibay, ed., *Cantares mexicanos,* fol. 30 r. and v.

3. The Spiritual Conquest: Perspectives of the
Friars and the Indians

1. Joaquín García Icazbalceta, *Bibliografía mexicana del siglo XVI,* A systematic catalogue of books published in Mexico from 1539 to 1600, with authors' biographies and other illustrations, p. 103.

2. Fray Toribio de Benavente Motolinía, *Historia de los indios de la Nueva España*, p. 188.

3. Ibid., p. 121.

4. Ibid.

5. *Cartas de Indias*, p. 65.

6. García Icazbalceta, *Bibliografía*, pp. 382–383.

7. Fray Bernardino de Sahagún, *Historia general de las cosas de Nueva España*, IV, pp. 350–361.

8. Durán, *Historia*, II, p. 102.

9. Ibid., pp. 79–80.

10. Bartolomé de las Casas, *Del único modo de atraer a todos los pueblos de la tierra a la verdadera religión*, p. 95.

11. Jacinto de la Serna, *Tratado de las idolatrías, supersticiones, dioses, ritos, hechicerías y otras costumbres gentílicas de las razas aborígenes de México*, p. 62.

12. García Icazbalceta, *Bibliografía*, p. 383.

13. Robert Ricard, *The Spiritual Conquest of Mexico*, a work about the apostolate and the missionary methods of the mendicant orders in New Spain from 1523 to 1572, p. 291.

14. Garibay, *Cantares mexicanos*, fol. 42 v.

15. Ibid., fol. 41 r.–42 r.

16. Francisco del Paso y Troncoso, *Epistolario de Nueva España*, X, p. 116.

17. Jacqueline de Durand-Forest, "Testament d'une indienne de Tlatelolco."

18. *Códice Ramírez*, p. 188.

19. León-Portilla, *La filosofía náhuatl*, pp. 130–133.

20. De la Serna, *Tratado*, p. 62.

21. León-Portilla, *La filosofía*, pp. 132–133.

22. Durán, *Historia*, II, p. 268.

23. Motolinía, *Historia*, p. 248.

24. Juan Ventura Zapata, *Crónica de Tlaxcala*, fol. 4 v.

25. León-Portilla, *La filosofía*, p. 130.

26. *Procesos de indios idólatras y hechiceros*, p. 20.

27. Sahagún, *Historia*, III, p. 271.

28. *Procesos de indios*, p. 21.

29. Muñoz Camargo, *Historia de Tlaxcala*, p. 165.

30. *Proceso criminal del Santo Oficio de la Inquisición y del fiscal en su nombre contra don Carlos, indio principal de Tezcuco. Secretario: Miguel López*, p. 49.

31. Ibid., p. 40.

32. Ibid., pp. 40–41.

33. Ibid., p. 41.

34. Ibid., p. 42.

35. Angel María Garibay K., "Temas guadalupanos. II, el diario de Juan Bautista."

4. Bartolomé de las Casas in the Indigenous Consciousness of the Sixteenth Century

1. Bartolomé de las Casas, *Tratados,* II, pp. 485–486.
2. Ibid., p. 487.
3. Ibid., p. 485.
4. In *Bartolomé de las Casas, 1474–1566, bibliografía crítica y cuerpo de materiales para su estudio,* Lewis Hanke and Manuel Giménez Fernández note certain documents in which help given by the Indians to Fray Bartolomé is alluded to. Thus, for example, they include the reference (p. 75) to a royal document of June 30, 1543, "conceding protection of arms to the caciques of the already named towns and those that helped Las Casas" in his missionary project in Guatemala (Archivo de Indias, Guatemala, 393, 2, 203 v. 205 r.). Marcel Bataillon, in *Etudes sur Bartolomé de las Casas,* pp. 160–162, refers to this same passage and gives the names of the four *caciques* thus rewarded.
5. The first to attend to this testimony, the letter of the principal Indians sent on May 2, 1556, to Philip II, was the tireless Don Francisco del Paso y Troncoso. While compiling materials for his *Epistolario,* he discovered it in the Archive of the Indies. The copy of this letter curiously disappeared from his papers, and thanks only to France V. Scholes could it be included, with others of indigenous authors that had been removed as well, in the appendices that accompany volume 16 and the last volume of the *Epistolario,* published in Mexico in 1942 (Document 439, pp. 64–66). Also, in Hanke and Giménez Fernández, *Bartolomé de las Casas,* p. 174, the existence of this letter is mentioned without any added commentary.
6. See Antonio María Fabié, *Vida y escritos de don fray Bartolomé de las Casas,* II, pp. 543–559.
7. See *Actas del Cabildo de la Ciudad de México,* VI, p. 128. Lewis Hanke has occupied himself with this theme on more than one occasion. See *Bartolomé de las Casas, letrado y propagandista,* pp. 87–88, where he records the commission from the *cabildo* received by the chronicler of the city, Don Francisco Cervantes de Salazar, to write, as a reply to Las Casas, a work in which the king's titles in New Spain were newly established.
8. Paso y Troncoso, *Epistolario,* VIII, p. 32.
9. Motolinía, *Carta al emperador,* p. 59.
10. See the letter that Don Antonio Cortés directs to Philip II on February 20, 1561, asking that the title of city and protection of arms be conceded to his town, Paso y Troncoso, *Epistolario,* XVI, pp. 71–74.
11. Edmundo O'Gorman, in Bartolomé de las Casas, *Apologética historia sumaria,* p. xiii.
12. Agustín Yáñez, prologue in *Fray Bartolomé de las Casas, doctrina,* p. ix.
13. Archivo General de Indias (Audiencia de Mexico 168); Paso y Troncoso, *Epistolario,* XVI, pp. 64–66. This letter is also conserved in the

Archivo de Indias, in the Náhuatl language in which it was originally written.

5. Cultural Trauma, *Mestizaje*, and Indianism in Mesoamerica

1. *Anales históricos de la nación mexicana*, II, fol. 34 (translation from Miguel León-Portilla, ed., *The Broken Spears: The Aztec Account of the Conquest of Mexico*, pp. 137–138).

2. *Libro de Chilam Balam de Chumayel*, pp. 119–120.

3. Toribio de Benavente Motolinía, *Memoriales o libro de las cosas de la Nueva España y de los naturales de ella*, p. 21.

4. Ibid., pp. 25–26.

5. Ibid., p. 28.

6. In many sections of his writings, Fray Bartolomé expresses his thoughts about this issue that was so important in his eyes. See *Del único modo*.

7. Gerónimo de Mendieta, *Historia eclesiástica indiana*, vol. I, prologue to vol. II.

8. The broad documentation in Náhuatl collected by Fray Bernardino de Sahagún is preserved in the *Códices matritenses* of the library of the royal palace and the library of the Academy of History, as well as in the *Códice florentino* of the Laurenzian Library of Florence. An analysis of the work of Sahagún is offered by Angel María Garibay K. in *Historia de la literatura náhuatl*, II, pp. 63–88.

9. Sahagún, *Historia*, I, pp. 28–29.

10. Mendieta, *Historia*, I, p. 52. Concerning this position of the Franciscans in relation to the indigenous populations, see John L. Phelan, *El reino milenario de los franciscanos en el Nuevo Mundo*.

11. George M. Foster, *Culture and Conquest: America's Spanish Heritage*.

12. See Sahagún, *Historia*, III, p. 352.

13. See Francisco A. de Icaza, *Diccionario autobiográfico de conquistadores y pobladores de Nueva España*.

14. Chimalpahin Cuauhtlehuanitzin, *Séptima relación*, fol. 213 r-v.

15. Concerning this, the indigenous informant Doña Luz Jiménez said: "The first we knew of the revolution was that one day Señor Zapata de Morelos arrived. . . . It was the first noble person who spoke to us in Mexican [Náhuatl]." See Fernando Horcasitas, *De Porfirio Díaz a Zapata, memoria náhuatl de Milpa Alta*, p. 105.

16. Concerning the thought and work of Manuel Gamio, see Miguel León-Portilla, "Algunas ideas fundamentales del doctor Gamio"; Juan Comas, "Manuel Gamio en la antropología mexicana."

17. With respect to the theory and practice of Indianism in Mexico, many evaluations from many different points of view have been expressed in recent years. For an evaluation of these perspectives, the following may be consulted: Gonzalo Aguirre Beltrán, "Comentario a la confrontación de problemas sobre el indigenismo en México"; Alfonso Villa Rojas, "El surgimiento del indigenismo en México."

18. Concerning the culture and experiences of the Yaqui, see Edward H. Spicer, "Yaqui"; and idem, *Cycles of Conquest.*

6. Conveying the Amerindian Texts to Others

1. Mendieta, *Historia,* prologue to vol. I.

2. Alonso de Zorita, *Breve y sumaria relación de los señores de la Nueva España,* pp. 112–113.

3. Sahagún, *Historia,* VI, chap. 19.

4. Zorita, *Breve y sumaria relación,* p. 113.

5. Ibid.

6. Las Casas, *Apologética,* II, p. 437.

7. Ibid., p. 438.

8. Francisco del Paso y Troncoso, ed., *Códice matritense de la Real Academia de la Historia,* Vol. 8, folio 32 r.

9. See, for instance, what Fray Diego Durán says about some of the songs of the Aztecs in his *Book of the Gods and Rites and the Ancient Calendar,* pp. 280–299.

10. Contributions dealing with the art and science of translation are extremely numerous. Bayard Quincy Morgan has prepared "A Critical Bibliography of Works on Translation." A series of international conferences have taken place during the last three decades devoted to what has been called automatic translation, machine translation or computerized translation.

11. Merce López Baralt, "Notas sobre problemas interpretativos ligados a la traducción: el caso de la literatura oral amerindia."

12. Daniel G. Brinton, *Rig Veda Americanus.*

13. For the most comprehensive evaluation of the contributions made by this remarkable Franciscan, see Munro S. Edmonson, ed., *Sixteenth Century Mexico, The Work of Sahagún.*

14. A description of the procedure adopted by Sahagún is offered by Luis Nicolau D'Olwer and Howard F. Cline, "Bernardino de Sahagún, 1499–1590," *Handbook of Middle American Indians,* 13, part 2, pp. 190–199.

15. Sahagún, *Historia,* III, p. 3.

16. Ibid., I, book 6, passim.

17. Angel María Garibay, ed., *Veinte himnos sacros de los nahuas;* Eduard Seler, "Die Religiosen Gesange der alten mexicaner."

18. In a note to the reader, before the text of book XII, the one that offers the indigenous testimonies about the Conquest, Sahagún wrote the following: "Although many have written of the conquest of this New Spain in Spanish, according to the account of those who conquered it, I desired to write it in the Mexican language, not so much to derive

certain truths from the account of the very Indians who took part in the Conquest, as to record the language of warfare and weapons that the natives use in it, in order that the terms and proper modes of expression for speaking on this subject in the Mexican language can be derived therefrom" (3, p. 21).

19. Fray Jerónimo de Alcalá, *La Relación de Michoacán*, p. 6.
20. Ibid.
21. For a bio-bibliographical sketch on Cristóbal de Molina, see Raúl Porras Barrenechea, *Los cronistas del Perú*, 1528–1650, pp. 275–286.
22. Cristóbal de Molina, "Relación de las fábulas y ritos de los Incas."
23. John H. Rowe, "Eleven Inca Prayers from the Zithuwa Ritual," p. 83.
24. Molina, "Relación," pp. 29–30.
25. Rowe, "Eleven Inca Prayers," p. 83.
26. Ibid., p. 85.
27. Ibid.
28. Molina, "Relación," p. 38.
29. Eugene A. Nida, "Science of Translation." In *Language, Structure, and Translation, Essays by Eugene A. Nida*, p. 95.
30. In his introduction to the *Carmina of Catullus*, Ruben Bonifaz Nuño describes the procedure he follows in his work as translator; in particular he tries to imitate as closely as possible the phonology of the Latin verse, pp. lxxxiv–lxxxvii.
31. *Codex Florentine.* The Archivo General de la Nación (Mexico) published a facsimile reproduction of this codex in which the texts collected by Fray Bernardino de Sahagún and the translation he prepared of them into Spanish are included.
32. *Codex Florentine;* Sahagún, *General History of the Things of New Spain*, book 6, *Rhetoric and Moral Philosophy*, p. 160.
33. "Pregnancy, Childbirth, and the Beatification of the Women Who Died in Childbirth," p. 87.
34. Alcalá, *La Relación de Michoacán*, p. 6.
35. Ibid.
36. Sahagún, *Historia*, I, p. 243, II, p. 300.
37. Ibid., I, p. 52; *Codex Florentine; General History*, Book 1, *The Gods*, p. 23.
38. In private conversation and in some lectures Garibay liked to make this pertinent comparison.
39. Eugene A. Nida, "Semantic Structure," pp. 104–106.
40. *The Book of Councel, The Popol Vuh of the Quiche Maya of Guatemala*, p. 22.
41. *Collection of Mexican Songs,* fol. 18 r. See also Miguel León-Portilla, *Native Mesoamerican Spirituality*, p. 118.
42. A fine rendition in English of this treatise has been published by Thelma D. Sullivan, "Náhuatl Proverbs, Conundrums and Metaphors Collected by Sahagún."

43. *Collection of Mexican Songs: Romances de los Señores de Nueva España.* Preserved in the Latin American Collection, University of Texas, Austin, fol. 19 v.-10 r. See also León-Portilla, *Native Mesoamerican Spirituality,* pp. 244–245.

7. Beyond Mesoamerica: *Norteño* Cultural Pluralism in the Pre-Hispanic and Colonial Periods

1. This is the translation of the expression in the Náhuatl language of *"in ixtlahuacan, in texcallan,"* "broad plains and rocky lands," where it was said that the vagabond Chichimecs ("barbarians") of the north lived.

2. Andrés Pérez de Rivas, *Historia de los triunfos de Nuestra Santa Fe entre las gentes más bárbaras y fieras del Nuevo Orbe, conseguidos por los soldados de la milicia de la Compañía de Jesús en las misiones de la provincia de Nueva España.*

3. Juan Matheo Mange, *Luz de tierra incógnita en la América septentrional y diario de las exploraciones en Sonora.*

4. See the text of the border treaty of 1832 in Edmundo O'Gorman, *Historia de las divisiones territoriales de México,* pp. 214–218.

5. With regard to this, see J. Fred Rippy, *The United States and Mexico,* pp. 126–167.

6. On the concept of a "physiographic province" and its application to the case of Mexico, see Jorge A. Vivó, *Geografía de México,* pp. 48–59.

7. Among others, the following works have been taken into consideration in preparing this part of the present chapter:

Ralph L. Beals, *The Comparative Ethnology of Northern Mexico before 1750; El norte de México y el sur de los Estados Unidos;* Spicer, *Cycles of Conquest.*

Also see the articles included in the *Handbook of Middle American Indians,* v. VIII, Ethnology, part two, Section v: Northwest Mexico, prepared by Edward H. Spicer, J. G. Grimes, T. B. Hinton, C. L. Riley, and E. R. Service, pp. 777–870 and 879–888.

8. Herbert Eugene Bolton, "The West Coast Corridor."

9. On Nuño Beltrán de Guzmán and his conquests, see José López Portillo and José Weber, *La conquista de Nueva Galicia.*

10. On the expeditions organized by Cortés, see J. Ignacio Rubio Mañé, *Introducción al estudio de los virreyes de Nueva España, 1535–1746,* II, pp. 246ff.

The actions of Mendoza in this field can be studied in Arthur S. Aiton, *Antonio de Mendoza: First Viceroy of New Spain.*

A classic work on Vázquez de Coronado is that of Herbert E. Bolton, *Coronado, Knight of Pueblos and Plains.*

11. Concerning this rebellion, see José López Portillo and José Weber, *La rebelión de Nueva Galicia.*

12. See Philip W. Powell, *Soldiers, Indians, and Silver: The Northward Advance of New Spain, 1550–1600.*

13. Among the most famous rebellions at this time are the following: that of the Indians of Guaynamota and Guazamota in Nueva Galicia, 1539; that of the Mixtón, 1541; those undertaken, between 1550 and 1561, by the Guachichiles, Guamaros, Zacatecos, and other tribes; those of the Chichimecs in the direction of Aguascalientes, 1575, 1593.

14. A broad vision of this is offered by Luis Navarro García in the first chapter of *José de Gálvez y la Comandancia General de las provincias internas.*

15. Concerning the Franciscan missions in the north, see Fernando Ocaranza, *Crónicas y relaciones del occidente de México.* On the Jesuit missions, Gerardo Decorme, *La obra de los jesuitas mexicanos durante la época colonial.*

16. See Lloyd J. Mecham, *Francisco de Ibarra and Nueva Vizcaya.*

17. Besides the already-cited work of Powell, see the synthesis offered by Spicer in chapter 11 of *Cycles of Conquest,* pp. 281–333.

18. José Arlegui, *Crónica de la Provincia de Nuestro Seráfico Padre San Francisco de Zacatecas,* p. 12.

19. Ibid., p. 15.

20. Ibid., p. 121.

21. Report of Father Nicolás Tamaral, *Misión de la Baja California,* pp. 216–217.

22. François Chevalier, *La formación de los grandes latifundios en México. Tierra y sociedad en los siglos XVI y XVII,* pp. 122–130.

23. Navarro García, *José de Gálvez,* pp. 405–406.

8. The Northwest since Mexican Independence

1. The estimates differ widely for the number of Mexicans who lived in the territories that came under U.S. domination. Richard R. Nostrand, in "'Mexican American' and 'Chicano': Emerging Terms for a People Coming of Age," p. 391, says: "By the time of the signing of the Treaty of Guadalupe Hidalgo (1848) and the purchase of land by James Gadsden (1853)—events marking the frontier's transition to United States political status—settlements were numerous and widespread and the Mexican population numbered over 80,000."

2. Such is the case of Articles VIII and IX of this treaty. Here we transcribe and italicize the most pertinent portions:

Article VIII. Mexicans currently established in territories formerly belonging to Mexico and that will lie in the future within the borders defined by the present treaty of the United States will be permitted to remain where they now live or relocate at any time to the Mexican Republic, *retaining within the territories indicated all the goods that they possess, or transferring them and passing their worth to whomever they wish, without having to pay any kind of contribution, obligation, or tax. . . .*

Article IX. Mexicans in the aforementioned territories who do not retain the status of citizens of the Mexican Republic, according to the stipulations of the preceding article, will be incorporated in the Union of United States and will be admitted at the appropriate time into the privilege of all the rights of United States citizens, according to the principles of the constitution; meanwhile, *they will be maintained and protected in the privilege of their liberty and property* and assured of the free practice of their religion without any restrictions.

3. Nostrand, "Mexican American and Chicano: Emerging Terms for a People Coming of Age," in *The Chicano*, Norris Hundley (ed.), Foreword by Miguel León-Portilla, p. 397. See also Manuel Gamio, *El immigrante mexicano, la historia de su vida*.

4. On the raids of the "barbarous Indians" and other border problems during this period, see Rippy, *The United States and Mexico*, pp. 172–176. Also, to understand the antecedents of this situation, Jack D. Forbes, *Apache, Navaho, and Spaniard*.

5. For example, see the collection of orders and decrees on the raids of "barbarous Indians" included in *Legislación indigenista de México*, special publication of the Instituto Indigenista Interamericano, Mexico, 1958, pp. 57–64.

6. See A. Woodward, ed., *The Republic of Lower California, 1853–1854, in the Words of Its State Papers, Eyewitnesses and the Contemporary Reporters*.

7. During this period gold mines were worked in the Northwest, in Nacozari and Altar, Sonora, and in Ocampo, Hidalgo, and Parral, Chihuahua. Silver mines in Batopilas, Artega and Parral, Chihuahua, and in Copala, Sinaloa. Copper mines in Santa Rosalía, Baja California; Cananea, Sonora; Barranca del Cobre, Magistral, and Chorreras, Chihuahua.

8. Herbert E. Bolton, "The Northward Movement in New Spain," p. 78.

9. *Sonora, Sinaloa y Nayarit, estudio estadístico y económico social elaborado por el Departamento de la Estadística Nacional, 1927*.

10. Figures from the Dirección General de Estadística, Mexico.

11. See W. Borah and S. F. Cook, "Marriage and Legitimacy in Mexican Culture: Mexico and California."

9. Beyond the Present-Day Mexican Border: The Navajo Cultural Experience

1. The series of lectures took place October 9–18, 1972, at the Navajo Community College, which thus inaugurated its program of visiting professors.

2. Aileen O'Bryan, *The Diné: Origin Myths of the Navajo Indians*, p. 101. For the myths about the various cosmic ages, see pages 1–13 of the same work.

3. Clyde Kluckhohn, *The Navajo*, p. 33.

4. The Navajo themselves have stories in which they allude very mean-ingfully to the mestizo character of the Nakai clan. The following is the transcription of a fragment of one of these stories: "There is a clan called the Mexican clan, *Nakai dinae'e.* This clan is closely related to the clan called *Tqo yah ha'tline* because a man from that clan captured a Mexican girl and the Spaniards captured an Indian girl. They planned to take the Mexican girl back to her people because the mother of the Indian girl grieved so greatly. They thought to exchange these girls, but the Indian girl escaped and returned; so they kept the Mexican girl and the clan *Tqo yah ha'tline* adopted her. She founded the clan *Nakai dinae'e"* (O'Bryan, *The Diné,* p. 119).

5. Kluckhohn, *The Navajo,* p. 41.

6. O'Bryan, *The Diné,* pp. 101–102.

7. Ruth Roessel, *Navajo Studies at Navajo Community College,* pp. 55–57.

8. "Philosophy of Navajo Community College," pp. 9–10.

Bibliography

Adams, Richard N. "Politics and Social Anthropology in Spanish America." *Human Organization* 23, no. 1 (1964): 1–4.

Aguirre Beltrán, Gonzalo. "Comentario a la confrontación de problemas sobre el indigenismo en México." *Anuario Indigenista* 30 (December 1970): 280–294.

———. "El indigenismo y su contribución al desarrollo de la idea de nacionalidad." *América Indígena* 29 (1969): 397–435.

———. *El proceso de aculturación.* Mexico City: National Autonomous University of Mexico (UNAM), 1957.

———. *Regiones de refugio.* Mexico City: Instituto Indigenista Interamericano, 1967.

Aiton, Arthur S. *Antonio de Mendoza: First Viceroy of New Spain.* Durham: University of North Carolina Press, 1927.

Alcalá, Jerónimo de. *La relación de Michoacán.* Edited by Francisco Miranda. Morelia: Fimax, 1980.

Alva Ixtlilxóchitl, Fernando de. *Obras completas.* 2 vols. Mexico City: Secretaría de Fomento, 1891–1892.

Anales de Cuauhtitlán. In *Códice Chimalpopoca.* Edited and translated by Primo Feliciano Velázquez. Mexico City: UNAM, 1976.

Anales del Museo Nacional de Arqueología, Historia y Etnografía. Epoch 1, vol. III (1886).

Anonymous. *Anales históricos de la nación mexicana.* Edited by Ernst Mengin. Corpus Codicum Americanorum Medii Oevi, vol. I. Copenhagen: Sumptibus Einar Munkrgaard, 1945.

Arlegui, José. *Crónica de la Provincia de Nuestro Seráfico Padre San Francisco de Zacatecas.* Mexico City: Imprenta de Cumplido, 1851.

Aubin, J. M. *Memoire sur la peinture didactique et la escriture figuratif des anciens mexicains.* Paris: E. Leroix, 1885.

Balandier, Georges. "The Colonial Situation." In *Africa: Social Problems of Change and Conflict,* edited by P. L. van der Berghe, pp. 36–57. San Francisco: Chandler, 1965.

Bataillon, Marcel. *Etudes sur Bartolomé de las Casas.* Paris: Centre de Recherches de l'Institut d'Etudes Hispaniques, 1965.

Beals, Ralph L. *The Comparative Ethnology of Northern Mexico before 1750.* Iberoamericana 2. Berkeley & Los Angeles: University of California Press, 1932.

Bolton, Herbert E. *Coronado, Knight of Pueblos and Plains.* Albuquerque: University of New Mexico Press, 1948.

———. "The Northward Movement in New Spain." In *Bolton and the Spanish Borderlands,* edited by J. F. Bannon, pp. 67–85. Norman: University of Oklahoma Press, 1964.

———. "The West Coast Corridor." *Proceedings of the American Philosophical Society* 91, no. 5 (December 1947): 426–429.

Bonfil, Guillermo. "Reflexiones sobre la política indigenista y el centralismo gubernamental de México." Paper presented at the 28th meeting, American Society of Applied Anthropology, Mexico City, 1969.

The Book of Councel: The Popol Vuh of the Quiche Maya of Guatemala. Translated by Munro S. Edmonson. New Orleans: Middle American Research Institute, Tulane University, 1971.

Borah, W., and S. F. Cook. "Marriage and Legitimacy in Mexican Culture: Mexico and California." *California Law Review* 54, no. 2 (May 1966): 965–979.

Brinton, Daniel G. *Rig Veda Americanus.* Philadelphia, 1890.

Cantares mexicanos. Edited by Antonio Peñafiel. Facsimile edition. Biblioteca Nacional de México, 1904.

Carmina of Catullus. Translated by Rubén Bonifaz Nuño. Mexico City: UNAM, 1969.

Cartas de Indias. Madrid: Ministerio de Fomento, 1877.

Caso, Alfonso. "Los ideales de la acción indigenista." In *Los centros coordinadores indigenistas.* Mexico City: Instituto Nacional Indigenista, 1962.

———. *¿Qué es el I.N.I?* Mexico City: Instituto Nacional Indigenista, 1955.

Chevalier, François. *La formación de los grandes latifundios en México. Tierra y sociedad en los siglos XVI y XVII.* Mexico City: Problemas Agrícolas e Industriales, 1956.

Codex Florentine. Manuscript 218–20. Palatina Collection, Medicean Laurenzian Library.

Codex Ramírez. Edited by Manuel Orozco y Berra. Mexico City: Leyenda, 1944.

Collection of Mexican Songs. Mexico: UNAM.

Comas, Juan. *La antropología social aplicada en México*. Mexico City: Instituto Indigenista Interamericano, 1964.

———. "Manuel Gamio en la antropología mexicana." *Anales de Antropología* 12 (1975): 47–65.

Cuauhtlehuanitzin, Chimalpahin. *Séptima relación*. Mexican manuscript 74, National Library of France, Paris.

———. *Troisième relation*. Edited and translated by Jacqueline de Durand-Forest. Paris: l'Hartmattan, 1987.

Decorme, Gerardo. *La obra de los jesuitas mexicanos durante le época colonial*. 2 vols. Mexico City: Robredo, 1941.

Dibble, Charles E. *Códice Xólotl*. Mexico City: UNAM, 1951.

D'Olwer, Luis N., and Howard F. Cline. "Bernardino de Sahagún, 1499–1590." In *Handbook of Middle American Indians*, edited by Howard F. Cline. XIII, part 2, pp. 190–199. Austin: University of Texas Press, 1973.

Durán, Diego de. *Book of the Gods and Rites of the Ancient Calendar*. Translated by Fernando Horcasitas and Doris Heyden. Norman: University of Oklahoma Press, 1977.

———. *Historia de las Indias de Nueva España y Islas de Tierra Firme*. 2 vols. and atlas. Mexico City: N.p., 1867–1880.

Durand-Forest, Jacqueline de. "Testament d'une indienne de Tlatelolco." *Journal de la Societé des Americanistes* 51 (1962): 129–158.

Edmonson, Munro S. *Sixteenth Century Mexico: The Work of Sahagún*. Albuquerque: University of New Mexico Press, 1974.

Fabié, Antonio María. *Vida y escritos de don fray Bartolomé de las Casas*. 2 vols. Madrid: N.p., 1874.

Forbes, Jack D. *Apache, Navaho, and Spaniard*. Norman: University of Oklahoma Press, 1960.

Foster, George M. *Las culturas tradicionales y los cambios técnicos*. Mexico City: Fondo de Cultura Económica, 1964.

———. *Cultura y conquista: la herencia española de América*. Jalapa: Universidad Veracruzana, 1962.

———. *Culture and Conquest: America's Spanish Heritage*. New York: Viking Fund, 1960.

———. "Guidelines for Programs of Community Development: *Public Health Reports* 70 (1955): 19–24.

Fray Bartolomé de las Casas, doctrina. Biblioteca del Estudiante Universitario, vol. 22. Mexico City: UNAM, 1941.

Gamio, Manuel. "Clasificación de las características culturales de los grupos indígenas." *América Indígena* 2 (1942): 17–22.

————. *El inmigrante mexicano, la historia de su vida.* Mexico City: UNAM, 1969.

————. *The Mexican Immigrant: His Life Story.* Chicago: University of Chicago Press, 1931.

————. *Mexican Immigration to the United States: A Study of Human Migration and Adjustment.* Chicago: University of Chicago Press, 1931.

Gamio, Manuel, et al. *La población del Valle de Teotihuacán.* 3 vols. Mexico City: Secretaría de Educación Pública, 1922.

García Icazbalceta, Joaquín. *Bibliografía mexicana del siglo XVI.* Edited by Agustín Millares Carlo. Mexico City: Fondo de Cultura Económica, 1954.

Garibay K., Angel María. *Cantares mexicanos.* 2 vols. Mexico City: UNAM, 1965, 1968.

————. *Historia de la literatura náhuatl.* 2 vols. Mexico City: Porrúa, 1953–1954.

————. "Temas guadalupanos. II, El diario de Juan Bautista." *Abside, Revista de Cultura Mexicana* 4, no. 2 (1945): 160–161.

————. *Veinte himnos sacros de los nahuas.* Indigenous Sources of Náhuatl Culture 2. Mexico City: UNAM, 1958.

Hamy, E. T. *Recherches Historiques et Archaeologiques.* Paris. Societé d'Anthropologie, 1885.

Hanke, Lewis. *Bartolomé de las Casas, letrado y propagandista.* Bogotá: Ediciones Tercer Mundo, 1965.

Hanke, Lewis, and Manuel Giménez Fernández. *Bartolomé de las Casas, 1474–1566: bibliografía crítica y cuerpo de materiales para su estudio.* Santiago de Chile: Fondo Histórico y Bibliográfico José Toribio Medina, 1954.

Horcasitas, Fernando. *De Porfirio Díaz a Zapata, memoria náhuatl de Milpa Alta.* Mexico City: UNAM, 1968.

Icaza, Francisco A. de. *Diccionario autobiográfico de conquistadores y pobladores de Nueva España.* 2 vols. Madrid: N.p., 1923.

Kennard, Edward, and Gordon McGregor. "Applied Anthropology in Government: United States." In *Anthropology Today: An Encyclopedic Inventory,* edited by William L. Thomas, Jr., pp. 832–840. Chicago: University of Chicago Press, 1953.

Kluckhohn, Clyde. *The Navajo.* New York: Doubleday, 1962.

Las Casas, Bartolomé de. *Apologética historia sumaria.* Edited by Edmundo O'Gorman, 2 vols. Mexico City: Instituto de Investigaciones Históricas, 1965.

————. *Del único modo de atraer a todos los pueblos de la tierra a la verdadera religión.* Edited by Agustín Millares Carlo and Atenógenes Santamaría. Mexico City: Fondo de Cultura Económica, 1942.

————. *Historia de las Indias.* Edited by Agustín Millares Carlo and Lewis Hanke, 3 vols. Mexico City: Fondo de Cultura Económica, 1951.

————. *Tratados.* 2 vols. Mexico City: Fondo de Cultura Económica, 1965.

León-Portilla, Miguel. "Acculturation and Ecosis: A Proposed Term to Express an Anthropological Concept." *Current Anthropology* 6, no. 4 (1965): 479–480.

————. "Aculturación y écosis." *Anales de Antropología* 2 (1965): 131–136.

————. "Algunas ideas fundamentales del doctor Gamio." *América Indígena* 20, no. 4 (October 1960): 295–303.

————. "Aztecs and Navajos, a Reflection on the Right of Not Being Engulfed." Weatherhead Foundation Occasional Paper. New York, 1975.

————. *The Broken Spears: The Aztec Account of the Conquest of Mexico.* Translated by Lysander Kemp. Boston: Beacon Press, 1972.

————. "Culturas en peligro." *Revista de Occidente,* no. 145 (April 1975): 1–15.

————. *La filosofía náhuatl estudiada en sus fuentes.* 3d ed. Mexico City: UNAM, 1966.

————. "Las Casas en la conciencia indígena del XVI." In *Conciencia y autenticidad históricas, homenaje a Edmundo O'Gorman,* edited by Leopoldo Zea and Miguel León-Portilla, pp. 169–76. Mexico City: UNAM, 1968.

————. "The Norteño Variety of Mexican Culture: An Ethnohistorical Approach." In *Plural Society in the Southwest,* pp. 77–114. New York: Weatherhead Foundation, 1972.

————. "El proceso de aculturación de los chichimecas de Xólotl." *Estudios de Cultura Náhuatl* 7 (1967): 59–84.

————. "Testimonios nahuas sobre la conquista espiritual." *Estudios de Cultura Náhuatl* 11 (1974): 11–33.

————, ed. *Native Mesoamerican Spirituality.* New York: Paulist Press, 1980.

Libro de Chilam Balam de Chumayel. Edited by Antonio Mediz Bolio. San José, Costa Rica: Ediciones del Repertorio Americano, 1930.

López Baralt, Merce. "Notas sobre problemas interpretativos ligados a la traducción: el caso de la literatura oral amerindia." *Sin Nombre* 10 (January–March 1980): 49–79.

López Portillo, José, and José Weber. *La conquista de Nueva Galicia.* Mexico City: Talleres Gráficos de la Nación, 1935.

————. *La rebelión de Nueva Galicia.* Tacubaya: Antigua Imprenta de A. Murguía, 1939.

Mair, Lucy. *Anthropology and Social Change.* London: Athlone Press, 1969.

Matheo Mange, Juan. *Luz de tierra incógnita en la América septentrional y diario de las exploraciones en Sonora.* Mexico City: Publicaciones del Archivo General de la Nación, 1926.

Mecham, Lloyd J. *Francisco de Ibarra and Nueva Vizcaya.* Durham: University of North Carolina Press, 1927.

Mendieta, Gerónimo de. *Historia eclesiástica indiana.* 4 vols. Mexico City: Salvador Chávez Hayhoe, 1945.

Molina, Cristóbal de. "Relación de las fábulas y ritos de los Incas." In *Las crónicas de los Molinas,* edited by Carlos A. Romero, pp. 1–87. Lima: Editorial Miranda, 1943.

Moore, John W. *Mexican-Americans: Problems and Prospects.* Madison: University of Wisconsin, 1965.

Morgan, Bayard Quincy. "A Critical Bibliography of Works on Translation." In *On Translation,* edited by Reuben A. Brower, pp. 268–293. Cambridge: Harvard University Press, 1959.

Motolonía, Toribio de Benavente. *Carta al emperador.* Mexico City: Jus, 1949.

———. *Historia de los indios de la Nueva España.* Mexico City: Editorial Salvador Chávez-Hayhoe, 1941.

———. *Memoriales o libro de las cosas de la Nueva España y de los naturales de ella.* Edited by Edmundo O'Gorman. Mexico City: Instituto de Investigaciones Históricas, 1971.

Muñoz Camargo, Diego. *Historia de Tlaxcala.* Mexico City: Secretaría de Fomento, 1892.

Navarro García, Luis. *José de Gálvez y la Comandancia General de las provincias internas.* Seville: Escuelade Estudios Hispanoamericanos, 1964.

Nida, Eugene A. "Science of Translation." In *Language, Structure, and Translation: Essays by Eugene A. Nida.* Stanford: Stanford University Press, 1975.

———. "Semantic Structure." In *Language, Structure, and Translation: Essays by Eugene A. Nida.* Stanford: Stanford University Press, 1975.

Nóguez, Xavier, ed. *Mapa de Tepechpan.* 2 vols. Mexico City: Enciclopedia del Estado de México, 1978.

"El Norte de México y el Sur de los Estados Unidos." Third Round Table, Sociedad Mexicana de Antropología, Mexico City, 1943.

Nostrand, Richard L. "'Mexican American'" and 'Chicano': Emerging Terms for a People Coming of Age." *Pacific Historical Review* 42, no. 3 (1973): 389–406.

O'Bryan, Aileen. *The Diné: Origin Myths of the Navajo Indians.* Washington, D.C.: Smithsonian Institution Bulletin 163, 1956.

Ocaranza, Fernando. *Crónicas y relaciones del occidente de México.* 2 vols. Mexico City: Robredo, 1937–1939.

O'Gorman, Edmundo. *Historia de las divisiones territoriales de México.* 3d ed. Mexico City: Porrúa, 1966.

Palerm, Angel. "Antropología aplicada y desarrollo de la comunidad." *Anuario Indigenista* (1969): 153–161.

Paso y Troncoso, Francisco del, ed.. *Códice matritense de la Real Academia de la Historia*. 16 vols. Madrid: Hauser y Menet, 1907.

———. *Epistolario de Nueva España*. Biblioteca Histórica Mexicana de Obras Inéditas, 2d series. 16 vols. Mexico City: Antigua Librería Robredo de José Porrúa e hijos, 1939–1942.

Pérez de Rivas, Andrés. *Historia de los triunfos de Nuestra Santa Fe entre las gentes más bárbaras y fieras del Nuevo Orbe, conseguidos por los soldados de la milicia de la Compañía de Jesús en las misiones de la provincia de Nueva España*. 2d ed. 3 vols. Mexico City: Luis Alvarez y Alvarez de la Cadena, 1944.

Phelan, John L. *El reino milenario de los franciscanos en el Nuevo Mundo*. Translated by Josefina Vázquez de Knauth. Mexico City: Instituto de Investigaciones Históricas, 1972.

"Philosophy of Navaho Community College." *Navaho Community College General Catalog, 1972–1973*. Many Farms, Arizona, 1972.

Porras Barrenechea, Raúl. *Los cronistas del Perú, 1528–1650*. Lima: Sanmartí, 1962.

Powell, Philip W. *Soldiers, Indians, and Silver: The Northward Advance of New Spain, 1550–1600*. Berkeley & Los Angeles: University of California Press, 1952.

"Pregnancy, Childbirth, and the Beatification of the Women Who Died in Childbirth." *Codex Florentine*, book 6, folios 128v–143r. Translated by Thelma D. Sullivan. Estudios de Cultura Náhuatl 6. Mexico City: UNAM, 1966.

Proceso criminal del Santo Oficio de la Inquisición y del fiscal en su nombre contra don Carlos, indio principal de Tezcuco. Secretario: Miguel López. Publicaciones del Archivo General de la Nación 1. Mexico City: Secretaría de Relaciones Exteriores, 1910.

Procesos de indios idólatras y hechiceros. Publicaciones del Archivo General de la Nación 3. Mexico City: Secretaría de Relaciones Exteriores, 1912.

Redfield, Robert; R. Linton; and J. J. Herskovits. "Memorandum on the Study of Acculturation." *American Anthropologist* 38 (1936): 149–152.

Ricard, Robert. *La conquista espiritual de México, ensayo sobre el apostolado y los métodos misioneros de las órdenes mendicantes en la Nueva España de 1523–1524 a 1572*. Mexico City: Editorial Jus, 1947.

———. *The Spiritual Conquest of Mexico*. Translated by Lesley Byrd Simpson. Berkeley & Los Angeles: University of California Press, 1966.

Rippy, J. Fred. *The United States and Mexico*. New York: F. S. Crofts, 1931.

Robbins, Richard H. "Identity, Culture, and Behavior." In *Handbook of Social and Cultural Anthropology*, edited by John J. Honigmann, pp. 1199–1222. Chicago: Rand McNally, 1973.

Roessel, Ruth. *Navajo Studies at Navajo Community College*. Many Farms, Az.: Navajo Community College Press, 1971.

Romances de los Señores de Nueva España, Poesía Náhuatl. Edited by Angel M. Garibay K. Mexico City: UNAM, 1964.

Rowe, John H. "Eleven Inca Prayers from the Zithuwa Ritual." *Kroeber Anthropological Society Papers,* nos. 8–9 (1953): 82–99.

Rubio Mañé, J. Ignacio. *Introducción al estudio de los Virreyes de Nueva España, 1535–1746.* 4 vols. Mexico City: UNAM, 1959.

Sahagún, Bernardino de. *Códice matritense de la Real Academia de la Historia.* Facsimile edition edited by Francisco del Paso y Troncoso. 3 vols. Madrid: Hauser y Menet, 1906–1907.

————. "Colloquios y doctrina christiana." In *La filosofía náhuatl estudiada en sus fuentes,* 4th ed., edited by M. León-Portilla, pp. 130–133. Mexico City: UNAM, 1974.

————. *General History of Things of New Spain.* Translated by Charles E. Dibble and Arthur J. O. Anderson. Monographs of the School of American Research. Santa Fe, N.M., 1969, 1970.

————. *Historia general de las cosas de Nueva España.* Edited by Angel María Garibay K. 4 vols. Mexico City: Porrúa, 1956.

Seler, Eduard. "Die Religiosen Gesange der alten mexicaner." In *Gesammelte Abhandlungen,* V, pp. 959–1107. 5 vols. Berlin: Behrend, 1902–1923.

Serna, Jacinto de la. *Tratado de las idolatrías, supersticiones, dioses, ritos, hechicerías y otras costumbres gentílicas de las razas aborígenes de México.* 2 vols. Edited by Francisco del Paso y Troncoso. Mexico City: Editorial Fuente Cultural, 1953.

Sonora, Sinaloa y Nayarit: estudio estadístico y económico social elaborado por el Departamento de la Estadística Nacional, 1927. Mexico City: Imprenta Mundial, 1928.

Spicer, Edward H. *Cycles of Conquest: The Impact of Spain, Mexico, and the United States on the Indians of the Southwest, 1533–1960.* Tucson: University of Arizona Press, 1962.

————. *Problemas humanos en el cambio tecnológico.* Mexico City: Editorial Letras, 1963.

————. "Yaqui." In *Perspectives in American Indian Culture Change,* edited by Edward H. Spicer, pp. 7–93. Chicago: University of Chicago Press, 1961.

Stavenhagen, Rodolfo. "Seven Erroneous Theses about Latin America." *New University Thought* 4, no. 4 (1966–1967).

Sullivan, Thelma D. "Náhuatl Proverbs, Conundrums, and Metaphors Collected by Sahagún." *Estudio de Cultura Náhuatl* 4 (1963): 93–177.

Tacitus. *Dialogus, Agirola, Germania.* Loeb Classical Library. Cambridge: 1939.

Tamaral, Nicolás. *Misión de la Baja California.* Madrid: Editorial Católica, 1946.

Torquemada, Juan de. *Monarquía indiana.* 2d ed. 3 vols. Mexico City: Porrúa, 1969.

Villa Rojas, Alfonso. "La responsabilidad de los científicos sociales. En torno a la nueva tendencia ideológica de antropólogos e indigenistas." *América Indígena* 29, no. 3 (1969): 787–804.
———. "Resultados de la orientación antropológica en la educación indígena en el México actual." *Anuario Indigenista* 29 (1969): 213–223.
———. "The Role of Anthropology in the Papaloapan Project." *Proceedings of the Inter-American Conference on Conservation of Renewable Natural Resources.* U.S. State Department Publication no. 3382. Washington, D.C., 1948.
———. "El surgimiento del indigenismo en México." In *¿Ha fracasado el indigenismo?* edited by Instituto Nacional Indigenista, pp. 229–243. Colección Sep-Setentas, no. 9. Mexico City: Sep-Setentas, 1971.
Vivó, Jorge A. *Geografía de México.* 4th ed. Mexico City: Fondo de Cultura Económica, 1958.

Woodward, A., ed. *The Republic of Lower California, 1853–1854, in the Words of Its State Papters, Eyewitnesses, and the Contemporary Reporters.* Los Angeles: Dawson's Book Shop, 1966.

Zapata, Juan Ventura. *Crónica de Tlaxcala.* Mexican manuscript 212, National Library of France, Paris.
Zorita, Alonso de. *Breve y sumaria relación de los señores de la Nueva-España.* Mexico City: UNAM, 1952.